More Than Play

More Than Play

*How Law, Policy, and Politics Shape
American Youth Sport*

DIONNE KOLLER

UNIVERSITY OF CALIFORNIA PRESS

University of California Press
Oakland, California

© 2025 by Dionne Koller

All rights reserved.

Library of Congress Cataloging-in-Publication Data

Names: Koller, Dionne, author.
Title: More than play : how law, policy, and politics shape American youth sport / Dionne Koller.
Description: First edition. | Oakland : University of California Press, 2025. | Includes bibliographical references and index.
Identifiers: LCCN 2024035558 (print) | LCCN 2024035559 (ebook) | ISBN 9780520399259 (cloth) | ISBN 9780520399266 (paperback) | ISBN 9780520399273 (ebook)
Subjects: LCSH: Sports—Law and legislation—United States. | Sports for children—Political aspects—United States.
Classification: LCC KF3989 .K63 2025 (print) | LCC KF3989 (ebook) | DDC 344.73/099—dc23/eng/20240804
LC record available at https://lccn.loc.gov/2024035558
LC ebook record available at https://lccn.loc.gov/2024035559

GPSR Authorized Representative: Easy Access System Europe, Mustamäe tee 50, 10621 Tallinn, Estonia, gpsr.requests@easproject.com

34 33 32 31 30 29 28 27 26 25
10 9 8 7 6 5 4 3 2 1

CONTENTS

Acknowledgments   vii

PART I. WHAT WE KNOW ABOUT YOUTH SPORT

Introduction   3

1. Definitions, History, and Data   11

PART II. THE LAW AND POLICY UNDERPINNING AMERICAN YOUTH SPORT

2. The Law of the Child and Family   33
3. The Law and Policy Approach to Sport   51
4. The Law and Policy Approach to Youth Sport   70
5. The Politics of Youth Sport   90

PART III. DISTRIBUTIVE CONSEQUENCES OF OUR CURRENT APPROACH TO YOUTH SPORT

6. The Youth Sport Surplus   109
7. Youth Sport's Beneficiaries   121

Conclusion   141

Notes   145

Selected Bibliography   193

Index   209

ACKNOWLEDGMENTS

Thank you to Maura Roessner, Sam Warren, Steven Baker, Stephanie Summerhays, and the University of California Press for supporting this book. This work is derived from an article I originally published in the *Yale Journal of Law and the Humanities*: "Identifying Youth Sport" (35, no. 1 [2024]).

I am so thankful for the enthusiasm for this project provided by my wonderful colleagues at the University of Baltimore School of Law, and I particularly appreciate the wisdom and feedback provided by Professors Gilda Daniels, Michele Gilman, Daniel Hatcher, Margaret Johnson, Nienke Grossman, William Hubbard, David Jaros, Robert Lande, Matthew Lindsay, Audrey McFarlane, Nancy Modesitt, Matthew Sipe, Amy Sloan, and Colin Starger.

I am also grateful for the support I received from the university and Deans Ronald Weich and LaVonda Reed, and appreciate the excellent research assistance from librarians Savannah Long and David Matchen, as well as Christina Charikofsky and Madeleine Songer. I am so fortunate for the insight and expertise that Adam Weissmann offered, and I likewise appreciate the discussions I had about youth sport and this work with my terrific students.

Finally, I benefited greatly from the considerable feedback while I was developing this project provided by Professor Janet Halley, the members of the spring 2022 scholarship working group of Harvard Law School's Children's Advocacy Project, Jane Fair Bestor, and Professors Timothy Davis, Jeremi Duru, Marc Edelman, Ryan Gauthier, John Holden, Nathan Kalman-Lamb, Steve Ross, Katharine Silbaugh, and Alfred Yen.

This book is dedicated to my family. I leave my children to determine what their youth sport experiences meant to them. For me, the best part was the time we spent together and the joy of seeing them feel a sense of accomplishment. In addition, my husband's skill as a youth sport coach has been surpassed only by his ability to love and support me as I wrote this book. And, finally, I want to thank my mom, who was the best youth sport parent a girl could ask for.

PART I

What We Know about Youth Sport

Introduction

In 2022, several parents brought suit against a gymnastics training center, alleging that their daughters had suffered physical and mental harm from "excessive conditioning" that, the parents asserted, was intended to punish their children in violation of the applicable "Safe Sport" policy. The court dismissed the claims. It held in part that the gym had no duty to protect the girls from the risks and harms that are considered "normal, routine, and customary during high-level competitive gymnastics training" and that are, in fact, "essential to gymnastics."[1] In addition, the court found that the girls' parents had signed valid waivers of liability barring their children from any recovery. As a result, whether or not the girls suffered harm, the law provided no remedy.

The result in *Campagna-McGuffin v. Diva Gymnastics Academy, Inc.* is neither anomalous nor limited to gymnastics, and it is easily justified under current legal doctrine. While the children and their parents believed the experience at Diva Gymnastics Academy amounted to an abusive punishment, the law told them it was just part of the sport. The policy underlying this case and the many others involving children in sport reflect the pervasive belief that participation in athletics provides important individual and societal benefits. As a result, the federal and state governments, as well as courts, generally seek to promote—and resist regulating—the activity we refer to as youth sport.

We rarely take the opportunity to ask what this experience actually is, likely because the answer seems obvious. We commonly assume that youth sport is a positive childhood experience to be encouraged and, of course, the necessary vehicle for reaching higher-level sport settings, whether intercollegiate, professional, or Olympic and Paralympic. The inspiration for this book came when I was giving a presentation on youth sport and outlining proposals for reform. A listener asked me a seemingly simple question: "What do you mean when you say youth sport? What is it?" What is it, indeed.

The answer, I found, is much more complex than common wisdom suggests. Since the time of the early Greeks, sport and healthy competition have been considered part of the "good life,"[2] and we often look to sport to develop character or teach essential lessons. Yet, at their core, sports are made-up games.[3] They are socially constructed, not naturally occurring or divinely given.[4] Social theorists argue, therefore, that we must avoid concluding that sport is always positive or virtuous, but instead view it as it is, shaped by societal systems that infuse sport with particular substance and significance. We should not, then, view sport narrowly or simplistically. To *know* sport fully, we must also understand the environment in which it operates.[5]

This effort in recent years has taken hold in nearly all sport settings, and we are starting to understand much more about today's athletic experiences, particularly for athletes. For instance, courts, Congress, and at least one federal agency are reexamining the structures of Olympic and Paralympic as well as intercollegiate sport that may contribute to economic and other forms of athlete harm.[6] Practices once seen as simply part of the game are being recharacterized as systems of power that can provide benefits for everyone but the athletes. Previously accepted, common training methods in elite Olympic and Paralympic Movement sports are now considered in some cases abusive. Individuals who have long been referred to as student-athletes, participating in their sports through the National Collegiate Athletic Association's (NCAA) "amateurism" model, are now being recast as workers with a claim to the substantial revenue their play generates.[7] At the core of these efforts is the belief that too much of the investment athletes put into their sport—physical, economic, mental—is being appropriated by others.

Yet this movement has, for the most part, not included youth sport. Youth sport, it is often asserted, is part of a healthy, ideal childhood, and nearly everyone—from the federal and state governments to parents—encourages children to take part. In this conception, youth sport is play with important future payoffs in the form of better physical and mental health, better educational outcomes, and a better society. With tens of millions of children participating, it would seem the conventional wisdom is true.

For decades, however, the youth-sport-is-good narrative has bumped up against a troubling reality. Most children quit by the time they reach adolescence, and they often do so because of what is frequently referred to as the professionalization of youth sport.[8] This process involves pressure to specialize in one sport at a young age,[9] overtraining in an effort to develop talent, and an emphasis on competition and winning.[10] The consequences of this approach include what the medical community has labeled an "epidemic" of (largely preventable) youth sport injuries.[11] Professionalization of youth sport also makes participation costly, so that millions of children, particularly children of color, those from economically disadvantaged households, and youth with disabilities, are unable to participate.[12]

Critics around the world, from sociologists to physicians, have taken on different aspects of professionalized youth sport. In the United States excellent books have been written about the current state of youth sport, vividly illustrating what professionalization looks like in the lives of children and their families and suggesting pathways for reform. Examples include Mark Hyman's *Until It Hurts*, Tom Farrey's *Game On*, and Linda Flanagan's *Take Back the Game*.

However, despite youth sport's cultural ubiquity, legal scholarship often neglects the activity.[13] Most sports law, children and the law, and family law textbooks give youth sport little to no mention. This is perhaps not surprising, given that the field of sports law itself has traditionally been marginalized and, as some note, has "only recently" been recognized as a legitimate area of scholarly focus.[14] This neglect is consistent with scholarly attention to sport generally, at least from a critical perspective. As a result, despite the significant and widely known consequences of our current approach, the system and the youth-sport-is-good narrative persists with little legal and policy scrutiny.

Accordingly, while we generally feel deeply familiar with sport, we may not understand the full picture when it comes to children's engagement with it. This is an epistemological issue, and it has significant implications for our law and policy approach to the activity. A recent example involving intercollegiate athletics illustrates the point. In 1984, the U.S. Supreme Court decided *NCAA v. Board of Regents of the University of Oklahoma*, an antitrust case challenging the NCAA's restraint on televising college football games.[15] Although the Court held that the NCAA violated antitrust law, it stated that "the NCAA plays a critical role in the maintenance of a revered tradition of amateurism in college sports. There can be no question that it needs ample latitude to play that role, or that the preservation of the student-athlete in higher education adds richness and diversity to intercollegiate athletics and is entirely consistent with the goals of the Sherman Act."[16]

Legally, this language is dicta—not necessary to resolve the case at hand and, therefore, not binding in future cases. The NCAA used it, nevertheless, largely to avoid antitrust liability in connection with its athlete eligibility rules for nearly four decades. Perhaps even more significantly, the NCAA used the language of the *Board of Regents* case to shape the cultural and policy narrative so as to position itself as a protector of a "revered tradition" and to argue that amateurism, emphasizing the notion that athletes must not earn any compensation connected to their status as an athlete, was not only a critical part of that tradition but the way college sport had to be. This was the defining knowledge of intercollegiate sport, and it seemingly had the Supreme Court's endorsement.

Our prevailing knowledge, however, did not reflect the full picture. Many legal scholars and other critics argued that the dominant narrative about intercollegiate sport concealed the power dynamics behind—and injustices that resulted from—the amateurism model.[17] This work helped create new knowledge and understandings about the NCAA's regulation of intercollegiate sport by identifying issues that made some of its features not only legally untenable but, for many, morally untenable as well. By the time the Supreme Court heard the case of *NCAA v. Alston* in 2021, it unanimously rejected the NCAA's arguments that were based on protecting this notion of amateurism. Instead, one justice in a concurring opinion referred to the model as a "massive money-raising enterprise" built and sustained "on the backs of student athletes who are not fairly compensated."[18]

Our knowledge of intercollegiate sport, therefore, went from valuing the NCAA's system as a "revered tradition" to viewing it—once we took account of the surplus distributions it produced—as, at least in some cases, exploitation. In this way, the period between the Supreme Court's 1984 and its 2021 opinion can be viewed as one of collective consciousness raising that helped us make better sense of the experience, and this altered understanding has been a catalyst for rethinking the law and policy approach to intercollegiate sport.[19]

Several important signs indicate a need to develop more fully our knowledge of youth sport and make better sense of that experience. First are the unequal power dynamics that we know, even under the best of conditions, exist in youth sport. Youth sport is an environment in which one party, the child who participates, does not stand on equal footing with the other actors in the athletic transaction. Thus, youth sport not only features the sponsor-coach-athlete hierarchy but also that of parent-child. Second, we now have much greater awareness of sexual and other forms of abuse in sport, often perpetrated against children. Finally, aside from cases of abuse, the data we have on youth sport tell a confusing story that the activity is, purportedly, beneficial and is an experience in which all children should take part, yet children in youth sport are often overtrained, are overcompeting, and, ultimately, are over it all because of burnout. Moreover, although it is believed to improve societal health and well-being, and although governments strongly endorse participation, many children do not have the opportunity to participate because of cost and lack of accessible programs.

With all this in mind, it is worth considering whether we have not yet been able to make greater sense of the complex phenomenon that is youth sport because we have not fully accounted for what, in the United States, youth sport is and who it is for. As a result, the under-the-radar dynamics that fuel the system continue operating, and the problems with the current approach persist as simply part of the game. These dynamics produce a kind of "asymmetrical disadvantage,"[20] in that children and, in some cases, their parents are unable to contextualize properly the youth sport experience. Children may respond to the challenges of the current system by quitting, concluding that they are not cut out to be athletes. Those who choose never to participate may believe they will not measure up, and so they do not wish to try—or they may internalize the message that they should choose youth sport and then feel like failures if they do not. Children without access to sport may suffer the frustration of seeing a system operate for millions of others, but not them. Moreover, parents may suffer the pain and frustration of engaging their children in a youth sport system that they see as having significant downsides but feel powerless to do anything about it. The gap in our knowledge about youth sport can, therefore, favor those with a stake in the current system's operation.

To be sure, across many academic disciplines, there is considerable research on, for instance, the benefits of physical activity for children and the problems with organized youth sport today. Some researchers have argued, however, that what is needed is an "integrated understanding" of youth sport,[21] and this book seeks more explicitly to put law and policy in the conversation. Specifically, I argue that our current approach to youth sport and its long-recognized challenges are shaped by the taken-for-granted, seemingly benign law and policy background conditions that green-light the system's continued operation. We cannot fully know American youth sport without understanding this link.

This book therefore seeks to go beyond what U.S. youth sport purports to be in order to explain the law and policy foundation for its operation and the distributional outcomes this structure permits. To do so, I employ a range of analytical tools drawn from critical theory, feminist legal theory, philosophy, law and economics, sociology, and political science that can help illuminate how law and policy help construct the youth sport system that operates in the United States today. While law and policy are my central focus, I am not using the tools of legal analysis, for instance, to apply law to the facts of this or that aspect of youth sport, analyze potential areas of liability for youth sport providers, or argue for statutory changes to address specific youth sport issues. This is not meant to be a treatise on the law of youth sport.

I am interested instead in creating a deeper understanding of the activity we call youth sport. The goal is for readers to see that the features of U.S. youth sport are no accident but are instead permitted by the interplay of law and policy choices privileging a range of actors with an interest in whether children take up sport and who claim a stake in the surplus value children's participation generates. This approach involves much more than play.

This book proceeds to explain youth sport by first reviewing what we currently know about it—both what we are told it is and what the relatively limited data show. I call this the traditional discourse around youth sport, and it is important to understand for two reasons. First, it serves as our collective starting point for what we believe we know about youth sport. Second, spotlighting the traditional discourse is important to help us situate what we know about youth sport not as divine truth about the way it must be but as a product of the legal background conditions that have created the current U.S. youth sport environment.

The analysis then moves to exploring the underappreciated but potent legal conditions that permit youth sport to operate as it does: namely, the interplay between the law and policy of sport and the law and policy of the child and family. Key to this is the largely privatized structure of youth sport that Congress endorsed through the Ted Stevens Olympic and Amateur Sports Act, and its rejection of the approach, common throughout the rest of the world, of a government agency with power to regulate. This largely privatized, unregulated system operates in partnership with parents, as the law's emphasis on parental authority and the presumption that parents act in their children's best interests (with the corollary that children have few rights) provides important legal insulation for the operation of youth sport. Finally, the prevailing ideology of our political and historical moment strongly influences the content of the youth sport experience. In this environment, the legal pillars of privatization and parental authority allow the values of the market to define the activity. From these conditions, we can more readily see that U.S. youth sport is, despite the conventional wisdom, a particular approach—and not necessarily the only or even the best method of engaging children in athletics.

With these conditions in mind, I then explain that what is key to fully understanding U.S. youth sport and why the system is resistant to change is tracing the surplus the current model generates and revealing its distributional effects. In doing so, I draw on the work of sports philosophers to demonstrate that the surplus created by children who participate is represented by the difference between *play*, an activity engaged in solely for the child's benefit, and sport, an activity that generates benefits not only for participants but also for others. The benefits are more than monetary, including values such as parental pride, national prestige, and general emotional boosts that persons connected to youth sport enjoy. The youth sport surplus can, therefore, be represented on a continuum, with children increasingly producing benefits for others as they move further away from play-based activities and deeper into the professionalized youth sport model.

Finally, I demonstrate how the surplus created by our approach to youth sport flows to a wide range of stakeholders, from the youth sport industry, sport regulators, and state and local governments to parents, sports fans, future elite athletes, sports medicine practitioners, and society at large. With this knowledge, we can move beyond the assumption that youth sport is somehow separate from systems of power in other sport settings that serve to appropriate value from athletes and, in some cases, lead to athlete harm. We can instead see youth sport as it is, which is a necessary part of the wider global sport system, with the same propensity exhibited by all other levels of sport to generate benefits for some at the expense of those who participate.

With this analysis in mind, I conclude with a hopeful message. As a former child athlete and as a parent who enthusiastically enrolled her children in sport, this book's intent is not to label youth sport as harmful or as an experience to be avoided or eliminated, or to suggest that youth sport providers have improper motives. Instead, I believe that once we truly know youth sport, beyond government slogans and romanticized images, we can finally pursue meaningful attempts at reform. Just as we are doing at the Olympic, Paralympic, and intercollegiate levels, we can seek law and policy changes that recalibrate youth sport in ways that center the well-being of those who participate, instead of perpetuating a system that primarily secures benefits for those who want them to.

CHAPTER ONE

Definitions, History, and Data

> Little league baseball has . . . encouraged our young people to direct their energies in healthful, competitive team sports; and participation in this sport by boys—and by their adult leaders—has helped to develop a feeling of fair play, community spirit and respect for the discipline of rules and decisions.
>
> Proclamation of Dwight Eisenhower establishing National Little League Baseball Week, June 4, 1959

To make greater sense of youth sport, we should begin by reviewing what can be considered our foundational knowledge of the experience. A following brief outline of the prevailing discourse,[1] history, and data on U.S. youth sport locates our collective starting point and sets the stage for understanding how law, policy, and politics shape the current approach.[2]

DISCOURSES OF YOUTH SPORT

All of us to varying degrees are steeped in the traditional discourses of youth sport.[3] An exploration of the activity, therefore, should begin by establishing what we are told about it. In short, the prevailing narrative is that children's participation in sport is highly beneficial and is an important part of a healthy childhood.[4] A relatively recent presidential statement on youth-sport participation represents well this long-held view:

> Each day across our country, thousands of coaches, parents, and teachers work to break down barriers to youth participation in sports to help young people improve their lives and empower them to reach their full potential. Sports and physical activity help children and adolescents improve cardiorespiratory fitness, build strong bones and muscles, lower the likelihood of obesity, reduce symptoms of anxiety and depression, and reduce the risk of

developing chronic health conditions. In addition, organized sports help our youth discover the importance of teamwork, social skills, hard work, determination, and the ability to overcome adversity. Students who participate in sports have up to 40 percent higher test scores and are 15 percent more likely to attend college. Unfortunately, despite the numerous benefits, youth sport participation has been decreasing.[5]

This statement and the many others like it reflect the prevailing conception of youth sport as a benefit that all children and families should seek—and position adults as its benevolent providers. It is also widely accepted that the primary challenges in youth sport are lack of access and, for those who are able to participate, retention, and that both issues should be addressed to increase sustained participation. These messages are evident in documents like the Department of Health and Human Services (HHS) National Youth Sports Strategy (NYSS). The NYSS's "Plan of Action" includes strategies to "keep youth in sports," such as urging "adults" to "encourage" children to "keep trying and keep playing."[6] Such admonishments supply the oft-repeated "truths"[7] about the activity.

DEFINING YOUTH SPORT

The prevailing message about youth sport participation assumes that we all understand what youth sport is, and in some sense we do. However, while there may appear to be a shared understanding of what is meant by the term, *youth sport* does not have a precise, consistent meaning, legally or otherwise. This imprecision has implications for data collection and, ultimately, our ability to make greater sense of the landscape.

To begin, it is helpful to start with what is meant by *sport*. As noted in chapter 6, the meaning of *sport* is something that prompts extensive philosophical debate. Moreover, sociologists explain that defining sport is challenging because "no single definition" can capture sport occurring "in all cultures at all times."[8] As a UNICEF Report on Children and Sport states, "Sport means different things to different people." For purposes of that study, sport was defined as "all forms of physical activity that contribute to physical fitness, mental well-being and social interaction. These include play, recreation, casual, organized or competitive sport, and indigenous sports or games."[9] Under this definition, sport can include, among other things, playground activity, swimming for fun or running for exercise, a pickup street hockey game, dance, or competitive basketball. Other activities, such as chess, cup stacking, or what are known as e-sports, prompt questions about whether they can or should be considered sport.[10]

Because of the many types of activities that can be classified as sport, sociologists generally use a broad definition. Thus, Jay Coakley offers a definition of sport as "physical activities that involve challenges or competitive contests." Coakley notes that this formulation embraces many different ways for individuals to participate, including (among others) organized competitive sports, team sports, individual sports, and collision sports, and different models through which they are conducted.[11]

As Coakley explains, the "power and performance model" of sport that is "dominant" in nations such as the United States is characterized by using physical skill to "push human limits" with the goal to win; demonstrating achievement through winning, which is said to be the result of "hard work and sacrifice"; risking physical harm and maintaining a "play with pain" attitude; seeking to exclude those who do not have sufficient ability; setting up a "chain of command" whereby athletes are controlled by sport sponsors and coaches; and an adversarial mindset in which other competitors are "to be conquered." Coakley points out that, while this model often serves as the benchmark for what counts as an authentic sport experience, other models exist, including one that emphasizes "pleasure and participation." This alternative approach to sport centers personal connection and empowerment, a tone of fun and well-being, inclusiveness, cooperative governance, and viewing competitors as cocreating the experience. While there are many ways to deliver sport, Coakley observes, the power and performance model is the one that enjoys the greatest popular and political support.[12]

We can also define sport with reference to its external goals and how it is delivered. David Ridpath explains that sports development can be broken down by context, so that elite development focuses on training athletes to cultivate talent and, ultimately, produce those with high-performance skills. Outside the elite setting, such as sport for the general population, development could rely on a different structure. Ridpath notes, however, that in the United States, there are "no standard definitions for overall sports-development and sports-delivery processes."[13]

Defining sport is not just an academic issue: it has significant implications for rights and resources and, therefore, poses an important legal question. For instance, in *Biedinger v. Quinnipiac University*, a federal appeals court held that cheer was not, as then operated by the university, a sport that mattered for Title IX purposes. The court specifically noted that the women who participated were "athletically able," but because the NCAA did not recognize it as a varsity sport, and the university did not treat it like one, cheer at that time did not merit legal recognition as a sport for purposes of the university meeting its obligations under Title IX.[14]

In light of the different ways sport itself is conceptualized, we can better appreciate the challenges in establishing a definition for youth sport. From a U.S. law and policy perspective, no clear category of activity is identified as youth sport. The federal government has stated that "youth sport is measured in a variety of ways" and there is no standard description that fully explains it.[15] State statutes reflect this variation. State legislatures provide definitions of youth sport and youth sport organizations for purposes ranging from concussion management, interscholastic sports, encouraging background checks for coaches, sales tax exemptions, and limiting youth sport sponsors' liability. In this context, youth sport is defined in different ways depending on the topic at hand.

For instance, an Illinois statute addressing youth sport concussions refers to a "sponsored youth sports activity" as being "any athletic activity, including practice or competition, for players under the direction of a coach, athletic director, or . . . leader of a youth sports league," with "youth sports league" defined as "any incorporated or unincorporated, for-profit or not-for-profit entity that organizes and provides sponsored youth sports activities" whether a public or private entity, "as well as any amateur athletic organization."[16] The Ohio legislature, for purposes of its youth sports concussion statute, defines "youth athlete" as "an individual who wishes to practice for or compete in athletic activities organized by a youth sports organization," and a "youth sports organization" as "a public or nonpublic entity that organizes an athletic activity" in which the athletes are not older than nineteen and are "required to pay a fee to participate. "[17]

Similarly, for sales tax purposes, Nebraska defines a "youth sports event" as one in which the activity is limited to persons under the age of nineteen.[18]

In contrast, in order to establish the employment status of certain coaches, South Carolina defines a "nonprofit youth sports organization" as one that, among other activities, provides "organized sports programs for persons under twenty-one years of age."[19] Montana, on the other hand, does not refer to an age but instead defines, in its sports-concussion statute, a "youth athlete" as "an active participant in an organized youth athletic activity," and focuses on "competition-oriented programs," with "organized youth athletic activity" defined as an "athletic activity organized or sponsored by a school district, nonpublic school, or youth athletic organization in which the participants are engaged in an athletic game or competition against another team . . . or in preparation for an athletic game or competition against another team, club, or entity."[20] Oregon, in encouraging youth sport sponsors to complete criminal background checks on coaches, states that a "youth sport activity" excludes school-based sports.[21] To encourage economic development through its sports authority districts, Iowa defines youth sport as nonprofessional and distinct from high school sports.[22] Thus, though offering a range of references to youth sport and youth athletes, state statutes clearly provide no consistent definition of the activity.

Also contributing to the challenge of identifying youth sport is the fact that no single governing body coordinates it. Other sport settings may be defined by the association, league, or other entity regulating the activity—a factor that heavily influences the internal rules and external laws that shape the experience. As a result, we can identify a particular type of sport simply by referencing the context in which participation occurs. Thus, there is professional sport, in which athletes are employees or independent contractors who earn income from their participation (e.g., the National Basketball Association and its affiliated teams; the Women's Tennis Association). Intercollegiate and interscholastic sports embed athletics in an educational institution, and participants are students (e.g., the NCAA and its member schools). Participants engage in Olympic and Paralympic Movement sport through the rules and structures created by the International Olympic Committee (IOC), the International Paralympic Committee (IPC), National Olympic Committees, and recognized International Sport Federations that have affiliate national governing bodies (NGBs) in participating countries (e.g., USA Swimming; U.S. Paralympics Cycling).

Youth sport, in contrast, does not have a defined context according to the level of play or a single regulatory body. As Ridpath notes, "What we have is a mishmash of several organizations that are educational, public, and private" that provide sport opportunities for children.[23] As a result, *youth sport* appears to describe only a sport experience in which a person legally a minor is the participant.

Using that as a guidepost, we can look to state law, which sets the age of majority. Almost all states set that age at eighteen,[24] as do countries in most of the world. For instance, under the United Nations Convention on the Rights of the Child, a child is defined as "every human being below the age of eighteen years" unless applicable law specifies otherwise.[25] Accordingly, if we simply use the generally accepted age of majority as a guide, we might define youth sport as any sport engaged in by children under the age of eighteen.

Yet, while eighteen provides a bright line between childhood and legal adulthood, the medical community describes individuals under the age of eighteen with more nuance, distinguishing between their developmental stages. For instance, the American Academy of Pediatrics refers to children, adolescents, and preadolescents.[26] While "under eighteen" as a catchall term obscures the different developmental phases minors go through on their way to legal adulthood, it also obscures the varied experiences that children may be having in sport. Individuals under age eighteen may participate in a variety of sport settings that afford them very different experiences, including more or fewer legal rights. Thus, children may participate in high school sports, they may compete as professionals in some sports, and some are Olympians or Paralympians. In this sense, the term *youth sport* does not necessarily mean sport for beginners or for those who are not performing at the elite level.

Youth sport also lacks precise meaning in that it often is referred to or included within what is called amateur sport. Scholars have noted that *amateur* is a "contested" and "complex" term with deep historical roots,[27] and I do not canvas here the substantial literature on the amateur ideology and its effects. For these purposes, it is enough to state that while there is not one fixed definition, amateurism as a concept arose in nineteenth-century England and was strongly connected to class and gender: an amateur athlete was a "gentleman" who engaged in activities like sport "for the love of them, doing them without reward or material gain, or doing them unprofessionally."[28] This philosophy of sport maintained that pure, authentic sport experiences—and athletes—were those untainted by commercial values.[29] Coakley similarly refers to amateur athletes as those whose eligibility hinges on earning no income in connection with their participation.[30] Moreover, as one legal scholar summed up, "The amateur receives no financial gain of any kind for his athletic prowess whether directly or indirectly. The amateur participates in sport for the glory of sport alone."[31] Sport sponsors, such as those who created the modern version of the Olympic Games and the NCAA's eligibility rules, distilled the concept of amateurism to mean that athletes training and competing in sport must do so without receiving any prohibited financial reward. As a result, one scholar has observed that the concept of amateurism is less about the love of the game than about "labor relations" between athletes and those who control their eligibility.[32]

Much of the athletic structure in the United States, put in place by sponsors such as the NCAA, the Amateur Athletic Union (AAU), and sport national governing bodies, was built on the requirement that participants meet these sponsors' definitions of amateurism, and the term is often used in connection with youth sport. For instance, some state statutes refer to "amateur youth sporting events," which Indiana defines as an event in which the participants are required to be under the age of eighteen and are prohibited from earning "direct or indirect compensation" for demonstrating their athletic skills.[33] Similarly, in exempting coaches from certain taxes, South Dakota refers to "youth or amateur sport," which the legislature defines as "any sport in which the participants are aged nineteen or younger and do not receive compensation for participation."[34]

But the concept of amateurism and rules that purport to describe it are not as tethered to a fixed definition as might be assumed. For instance, the Supreme Court's 2021 opinion in *NCAA v. Alston* stated that "the NCAA's conception of amateurism has changed steadily over the years" and there was no "coherent definition" of it.[35] Similarly, the Ted Stevens Act, which established the modern version of the U.S. Olympic and Paralympic Committee (USOPC), speaks of "amateur athletes" and "amateur athletic competition." The statute defines an "amateur athlete" as "an athlete who meets the eligibility standards established by the national governing body or paralympic sports organization for the sport in which the athlete competes."[36] An amateur athlete under this definition is not necessarily a person who foregoes compensation or who is of specific ability level or age but only one who meets the terms of participation set by the sports regulator. As the U.S. Olympic "Dream Team" history shows, *amateur* in this context now has little independent meaning.

It appears, however, that Congress, in the Ted Stevens Act, intended the term *amateur athletics* to encompass sport for children, as grassroots youth sport participation was considered the base of the Olympic and Paralympic developmental pyramid. For instance, the statute identifies the purposes of the USOPC as, among others, to "develop amateur athletic activity" and encourage "amateur athletic activities" for women, persons with disabilities, and racial and ethnic minorities. In connection with these mandates, the statute defines an "amateur sports organization" as "a not-for-profit corporation, association, or other group . . . that sponsors or arranges an amateur athletic competition."[37] This conception would include several different types of athletic sponsors, including local sport organizations; education-based sports programs, including high school and college sports; adaptive sport organizations; Olympic and Paralympic sport organizations that regulate competitions featured on the Olympic and Paralympic menu; pay-to-play private sport clubs, such as the AAU; charitable community sport organizations such as the YMCA; and sport conducted through the governance of national sport organizations that are not currently part of the Olympic and Paralympic lineup, such as USA Lacrosse.

With the exception of K-12 school-based programs, none of these "amateur" sport settings are explicitly limited to children. However, it is assumed that children are the focus. For example, legislative history connected to the Ted Stevens Act shows how the USOPC requested that Congress provide sufficient federal funding to help generate "public awareness of the benefits of amateur sports and to expose a greater number of our youth to these wholesome activities."[38] Ultimately, then, while we have cultural familiarity with the notion of amateur sport—and, perhaps, some intuitive sense of what is meant by the term—it does not provide a clear-enough meaning for youth sport to enable a full account of the territory.

We might, then, identify youth sport in the United States by what it is not. It is not professional sport (though children under the age of eighteen may in fact be professional athletes). It is not intercollegiate sport (though individuals under age eighteen may participate on such teams). Youth sport also is not free, unsupervised play or physical-literacy instruction. Medical and other researchers have, therefore, defined youth sport with reference to its structure. For instance, the American Academy of Pediatrics' clinical guidance on youth sport defines the activity as organized sport, defined as "physical activity that is directed by adult or youth leaders and involves rules and formal practice and competition. School and club sports are included in this definition. Physical education classes at schools" are not.[39]

Sociologists suggest another method of defining youth sport, by connecting it with its goals. From this perspective, Coakley observes that there are three discernable models for constructing youth sport according to the outcomes to be achieved. First is a "skills and excellence" model that emphasizes development of talent to progress children up a competitive ladder to higher levels of sport. Coakley reports that this approach is the one most emphasized in the United States. The second model has as its goal "physical literacy and lifelong participation." This approach emphasizes children engaging in physical activity to improve overall well-being. The third model has the goal of "personal growth and development." This strategy uses sport as an intervention in the lives of children deemed disadvantaged, such as those living in low-income and urban settings, whom policy makers and others believe could benefit from sport.[40]

Given the many possible conceptions of youth sport and no standard definition, I use the term *youth sport* here to refer to *athletic activity engaged in by persons under the age of eighteen through organized programs at what is often called the grassroots, or entry, level that seek to develop talent through the skills and excellence approach*. This definition captures my intent to analyze the law and policy structure and distributive outcomes of what is, in effect, the children's version of the power and performance model dominating American sport. This environment includes schools; recreational leagues; what private sector sport sponsors label "travel" teams, "club" teams, and "select" teams; and organizations that may or may not be affiliated with the U.S. Olympic and Paralympic Movement. Because youth sport occurring in these different settings may be subject to varying legal treatment, I highlight the differences where relevant.

HISTORY OF YOUTH SPORT

With this conception of youth sport in mind, briefly reviewing the history of its development can help us contextualize what we know about youth sport today. Sport scholars mark the beginning of adult-supervised, organized youth sport in the late 1800s, after the Civil War. As David Wiggins explains, taking a more structured approach to sport was part of the overall modernization of society, and groups such as the Muscular Christians saw sport for children as a way to address the societal transformation brought about by the increasingly industrial economy and immigration.[41] Programs were primarily sponsored by local governments, churches, and schools, and the goal was to teach children American values, keep them out of trouble, and help them become economically productive citizens. Youth sport advocates also hoped to ensure that boys learned masculine values.[42] Youth sport was intended primarily for white boys, not white girls or Black children.[43]

The development of youth sport programs coincided with other Progressive-era reforms aimed at children (further explained in chapter 2). Sport participation, therefore, fit well within the mood of the time, which was to intervene in the lives of children to shape them, save them, protect them, and otherwise ensure they became ideal American citizens in the developing industrial economy. The emergence of youth sport also fit within the overall trajectory of sport, coinciding with the emergence of the concepts of amateurism and the amateur athlete.

Yet, as with other Progressive-era initiatives aimed at children, the youth sport movement had its downsides. Wiggins notes that, as early as the 1920s, "private businessmen" who sold sport participation as a way to keep boys out of trouble and on the path to success were not careful to ensure programs were developmentally appropriate. Programs emphasized competition and winning so that youth sport became "a means to an end rather than an end in itself." Throughout the 1940s and 1950s, Wiggins explains, organized youth sport participation continued growing, prompting critics, including health care and physical education experts, to object that youth sport programs too heavily stressed, among other things, playing to win, sport specialization, and unhealthy levels of training while not ensuring appropriate coaching. Critics argued that these issues, along with increased commercialization and problematic parents, meant that adult-organized youth sport needed reform.[44]

The calls for reform, however, did not lead to substantive change in the way most youth sport programs were conducted. As Wiggins states, by the 1950s, the Cold War prompted significant government concern over children's physical fitness and our military readiness.[45] As discussed in chapter 4, the federal government at this time began strongly encouraging youth sport participation. A 1962 Kennedy administration statement reflects this view: "More than 10 million of our 40 million school children are unable to pass a test which measures only a minimum level of physical fitness, while almost 20 million would be unable to meet the standards set by a more comprehensive test of physical strength and skills. . . . These figures indicate the vast dimensions of a national problem which should be of deep concern to all of us."[46] It was during this time, as scholars have documented, that a "fundamental philosophical and political reorientation" took place, moving from an emphasis on promoting broad-based health and fitness to producing elite athletes. In this period, "the character of children's play" changed.[47] Youth sport programs met the moment and continued to grow,[48] though they remained highly segregated. While Black boys had some access to integrated, private, organized youth sport in northern states, they participated in sport on segregated teams in the South. Girls still largely remained excluded from sport.[49]

During the civil rights movement of the 1960s and early 1970s, courts and legislatures began to grant children some, albeit limited, rights in a variety of areas,[50] and there was a push to include all children in sport. Moreover, the women's rights movement and Title IX, enacted by Congress in 1972 to prohibit discrimination on the basis of sex in federally funded education programs, including school sports programs, opened up sport to much greater numbers of girls. Thus, during the 1970s and 1980s, as Coakley notes, youth sport participation was solidified as an important "part of the process of growing up."[51]

This expansion in youth sport participation coincided with the emergence of sports medicine as a field. The National Athletic Trainers Association and the American College of Sports Medicine were both founded in the 1950s.[52] By the 1990s, Jack Berryman and Roberta Park point out, more than eighty groups claimed involvement in the field, and the medical side of sport was as widely defined as sport itself, with the label "sports medicine" embracing medical support of athletes, "therapeutic exercise," and exercise to prevent disease.[53] Kathleen Bachynski has documented the growth of sports medicine as a discipline in response to the dangers of the game of youth football, explaining that medical supervision, not elimination of the game, became the preferred solution.[54] Sports medicine has developed to the point that team doctors and athletic trainers are now a standard part of professional, intercollegiate, and, increasingly, even some high school sports.[55]

Coakley attributes the growth in organized youth sport participation over the past several decades to a number of factors, including the greater frequency of parents working outside the home and the need to ensure supervision for their children, as well as the continued growth of professional and elite sport as an important part of American society.[56] Today, youth sport programs are usually operated by private, not government, entities, something commonly referred to as the pay-to-play model.[57] Publicly supported free or subsidized recreational youth sport opportunities have largely "disappeared."[58]

THE DATA ON YOUTH SPORT

Growth in participation over the past fifty years has spurred greater scholarly attention to youth sport.[59] However, with such an expansive landscape and no standard definition of what youth sport is,[60] data collection is difficult and findings incomplete. Nevertheless, the government and private entities have attempted to gather information that can help us understand, at a minimum, the scope and trends of U.S. youth sport today.

Data on American youth sport can be situated within the context of the overall global sport industry. Economists estimate that the U.S. sports industry makes up "half the world's sports revenue."[61] Sports-marketing professionals include youth sport within the larger picture of U.S. sports consumption, and they estimate revenue for the entire U.S. sports industry at over $430 billion,[62] with youth sport accounting for $15-$19 billion.[63] Studies show that 86% of Americans think of themselves as sports fans, with 92% of men and 80% of women identifying as such. Nearly 90% of sports fans follow more than one sport or team, and 24% of Americans surveyed label themselves "intense" fans.[64]

Scholars note that developing as a sports fan begins in childhood, and that participating in sport programs which emphasize talent development, competition, and winning leads to a desire to follow elite athletics as an adult.[65] Polls of children ages seven to eleven show that most consider themselves fans of major professional and college sports. Most sports fans report that they are willing to pay to ensure they get the sports content they desire.[66] Moreover, research shows that "about 63 percent of American families whose kids are involved in sports spend from $100 to $499 per child per month on sporting activities. Another 18 percent pay $500 to $999 per month and about 11 percent spend $1,000 to $1,999. And 8 percent report spending $2,000 per month or more, amounting to $24,000 per year."[67]

While there is a considerable amount of information relevant to sports marketing, that on youth sport itself is less fulsome. Youth sport data can be broken down between sport occurring in schools and outside schools. The National Federation of State High School Associations (NFHS) is the private national entity that promotes and supports state high school athletic associations, and as part of this effort, NFHS collects yearly data on interscholastic sports programs. The NFHS reports that high school sports programs, the majority of which are through public schools, serve nearly 8 million adolescents, with 7.9 million boys and girls participating in 2018-19, prior to the COVID-19 pandemic, and 7.6 million in 2021-22. In 2021-22, the number of boys participating was 4,376,582, and the number of girls 3,241,472. The number of participants has grown, particularly for girls, since data were first collected in 1971-72, when the total number of participants was 3,960,932, with slightly more than 3.6 million boys and nearly 300,000 girls.[68] However, in all states, the number of girls who participate in interscholastic sports remains lower than the number of boys.

The NFHS data show that across the country there is a wide variety of sports offered, including traditional ones such as basketball, football, and cross-country and more recent offerings, such as mountain biking and rock climbing. Sixteen different adapted sports were offered for athletes with disabilities, ranging from corn toss and floor hockey to volleyball. The most popular boys' sports, in terms of numbers of participants and school sponsors, are football, basketball, and track and field; the most popular girls' sports are track and field, volleyball, soccer, and basketball.

Researchers have identified important issues within high school sports. For instance, high schools in economically privileged areas offer more and better sport participation opportunities than schools that draw students from "under-resourced households."[69] The Women's Sports Foundation (WSF) further reports that "far fewer athletic opportunities are available to students" in what are defined as "heavily minority schools" than in "heavily white" institutions. Thus, the WSF reports, "in a typical heavily minority school, there are only 25 spots available on sports teams for every 100 students; in a typical heavily white school, there are 58 spots available on sports teams for every 100 students." This disparity also impacts differences in opportunities for boys and girls, as the WSF reveals: "In a typical heavily white high school, girls had 82% of the athletic opportunities that boys had. In a typical heavily minority school, girls had only 67% of the opportunities."[70]

In addition, research by GLSEN (formerly the Gay, Lesbian, and Straight Education Network) focused on the experiences of LGBTQ students in school sports shows that students who identify as LGBTQ often avoid "school spaces associated with sports" because these students feel "unsafe." Thus, over 43% of LGBTQ students reported that they avoided school locker rooms, and 25% avoided school athletic facilities. GLSEN concluded that although LGBTQ students may benefit from school sports participation, they are not as likely to participate, because they view the sports environment as "unsafe and unwelcoming."[71] Researchers similarly report that children with disabilities often find school-based athletics and physical activity programs unwelcoming and inaccessible.[72]

Finally, researchers report that concussions remain a significant issue in high school sports. Most sport concussions occur in youth sport, with traumatic brain injury accounting for "8.9% to 12.6% of all athletic injuries in U.S. high schools." These data, however, are believed to be an underrepresentation of the full problem, as most high schools do not have staff who could accurately identify a concussion injury, because approximately "two-thirds of high schools" do not have a dedicated certified athletic trainer, and as many as one-third have no athletic trainer with experience spotting concussions.[73]

Much of the data on youth sport outside school are collected by the private sector, from groups such as the National Sporting Goods Association, the Sports and Fitness Industry Association,[74] the National Council of Youth Sports, and the Physical Activity Alliance (PAA). The National Council of Youth Sports states that about 60 million children between the ages of six and eighteen participate in youth sport.[75] The PAA gives the United States a grade of *D-* for children's overall physical activity, and a *C* for overall organized sport participation.[76]

The U.S. Department of Health and Human Services reports that, as of 2017, 58% of children aged six to seventeen participated in sport.[77] The HHS Office of Disease Prevention and Health Promotion, through its Healthy People 2030 program, states that in 2020–21 50.7% of children aged six to seventeen participated "on a sports team or took [a] sports lesson" in the previous year, down from 58.4% in 2016–17.[78] All research shows that sport participation rates are lower for girls, racial and ethnic minorities, children from "lower income households," youth with disabilities, and minors who identify as lesbian, gay, bisexual, or transgender.[79] The National Youth Sports Strategy states that 76 percent of children from socioeconomically privileged households participate in sports, while only 41 percent of those from "households at less than 100 percent of the poverty threshold" do.[80]

An Aspen Institute survey shows that the average participating child dedicated nearly twelve hours per week to sport, with some children spending up to sixty hours per week.[81] Research also shows that 80% of parents who enrolled their children in competitive activities, most commonly youth sport, believed that the more they financially invested in their child's participation, the "more they believed it would lead to a future financial payoff."[82]

Youth sport coaching is "dominate[d]" by middle-class men, and most youth sport coaches have no specific education or training, instead relying on their own understandings about sports development.[83] Research from the Aspen Institute found that fewer than half of all coaches are trained in basic first aid and CPR, and only about one-third are trained in injury prevention, concussion management, physical conditioning, sports skills and strategies, or athlete motivation.[84] Sport scholars observe that the "adults who control" youth sport programs generally show little interest in training and learning coaching techniques because of the pervasive view that participation alone leads to positive results.[85]

Researchers also explain that most youth sport experiences are institutionalized, encourage sport specialization, favor those whom coaches believe are the most talented athletes, and exclude those who do not immediately contribute to winning.[86] These attributes are part of what Coakley calls the skills and excellence model and contribute to the professionalization of the activity.[87] Consistent with this approach, the professionalization of youth sport has three primary characteristics: an emphasis on winning and identifying talent, specialization in one sport at a young age, and year-round training.[88]

The NYSS finds significant "barriers to entry" that prevent children from participating in sport, including lack of access to safe play spaces, lack of transportation, cost, and "lack of interest [in] or knowledge" of the benefits.[89] Retention is also an issue, as most children who participate in sport quit.[90] The biggest factor, according to surveys, is "lack of fun"; other factors include long-term participation costs, "stress and burnout," "overuse injuries," and increasingly competitive environments as children progress.[91]

RESEARCH ON THE YOUTH SPORT EXPERIENCE

One of the primary reasons cited by the federal government to encourage sport participation is that consistent exercise provides "indisputable" health benefits.[92] The NYSS lists numerous additional gains from sport participation, ranging from increased "confidence" and "self-esteem" to lower risk of suicide and "improved life skills." The NYSS also states that sport participation by adolescents can bolster mental health, reduce "youth violence and crime," and help "develop social and interpersonal skills," as well as yield "cognitive and academic benefits."[93] The follow-up to the NYSS, the "President's Council on Sports, Fitness, and Nutrition Science Board Report on Youth Sports," states that youth sport provides "distinct societal benefits" and is "one of the most powerful ways to promote health habits for a lifetime."[94] The Centers for Disease Control and Prevention also promotes youth sport as part of its "Active People, Healthy Nation" public health initiative, and the Government Accountability Office issued a report specifically touting the benefits of physical activity and youth sport in curbing childhood obesity, among other short- and long-term gains.[95] Other government reports and initiatives trumpet youth sport as providing numerous benefits to children and highlight youth sport's effectiveness in preparing children to become productive participants in the labor market.[96] Government officials also have cited the benefits of sport to explain the importance of Title IX enforcement and girls' participation in sport.[97]

The American Academy of Pediatrics (AAP), in reviewing the "perceived benefits" of organized youth sport, states that organized youth sport participation "can be" important to children's overall health and well-being. Specifically, the AAP finds, organized sports participation helps build motor skills, and sports participation "is associated" with the development of life skills. Youth sport participation "correlates positively with" mental health, "has a positive influence on" emotional regulation and the development of self-esteem, and "appears to have" an effect on protecting against suicide. The AAP concludes that participation in a sports team also is an important way for children to form their social identities and "may lead to" lifelong health benefits. The AAP also avers that organized youth sport participation can improve well-being for children with disabilities. Moreover, children involved in organized youth sport have higher levels of physical exertion than children who are not athletic, so organized youth sport "may be" a strategy for decreasing childhood obesity.[98]

The AAP report states that participating in organized youth sport risks early sport specialization that leads to overtraining and, eventually, burnout. Scholars and sports medicine specialists have also identified youth sport injuries as a "major public health challenge,"[99] with overuse injuries a "particular concern."[100] A heavy focus on sports can also be socially isolating for the participant and undermine the development of social skills. While adolescents who participate in organized youth sport "appear less likely" to smoke or use illegal drugs, the AAP states that they are "more likely" to consume alcohol, engage in binge drinking, or use performance-enhancing drugs such as anabolic steroids, and adolescent males involved in sport are "more likely" to be prescribed opiate medication and misuse it than peers who are not. Some who participate in certain youth sports "may engage in" what are deemed "unhealthy weight control practices." The AAP notes that some parents and coaches target children who participate in sport with an unhealthy amount of pressure and influence, and that bullying and hazing are "common" in youth sport.[101]

Importantly, the AAP admits that "much of the research" on the benefits of organized youth sport "has largely been observational in nature" so that while it "may show statistically significant correlations, it cannot necessarily establish causality."[102] Further, scholars explain that research on the association between sports participation experiences and positive outcomes such as "building character" has produced "inconsistent and misleading" results due to numerous oversights, including the fact that sport participation is self-selected and the character development that may occur through sport participation may also occur in other activities.[103] As a result, the benefits of organized youth sport participation are not a guaranteed outcome of participation but instead depend on the quality of the experience.[104]

Some of the research needed on youth sport, scholars report, is lacking. While scholarship on youth sport has expanded, Daniel Gould asserts that "it is imperative that the most critical issues involved in youth sport be studied."[105] The Department of Education has noted, for instance, that there is not enough research on ways to increase access to physical activity and sports programs for children with disabilities.[106] Some scholars highlight a continuing need for greater critical analysis of "sport as the universal panacea": this view of sport still prevails though the research to back it up is insufficient. This is especially true where it is not clear which definition of sport is being used.[107] Michael Messner and Michela Musto point out that additional research is needed on children who do not participate in sports.[108] Moreover, scholars suggest that research can provide recommendations for changes to make youth sport safer and to better understand its long-term health effects.[109]

Further, Gould describes a range of psychological issues that need greater research attention, such as how to coach children who lack foundational physical skills and how best to motivate young athletes. Gould also suggests research is needed to understand better how youth sport affects mental health, how to construct youth sport to increase access, and how best to meet children's developmental needs and ensure that positive values and life lessons are in fact transmitted through the youth sport experience, as well as preventing abuse by parents and coaches.[110]

To reach the commonly cited goals of greater participation and retention in youth sport, numerous organizations have called for reform.[111] As the Aspen Institute's Sport and Society program concluded, the United States has "a de facto youth sports system that is dysfunctional at best, broken at worst."[112] In describing U.S. youth sport through its history and the prevailing policy discourse, then, one might say that it is an important part of a healthy childhood and that all children should participate. From the view of the millions of children who quit or never even seek to play, we might simply identify it as not "fun."[113] But understanding grassroots youth sport should not end there. As the following chapters show, our current approach to engaging children in sport is the product of law and policy choices—including the choice *not* to regulate—that provide the "legal permissions" under which our current system operates.[114]

PART II

The Law and Policy Underpinning American Youth Sport

CHAPTER TWO

The Law of the Child and Family

> Physical activity and participation in sports are central to the overall health and wellbeing of children. . . . Sports and physical activity can introduce young people to skills such as teamwork, self-discipline, and sportsmanship. Lack of recreational activity, on the other hand, may contribute to making young people more vulnerable to gangs, drugs, or violence.
>
> "Memorandum on Enhancing Efforts to Promote the Health of Our Young People through Physical Activity and Participation in Sports," President William J. Clinton administration, June 23, 2000

The history, data, and prevailing discourse concerning U.S. youth sport put the family and child at the center of the activity, as it is assumed that sport participation will enter a child's life after families are made aware of the benefits and, therefore, choose to participate. This has important implications for the way the law conceptualizes grassroots youth sport and the government's relationship to it. This chapter, accordingly, begins exploring the full contours of the legal and policy permissions that greenlight our current approach by highlighting the themes in the law concerning the child and family that are most relevant to the youth sport experience.

Several concepts in the law of children and families set the stage for our current system of organized grassroots youth sport and enable it to thrive. First, U.S. law traditionally conceives of the family as a private realm in which the government should usually not interfere. The law, therefore, recognizes parents as having primary authority for raising their children and ensuring their well-being, and presumes that, in most cases, parents act in their children's best interests. Second, the state has the authority to regulate children and families in order to protect children from harm or achieve other policy goals. Finally, I highlight the policy choice to provide children with few legal rights.

LEGAL HISTORY

The U.S. Supreme Court has long held that children's status under the law is "unique" and "special" due to both children's needs and parents' rights.[1] Accordingly, many rights enjoyed by adults are limited for or denied to children.[2] This unique and special status, however, has produced a legal landscape that some scholars assert is complicated to the point that it may even appear "incoherent."[3] To understand the law's approach to children, it is helpful to begin with a brief history of its development.

Huntington and Scott explain that until the late 1800s the state had very little role in regulating the family. Fathers had "property-like" rights over their children and had the power to shape nearly every dimension of their children's lives.[4] Progressive-era reformers argued successfully to change this approach, asserting that the state, acting as parens patrie, should take steps to ensure children's well-being. States responded by enacting initiatives aimed at protecting children, including legal reforms such as juvenile courts, which aimed to reform children, not punish them; laws prohibiting child abuse and harmful child labor; and laws requiring children to attend school. The law at that time manifested an expectation that either parents or the government would promote children's well-being; the law did not recognize children as having their own rights and interests.[5]

During the civil rights era of the 1960s and 1970s, Huntington and Scott explain, reformers sought greater rights for children. Supreme Court decisions reflected the trend, as the Court held that children possessed at least some constitutional protections in, for instance, juvenile court proceedings and political speech in school. States also recognized rights for adolescents, for example, to access certain types of medical care.[6] With the turn of the twenty-first century, scholars also began to highlight the significant harm inflicted by traditional state interventions aimed at "saving" children from what were thought to be dangerous or neglectful family situations, particularly because of the significant race and class bias incorporated in these efforts.[7] As a result, scholars have explained, there has been, and continues to be, considerable rethinking of what was commonly referred to as the "child welfare system," including child removal and foster care.[8]

Scholars assert that what is now emerging is a new law and policy paradigm that has as its central purpose legal regulation of children and families to promote children's "well-being."[9] Yet, while the law of the child and family may currently be trending toward new understandings of children and their needs, youth sport is not part of the conversation. The long-standing belief that sport is part of a good childhood, coupled with traditional legal support for parental authority and respect for family privacy, likely explains why child advocates and scholars have not made youth sport a significant target for policy change.

PARENTAL AUTHORITY IN A PRIVATE SPHERE

Understanding the law of the child begins with appreciating the traditional legal view that the family is a private sphere, with parents in the best position to steward their children's lives. The Supreme Court has emphasized that "the realm of the family" is "private" and the state may not interfere or "question the ability" of parents to determine the particulars of a child's upbringing unless the parent is deemed unfit.[10] This principle rests on two primary justifications: parents are most likely to act in their child's best interests, and parents enjoy an independent, constitutional liberty interest in raising their children.[11]

There are, of course, many benefits to this approach. For instance, scholars have explained that protecting the privacy of the family from state intrusion "provides family members with a place to develop themselves both as an individual and as part of an entity."[12] The private family can help foster the development of the parent-child relationship, usually the most important relationship in a child's life.[13] Further, emphasizing family privacy and integrity as a buffer against state intervention can be critical to protecting families, particularly families of color and families experiencing poverty, from the harm of, for instance, unwarranted child removal.[14] As the Supreme Court stated in *Santosky v. Kramer*, "Freedom of personal choice in matters of family life is a fundamental liberty interest protected by the Fourteenth Amendment."[15]

Thus, the Supreme Court has stated, "for centuries it has been a canon of the common law that parents speak for their minor children."[16] However, while the law's emphasis on family privacy has obvious upsides, there are also drawbacks. Dailey and Rosenbury observe that sweeping parental authority can be traced to "the common law system of coverture," which through the nineteenth century set the rules for legally married men and women.[17] Under the doctrine of coverture, the husband was the only member of a family with legal status, and the law deferred to husbands' authority in the home. As Dailey and Rosenbury explain, fathers during this time legally controlled "almost every aspect of [their] children's lives," including putting them to work, putting daughters into marriages, and punishing them, even, in some states, if such punishment resulted in the child's death.[18]

Frances Olsen observed that these family conditions, occurring in what was purportedly the private family realm, in fact had the endorsement of the state, so that the government's hands-off approach to family matters was hardly neutral. For instance, as nineteenth-century feminists asserted, the state's choice to view the family as "private" and not subject to intervention amounted to granting husbands a right to dominate their wives and, therefore, de facto state approval of the "social roles" within the family that rested on a common understanding of acceptable family operations.[19] The state's preference to stay out of the family, Olsen argues, must therefore be evaluated with reference to these pervasive, though often unstated, assumptions. With this in mind, it is apparent that the state's nonintervention principle in fact worked as a tool to thwart policy initiatives that would change the "status quo," with the status quo then enjoying the appearance of natural inevitability and not a condition permitted by the state's inaction. These critiques of the state's choice to allow families to operate without government interference helped advance women's rights.[20]

The notion of the private family, however, remains firmly in place with respect to children, so the law's reliance on parental authority, scholars argue, acts to assign children "to the private sphere and hence legal obscurity."[21] Thus, today, both parents enjoy a constitutionally protected interest in controlling their child's upbringing.[22] The law assumes that this control benefits children, as parents—because of their love for and deep understanding of them—will naturally advance their children's interests.[23] Relatedly, courts often assume that the interests of parents and their children align.[24] The law in this way also respects what the Supreme Court has recognized as parents' own right to determine how their children are raised.

The Supreme Court has emphasized these rationales in several cases involving children. In *Troxel v. Granville*, the Court's plurality opinion stated that "the interest of parents in the care, custody, and control of their children . . . is perhaps the oldest of the fundamental rights and liberty interests." The Court further averred that "there is a presumption that fit parents act in the best interests of their children."[25] Similarly, in *Parham v. J. R.*, the Court observed: "The law's concept of the family rests on a presumption that parents possess what a child lacks in maturity, experience, and capacity for judgment required for making life's difficult decisions. More important, historically it has recognized that natural bonds of affection lead parents to act in the best interests of their children."[26] The Supreme Court, therefore, considers deference to parents a cornerstone of our commitment to freedom, individual liberty, and keeping the state out of private households.[27] Thus, as scholars point out, while the law has evolved so that children are not their parents' property, the government and courts "generally embrace parental rights as the appropriate starting point for protecting children's interests."[28]

U.S. law, as a result, grants parents "broad legal authority and discretion" to control all aspects of a child's upbringing,[29] so that the emphasis on parental authority covers a wide range of issues, from determining the child's educational path to the exercise of religion.[30] Parents may limit children's access to the internet or other family members and have considerable latitude in disciplining their child, even physically.[31] Parents may put their children of any age to work in family businesses; if children engage in non-family work for pay, parents may take the earnings.[32] Although there are exceptions, parents also have discretion to seek or refuse medical treatment on behalf of a child.[33] As Dailey and Rosenbury summarize, children have "limited to no control over their associates, labor, or bodies."[34]

In sum, the law's emphasis on parental authority is linked to parents' right to raise their children as they choose and is based on the assumption that parents will, in most instances, act in their children's best interests.

Parental authority, then, is often viewed as important to protecting the private family sphere from state intrusion. Some scholars, however, have emphasized that this view "perpetuates the myth" that the state does not already regulate family life.[35]

STATE AUTHORITY TO PROTECT CHILDREN

Although the law endorses parents' right to make a broad range of decisions for their child, the Supreme Court also has recognized a role for the state in protecting a child's well-being. This power stems from states' inherent police powers to advance their citizens' health and welfare and from the states' parens patrie power to protect its vulnerable citizens, including children.[36] The bedrock case of *Prince v. Massachusetts* (1944) illustrates the principle. In *Prince*, a nine-year-old child's aunt and guardian was convicted of violating the state's child labor law by allowing the child to sell magazines on the street in the evening. The Court upheld the conviction, explaining that the state had the power to protect the interests of children and, indeed, "the whole community" by ensuring that children are not subjected to abuse and are provided the support to develop "into free and independent . . . citizens." Thus, while the Court acknowledged that there is a "private realm of family life which the state cannot enter," the state possesses significant power to limit parental authority in order to ensure a children's well-being; thus the family may be regulated when it is in the "public interest."[37]

The Supreme Court has, therefore, upheld regulations that the state promulgates to protect children in a range of areas, even where the risk of harm is not fully clear or might be subject to debate. For instance, in *Ginsberg v. New York* the Supreme Court upheld a state statute that prohibited the sale of material to minors under the age of seventeen that the statute defined as obscene.[38] The Court reasoned that, while parents' authority to rear their children is "basic in the structure of our society," the state also has its own interest in "the well-being of its youth" and protecting children from harm. As Silbaugh points out, this reasoning applies to a host of other state regulations intended to promote children's welfare, such as requiring children to attend school, prohibiting child labor, regulating child marriage, prohibiting and responding to child abuse and neglect, mandating vaccinations, prohibiting the sale of alcohol and tobacco to minors, imposing curfews that prohibit children from being out in public at a certain time without adult supervision, and making bicycle helmets and car seats mandatory.[39]

The Supreme Court also has recognized that parental authority is not absolute in areas where parents have a conflict of interest with their child or otherwise might not act in their child's best interests. For instance, in *Parham*, the Court explained that, while the law presumes parents act in their children's best interests, this is not the end of the analysis, as "experience and reality" may rebut that presumption.[40] The *Parham* case was a challenge to a state procedure permitting parents to commit their child to a psychiatric institution. While emphasizing that parental authority and discretion is most important, the Court noted that parents may not always act in their child's best interest, so that, in cases where the child's physical or mental well-being may be in jeopardy, the state may intervene. As a result, the Court held that parents do not have final, unreviewable authority to commit their child to a mental health facility and that the decision must receive some level of neutral review outside the family. It is clear, then, that while parents have substantial authority to shape their children's upbringing, the state also has a legally recognized interest in protecting and regulating the children who will become our future citizens.

FEW RIGHTS FOR CHILDREN

In addition to the independent interests of parents and the state in shaping children's lives, the law supports the role of parents and the state because children are assumed to lack the maturity to act properly for themselves. For instance, in *Parham*, the Court noted that "most children, even in adolescence, simply are not able to make sound judgments concerning many decisions."[41] Thus, because of children's immaturity, courts and policy makers generally presume that children lack the capacity to make decisions in their best current and future interests, that children are vulnerable and subject to coercion and improper influences, and that greater rights for children would undermine the authority of parents.[42] The result is that the law frequently speaks of children's vulnerability and need for protection from harm and does not grant children the full scope of rights that adults enjoy.

This is evident, for instance, in the fact that the law has long held that contracts entered into by minors are voidable and, therefore, that contractual obligations undertaken by persons under eighteen may be affirmed or rejected when the child reaches adulthood.[43] The reason for this principle, courts explain, is that "the law should protect children from the detrimental consequences of their youthful and improvident acts" and the law should protect children from adults who might take advantage of their "youth and inexperience."[44] In tort law, negligence is usually determined with reference to a child's age, intelligence, and experience, and most states recognize that children under certain ages are not capable of negligence.[45] Moreover, in the criminal law context, the Supreme Court has also recognized that children are different from adults and should enjoy greater protection from the law as a result. For example, the Court has held it unconstitutional to sentence minors to death and to sentence them to mandatory life without parole.[46] In the latter case (*Miller v. Alabama*), the Court cited children's lesser "moral culpability" because of their immaturity, so that a mandatory life sentence was not justified. The Court stated that in considering such a sentence, the state may not adopt procedures for all cases that deem the characteristics of youth and the child's particular circumstances irrelevant.

The Supreme Court has recognized children's lack of maturity and particular vulnerability in the context of sport.[47] In *Brentwood Academy v. Tennessee Secondary School Athletic Association*, the Tennessee high school athletic association, which the Court, in a previous case, held was a state actor subject to constitutional limits, sanctioned a member high school for violating association rules against recruiting players.[48] The violation occurred when the school's football coach sent a letter about spring practices to incoming eighth-grade students who had committed to the school but not yet enrolled. The school challenged the sanction, claiming its communication was protected by the First Amendment. The Court rejected the school's argument, noting that the purpose of the association's rule was, among other things, to protect middle-school students from "exploitation."[49] The Court stated that "the dangers of undue influence and overreaching that exist when a lawyer chases an ambulance are also present when a high-school coach contacts an eighth grader."[50]

Similarly, the Supreme Court in *Santa Fe Independent School District v. Doe* held that it was unconstitutional for a high school to permit students to lead a prayer before football games. The majority opinion emphasized that students, particularly athletes and others who are required to be at the game, would feel "immense social pressure" to join the pregame prayer, which coerced students in attendance to participate in an impermissible act of religious expression.[51]

In recent years, however, the Supreme Court has shown less willingness to recognize children who participate in sport as being particularly subject to coercion and undue influence, at least in the context of an adult's First Amendment Free Exercise and Establishment Clause claim. In *Kennedy v. Bremerton School District,* the Court rejected the argument that a high school football coach should be prohibited from praying at the fifty-yard line after games, and while still on duty, because it could be coercive to athletes.[52] The majority reasoned that there was no evidence students were required to participate. The dissent, however, focused on the vulnerability of children, especially those who participate in sports, stating that a coach has "unique coercive power" over young players, as athletes generally seek the approval of their coaches and could feel pressure to participate in postgame prayer to ensure that they remain in the coach's favor, which could affect allocation of playing time. In a situation where the coach led the prayer ritual immediately after the team concluded a football game, it is not enough, the dissent argued, to state that the coach never required the students to pray.

Like the Court in *Bremerton,* courts and legislatures recognize that individuals under the age of eighteen have, in some contexts, at least some level of maturity. Many states permit adolescents to consent to certain medical treatments or to access birth control.[53] Moreover, despite some constitutional limits, courts and legislatures often recognize that minors may form an intent to commit crimes and, therefore, possess the maturity to be tried as adults.[54] In addition, minors are not presumed to be incapable of waiving their constitutional rights to, for instance, remain silent or obtain legal counsel.[55]

Nevertheless, despite some willingness to accept that children, or at least older adolescents, may have sufficient maturity in certain contexts, and despite the efforts of the children's rights movement, courts and policy makers have not been willing to extend children the full range of rights provided to adults. Scholars note that courts and policy makers remain "ambivalent" about providing children with rights,[56] so that law and policy continues in most cases to conceptualize children as subject to the authority of either their parents or the state.[57] Some scholars have, therefore, characterized children as a "voiceless minority," and, while different approaches have been used to address their interests, providing children with greater rights is generally not one of them, so that the notion of children as subjects in their own right still garners too little attention from courts and legislatures.[58] As Dailey and Rosenbury state, "One need not master the field of children and law to recognize that our legal system denies children basic personal, social, and political rights."[59]

THE CHILD LABOR EXAMPLE

All of these law and policy themes—family privacy, parental and state authority, and few rights for children—produce inconsistencies and tensions in the law of the child and family that contribute to the overall perception that the legal doctrine is almost to the point of being, in some scholars' words, incoherent. This condition is readily apparent in the law and policy approach to child labor.

The history of child labor regulation is complex. At least one historian has observed that the drive to ban child labor and the resulting law and policy framework has its roots in the North-South divide over slavery and the transition to a capitalist, industrial economy.[60] For purposes of the analysis here, I limit the description to aspects of child labor regulation most relevant to understanding the law and policy approach to youth sport.

Child labor statutes, in some respects, take a strong protective approach by not only prohibiting businesses from hiring certain child workers but doing so in most cases without recognizing any authority for parents to permit their child to work outside the home. Legislatures assume that, given the impact on family finances, parents may put their interests and those of the household over their child's, so that employers are not the only parties that potentially could exploit children's work.[61]

However, the law's concern for children being harmed through oppressive work is also limited, so that types of work that may pose some of the greatest risks of harm, such as agriculture, are largely unregulated. As one scholar has observed, "Today, the mention of 'child labor' brings forth nostalgic recollection of a distant struggle and the self-satisfied perception that, at least here in the United States, we have abolished this ancient evil."[62] This is not fully the case.

There is a long history in the United States of children working, and the development of child labor law demonstrates the difficulty of regulating an activity engaged in by children that can be, at its best, an important childhood experience while also posing the risk of, at its worst, significant exploitation and harm. Paid employment may, in many ways, benefit individuals under the age of eighteen by providing income, teaching life lessons, and developing future job skills. Yet child labor can also have significant downsides, including academic harm, workplace health and safety risks, and exposure to sexual harassment or other forms of abuse. Many children have been injured or even killed in the workplace.[63]

The potential harm from children's employment, historians have shown, became an important political issue at the beginning of the twentieth century, with reformers seeking federal and state interventions and even a constitutional amendment.[64] Children regularly worked long hours on family farms, in mines, in factories, and at other hazardous industrial jobs, and, despite the risks, many parents supported their children's work as necessary to earn income for the family. Hugh Hindman estimates that in 1900 over 20% of all children aged ten to fourteen, and a little over 30% of fourteen- and fifteen-year-olds, were in the workforce.[65] Concerns over the nature of this work, along with the drive to put children in school, set child labor among the areas of focus for Progressive-era reforms aimed at children.[66]

In 1938, Congress enacted, and the Supreme Court subsequently upheld, the Fair Labor Standards Act (FLSA), which included a provision prohibiting "oppressive child labor."[67] The purpose of FLSA's child labor provisions, according to the Department of Labor (DOL), is "to ensure that when young people work, the work is safe and does not jeopardize their health, well-being or educational opportunities."[68] Oppressive child labor is defined by both the statute and DOL regulations, and what counts as legally oppressive depends on a combination of a child's age and the type of job.[69] In general, the minimum employment age is sixteen, though some employment of children fourteen to sixteen is permitted if it does not interfere with school.

Children under eighteen may not hold jobs the DOL has deemed hazardous, such as mining, forestry, and working with radioactive materials.[70]

Today, the FLSA and state laws together regulate child labor, and they have made an enormous impact. For instance, Hindman reports that by 1940 only a little over 5% of fourteen- and fifteen-year-olds were in the workforce, and by 1967 the Department of Labor defined the labor force as individuals who are sixteen and older. Much work done by children today is considered beneficial to their development, not oppressive, as children under sixteen often perform work within their communities, such as babysitting, lawn and pet care, or retail or food service. Most of these children work during the summer, and not for an excessive number of hours. Indeed, because of the benefits of such employment, Hindman states, the "child labor problem has been redefined" to focus on *lack of* employment for children, especially those from socioeconomically disadvantaged families.[71]

However, while the FLSA and state statutes had a dramatic impact on protecting children from what may be the worst forms of child labor, gaps in the law mean a significant number of children still engage in burdensome, even dangerous work. First, as Wood points out, while proponents of child labor regulation convinced Congress to legislate toward that end, "child labor was assigned a much narrower definition than reformers sought."[72] The FLSA also does not have a strong mechanism for enforcement, as it provides no private right of action for children or parents to seek redress for violations, and scholars have found DOL and state enforcement mechanisms to be "inadequate."[73] The media have reported that thousands of children are employed illegally, working in hazardous conditions and beyond permissible hour limits, and many states in recent years have taken steps to roll back child labor protections.[74] Children are still employed illegally in the apparel industry, for instance, through home-based sweatshop networks, and one of the most significant child labor issues is work in agriculture. Due to FLSA's exemptions and little state regulation, hundreds of thousands of children, some very young, regularly perform hazardous work in the commercial agriculture industry.[75]

In both agriculture and industry, a significant gap in child labor law is leaving unregulated work that occurs in the privacy of families under the direction of parents. This work is therefore not illegal, but that does not mean it is not, fundamentally, work. As Hindman notes, children's activity does not become labor only when the law declares it as such.[76] In this sense, much work that occurs within the family, either on family farms, family businesses, or elsewhere under the direction of parents, is not considered a policy problem because of the traditional assumption that parents have the authority to direct their children's upbringing and will act in their children's best interests.

Commentators have highlighted this issue in the context of what they identify as a new form of child labor, a form not often considered to be work at all: performing as social media influencers.[77] As observers have pointed out, while social media influencing by children is a relatively new phenomenon, it is similar to what has long occurred in the entertainment industry. Children working as performers were specifically exempted from FLSA, which explicitly does not apply to children "employed as an actor or performer in motion pictures or theatrical productions, or in radio or television productions."[78]

Whereas early drives to regulate child labor focused on harms to children, particularly girls, who associated with performers,[79] Congress had two justifications for ultimately excluding children working as performers from the protection of federal labor law. First, Marina Masterson explains, Congress assumed that acting and performing were not akin to harmful child labor but were experiences that benefited children by allowing them to cultivate their "talents." Child actor Shirley Temple was at the height of her popularity when Congress enacted the FLSA, so that limiting or prohibiting children from working as entertainers would have included her. This policy choice became known as the Shirley Temple Act. States were, therefore, left to determine whether and how to regulate child actors' work, and there is no uniformity. California and New York, for example, provide children with robust protection; other states offer none.[80]

Commentators have pointed out these gaps, as today's social media landscape offers new opportunities for children to perform and this activity is seemingly not covered by state child-actor provisions.[81] Social media influencers are individuals who create interest in a product or service by posting about it on social media. Children under the age of thirteen are a particularly effective type of marketer, now referred to as a "kidfluencer," within the larger, billion-dollar influencer industry. They earn income for creating social media content by, for instance, posting videos of themselves using products such as toys or games, eating certain foods, or wearing certain clothes. The work can be particularly lucrative, as one eight-year-old reportedly earned $26 million in one year for supplying content that reviewed toys.[82]

Parents are key to the kidfluencing arrangement, as they direct nearly every aspect of the exercise, from organizing the photos and filming, to instructing their children in what to do and say and, ultimately, delivering the posted content. Accordingly, unlike a child acting on Broadway or in television or movies, performing for social media content is usually done in the home, not a workplace, and so it occurs under the supervision of parents, not employers. As Masterson explains, "Parents . . . have almost complete control over the conditions of the child's work."[83] In this environment, parents of social media kidfluencers often assert that what their child is doing is not labor but play. Of course, because of the potential earnings involved, this "play" is often assumed to be for a child's future benefit.[84]

Child advocates point out, however, that with social media influencing, what might at one time or in some contexts be considered play is now work, as children must deliver content on a set schedule, with some appearing in hundreds of posts every year. This trend poses the risk that parents will exploit their children by monetizing them or by using their children for fame and celebrity. Advocates cite other risks as well.[85] Further, the law's emphasis on parental authority means parents have considerable freedom to determine how their children interact with social media and who claims the earnings. Assumptions about what counts as burdensome work and what is merely developing children's interests and talents—and the notion that parents have the authority to act in what they view will promote their children's well-being—mean that the thriving kidfluencing industry often operates with little regard to the children at the center of the enterprise.

The example of child labor regulation, then, exemplifies well the competing interests, traditional assumptions, and blind spots in the way law is applied to children. Children working is not in all contexts harmful and, indeed, may provide the young workers with important developmental benefits. Moreover, leaving significant types of work, such as that occurring within the privacy of the family, unregulated, and entrusting parents to ensure their child's welfare, is hardly irrational. Where parents may be strongly incentivized to act in their own self-interest, federal and state governments have, in at least some areas, stepped in and exercised regulatory power.

Yet the child labor example also illustrates the difficulties, as well as our collective conflict of interest, when it comes to the law and policy approach to children. Regulating child labor requires drawing policy lines between what counts as problematic work and what is deemed developmentally appropriate. The lines, of course, are always drawn by adults. With few independent rights of their own, children's lives and labor are therefore subject to power structures they have little ability to change.

The law's treatment of child labor also shows that the presence of parents often converts what may be a significant issue for children's health and well-being into just another private family matter, so that the law, in effect, allows parental authority and a parental presence possibly to erase children's reality. This inevitably leads to regulatory gaps, and it is perhaps not surprising that these gaps are prone to occur in areas where the benefits society enjoys from children's efforts, from harvesting our food to simply entertaining us, may drive our determinations of whether the activity in question fosters or hinders children's well-being.

YOUTH SPORT AND THE LAW OF THE FAMILY AND CHILD

The child labor example shows that the law of the child and family can both ensure children can engage in work experiences with important developmental benefits, *and* leave them potentially exposed to harm. The prevailing approach to youth sport features the same dynamic.

To begin, parental authority certainly extends to the decision to enroll a child in sports, even sports that could cause serious injury or death, such as football, cheerleading, ice hockey, or gymnastics.[86] Sociologists explain that organized grassroots youth sport grew with changes in understandings of and approaches to raising children, including the notion that being a "good parent" includes placing children in adult-led activities in which children can be properly supervised and kept "out of trouble."[87] Youth sport programs, in this view, are thus part of parents' "control over their children."[88]

Legally, then, parents have wide authority over whether and how their children engage with sport. As Carrington and Andrews state, "For the most part we are introduced to certain sports (and not others) at a young age and encouraged to play (or not) by significant others such as parents and teachers and coaches."[89] Parents ultimately decide whether their child will participate and, if so, in which sport, and parents provide the funding, transportation, and other logistical support.[90] In addition to enrolling their children, parents largely decide issues raised by a child's participation in sport. Parents have the authority, for instance, to consent not just to necessary medical treatment for sports injuries but treatment designed to enhance athletic performance. Parents may legally decide to "redshirt" their child—that is, delaying the start of kindergarten or repeating eighth grade to delay entering high school—to get an advantage in sports.[91] Parents have the authority to switch schools, or to remove a child from school altogether and homeschool, in order to seek more or better athletic training.[92] In addition, in most states, parents have the right to waive tort claims on behalf of their children who participate in sport.[93]

While the law gives parents considerable authority over their children's lives, assuming that parents act in their children's interest in the first place, such a presumption, Dailey and Rosenbury note, "reflects an overly romanticized vision of the parent-child relationship." The law's presumption that parents always act in their children's best interests

> wrongly elevates parental love above all else. . . . Parents do provide essential love and care, along with the profound sense of security and safety that only loving caregivers are able to provide. But despite that love, or perhaps because of that love, parents do not always see their children as separate people. . . . [P]arents are sometimes unable to acknowledge how their children's interests may depart from their own, even when parents believe they are acting to further their children's interests. In some circumstances, children may be treated as extensions of parental egos or used to satisfy parental needs and desires.[94]

This is undoubtedly true in youth sport. Katharine Silbaugh describes the issue with respect to statutes meant to address the problem of traumatic brain injuries, or concussions, in youth sport. Researchers have found that children "are especially vulnerable" to sport concussions because of their physical immaturity.[95] Moreover, sport concussions present a particular risk for children because coaches and parents often do not have sufficient skill or knowledge to detect an injury and most children participate in sport without a doctor or athletic trainer present.[96]

Concussions in sport, especially those suffered by children, became a prominent media and policy focus nearly two decades ago when numerous powerful narratives of harm involving both professional and youth players triggered a legislative response.[97] The injured player most widely credited with providing the impetus for state legislation was Zackery Lystedt.[98] In 2006, Lystedt suffered a concussion after making a routine tackle during a school football game. Coaches allowed Lystedt to return to the game, and he suffered a severe brain injury that left him with permanent disabilities. In the years following the injury, the Lystedt family successfully lobbied for passage of the "Lystedt Law" in Washington State, which served as a model for other state statutes.[99] All fifty states and the District of Columbia today have statutes aimed at youth sport concussions.[100]

Youth sport concussion statutes include three core features.[101] The first is promoting awareness. The statutes in varying degrees mandate that athletes, parents, and coaches be educated about the dangers of concussions, such as by signing a concussion awareness form.[102] Second, the laws typically require that an athlete be removed from play if they suffer or are suspected of having suffered a concussion. Finally, the statutes usually mandate that athletes may not return to play fewer than twenty-four hours after being removed for a concussion and not until receiving sufficient medical clearance.[103]

Silbaugh argues that the emphasis on parental authority evident in youth sport concussion statutes protects sports that frequently cause concussions, such as football, more than it serves to protect the children who play.[104] In the youth sport setting, Silbaugh explains, it is widely known that many parents lose their ability to make decisions solely in their child's best interests as they get emotionally involved in the child's sports participation, and most parents do not have the training necessary to diagnose a head injury. Nevertheless, youth sport concussion statutes, in claiming to defer to parental authority, emphasize informing parents of the risks of concussions, not regulating sport. Moreover, Silbaugh points out, notifying parents of the harms of sport concussions may legally strengthen a youth sport sponsor's defense that the parent, on behalf of the child, assumed the risks of the game, including head injury. While numerous states regulate to protect children from various potential harms, including those they assume parental judgment alone would be ineffective in avoiding, states have taken a different approach regarding head injuries in youth sport. Thus, while the statutes may "formally" be aimed at injury prevention, in reality, they operate to protect sports providers from liability. Silbaugh further argues that relying on unchecked parental authority in this context means that "parents contribute legitimacy to children's risk more than they . . . prevent harm" to the children who play.[105]

In sum, the law of the child and family includes powerful doctrines and assumptions that can greatly benefit children and their families. It also includes doctrines and assumptions that can obscure children's real experiences or even contribute to their harm. Because of their lack of full maturity, and without full legal rights of their own, children must rely primarily on parents or guardians and, in some cases, the state to act in their best interests. These circumstances operate in what the law presumes is a protected private family sphere, where rosy views of an alignment of parent and child interests can obscure children's present needs and preferences. Policy makers may, therefore, effectively endorse certain social arrangements by adopting a "neutral" stance and declining to take regulatory action. As the following chapters explain, the romanticized notion of closely aligned child and parent interests works with the law's romanticized vision of sport. Specifically, the law of the family and child and the law of sport together create an environment in which the grassroots youth sport experience is largely left to parents and the private sector to define.

CHAPTER THREE

The Law and Policy Approach to Sport

> As little as possible.
>
> > Senator John McCain, when asked how much the government should be involved in sport (2014)

Like the law and policy of the child and family, the law and policy of sport also gives a green light to the prevailing approach to engaging children in athletics. Legislatures and courts tend to see sport through the same traditional lens that was applied to the family: as a private sphere that the government should not regulate. Legislatures and courts therefore usually take a hands-off approach to sport, preferring instead to defer to private sponsors responsible for managing the operation of the games and the athletes who participate. Yet, while it is clear that sports leagues and administrators would like to avoid *regulation*, they in fact enjoy substantial law and policy *support* for their operations.

THE HANDS-OFF APPROACH

One way to view the law and policy approach to sport is that it takes the perspective of a sports fan. The law has traditionally viewed sport at its best, or at least seen the best in those who sponsor sport for our enjoyment. Baseball's long-standing antitrust exemption provides an abiding example. In 1922, the U.S. Supreme Court ruled unanimously in *Federal Baseball Club v. National League* that the business of professional baseball was not subject to antitrust law, even though Congress had not deemed it exempt.[1] The Court upheld its analysis in 1953, and again in 1972 in *Flood v. Kuhn*. The opinion in

Flood famously begins with an entire section dedicated to recounting the highlights of baseball's beginnings with a list of "celebrated" players who "provided tinder for recaptured thrills, for reminiscence and comparisons, and for conversation and anticipation in-season and off-season." Although the Court held that professional baseball as it then operated would clearly be covered by antitrust law, it stated that it would not subject the game to such scrutiny because of baseball's "unique characteristics and needs."[2]

Similarly, in a Title IX case, a federal appeals court began its opinion by describing the "magic" of college sports for both the athletes who participate and the universities for which they compete. The court stated that colleges and universities "nurture the legends, great or small, inhering in their athletic past, polishing the hardware that adorns field-house trophy cases and reliving heroic exploits in the pages of alumni magazines."[3] Sport is so beloved and so respected as an institution that at least one legal scholar has written about the countless sports references included in judicial opinions.[4]

The law's often romantic view of sport informs a traditional policy preference for the government to stay out of it. Senator McCain's comment reflects the common wisdom the less government involvement, the better—whether by the courts, Congress, state legislatures, or executive branch agencies,[5] and the law of sport generally evidences considerable deference to sports sponsors and regulators to structure and manage the sport experiences within their jurisdictions. A substantial amount of law in areas such as contracts, torts, labor, antitrust, and civil rights certainly applies to sport at all levels. Yet, given how much sport is part of American life, there is surprisingly little law aimed at regulating it. Thus, U.S. sport is usually viewed as a matter of private, individual choice, not public policy.[6]

The hands-off approach to sport has even influenced academic debates about whether sports law is an area of scholarly merit. For instance, in analyzing whether sports law is an academic field, Burlette Carter explains that the area traditionally has been "removed from the things that make a field a field" because of the lack of litigation establishing a specific common law and the lack of "legislative and administrative action" sufficient to create a statutory and regulatory framework. This near vacuum is not an oversight, Carter asserted, but is "deeply rooted in our assumptions about the nature of sports, the nature of those who participate in it, and our resulting treatment of both in the law."⁷

The notion of sport as special, and the government's preference to stay out of it, may be attributed at least in part to the development of much of sport around the concept of amateurism. The Supreme Court has explained that "neither the conduct nor the coordination of amateur sports has been a traditional government function."⁸ Entities such as the NCAA and AAU were formed as private, voluntary organizations that effectively exercised monopoly power over sport within their claimed jurisdictions, and the federal government and courts stayed out of their affairs. The 1930 case of *Gray v. Ferris*, involving a challenge to an AAU athlete-eligibility determination under their rules of amateurism, reflects the sentiment. Highlighting the AAU's important role in coordinating U.S. sport, the New York court stated that the case presented "a question of grave importance" to the AAU's authority. The court predicted that if the athlete plaintiff's request for relief were granted, the "power of the . . . [AAU] to supervise, govern, and protect amateur athletics would be nullified and destroyed."⁹

The hands-off approach was, therefore, not simply a technical legal matter. It was tied to preserving the concept of amateurism and the notion of sport in its purest form as contests between athletes who participated not for commercial reward but for love of the game. In the 1940s, for instance, then-IOC vice president Avery Brundage called the concept of amateurism essential to the existence of the Olympic Games: "Abandonment of these principles will sound the death knell of the Games."¹⁰ Similarly, in *Santee v. Amateur Athletic Union*, which considered an athlete's challenge to an AAU eligibility determination, the New York court described the AAU as "a voluntary, unincorporated association whose objective . . . is to encourage and foster athletics for sport's sake." The court rejected the athlete's request for relief, stating that by violating the AAU's eligibility rules the athlete could not claim "the halo of amateurism."¹¹ After World War II, the government readily supported the AAU and upheld the perspective that Congress and the courts should stay out of its affairs because of Cold War politics; in this way, historian Joseph Turrini explains, the American system could be seen as a "product of capitalist democracy" in contrast to the Soviet Union's communist sport system.¹²

Similarly, the Colorado court in *Bloom v. NCAA* suggested the hands-off approach was also necessary to maintain what is special about sport. In denying the athlete's claim, the court referred to the NCAA using the Supreme Court's oft-quoted language in *NCAA v. Board of Regents*, as "'the guardian of an important American tradition,' namely, 'amateurism in intercollegiate athletics.'" The court further stated that, through the amateur tradition, "college sports provide an important opportunity for teaching people about character, motivation, endurance, loyalty, and the attainment of one's personal best—all qualities of great value in citizens."[13] The federal court of appeals in *Berger v. NCAA* reinforced this view. In denying the athletes' argument that their participation in college sport was covered by the federal Fair Labor Standards Act, the court held that NCAA rules prohibiting college athletes from earning income from their participation "define what it means to be an amateur or a student-athlete, and are therefore essential to the very existence of [intercollegiate sport]."[14]

The hands-off approach is perhaps most prominently evidenced by the fact that, unlike most nations, the United States does not have a ministry, department, or similar government agency tasked with overseeing sport.[15] Congress rejected that approach when it enacted the Ted Stevens Act. While Congress and the courts have historically allowed entities such as the NCAA and AAU to manage sport with little government oversight, Congress finally stepped in when disputes over different sport sponsors' jurisdictions and athlete eligibility rules kept too many talented athletes off teams representing the United States in international competition. In 1975, President Gerald R. Ford established a commission to study and propose solutions to the "problem" of relatively weak U.S. showings in major athletic events, including the Olympics. The President's Commission on Olympic Sports found that the United States was "in severe trouble" in that our sport system did not demonstrate that the United States was "a major power" in international sport, and recommended that Congress take action.[16] Specifically, the commission urged Congress to create a single entity responsible for coordinating Olympic and so-called amateur athletics in the United States, though it explicitly excluded education-based sports programs so that the NCAA could continue regulating intercollegiate sport. The commission made it "'clear that it did not want the Federal Government running amateur athletics.'"[17] The uniquely American approach to U.S. sport that the commission outlined, I have argued elsewhere, manifested the period's "Cold War mentality."[18] The goal was to stimulate "'individual athletic achievement' and Olympic success through the free market and not federal regulation."[19] To achieve this goal, the United States needed to "rely on its greatest strength, free enterprise," to construct a successful sports system.[20]

Congress responded to these recommendations by enacting the Amateur Sports Act of 1978 (later renamed the Ted Stevens Act), in effect codifying the hands-off approach. The statute chartered the modern version of the USOPC as a private, nonprofit patriotic corporation.[21] Congress granted the USOPC—along with private national sport-governing bodies that the USOPC would oversee—with the exclusive authority to regulate U.S. participation in Olympic and Paralympic Movement sport.[22] The Congressional Research Service describes this authority as amounting to a "functional monopoly."[23]

The USOPC is, by design, unique within the worldwide Olympic movement in that it receives no government support.[24] Instead, to fund its ambitious mission, Congress granted the USOPC the "exclusive right" to raise revenue by licensing the Olympic trademarks.[25] Moreover, as chapter 4 discusses further, because of the ultimate connection of grassroots youth participation to our country's success in international sport, Congress made it part of the USOPC mission.[26]

The Ted Stevens Act also provided for limited future government involvement in the U.S. Olympic Movement by circumscribing the role for courts. Congress rejected a proposal to include in the statute an "Amateur Athletes Bill of Rights," and the statute explicitly provides that it creates no legal cause of action that would permit an individual to bring suit for violation of its provisions.[27] It preempts state law claims based on athlete eligibility or related to athlete participation.[28] Instead, disputes under the act are resolved through private arbitration. Congress also denied courts jurisdiction to grant an injunction allowing an athlete to compete in the Olympic Games within twenty-one days of the start of the games.[29] Courts have recognized a cause of action under the statute only in the limited case where athletes or others allege that the USOPC or an NGB have not followed its own rules.[30] Moreover, the Supreme Court has held that, despite its high-profile public purposes, the USOPC is a private entity and not a state actor, so the Constitution does not apply to its actions.[31]

Like the USOPC, the United States Anti-Doping Agency (USADA), the entity that provides performance-enhancing drug testing and results management for U.S. Olympic and Paralympic Movement sports, is also a private, nonprofit corporation and not a government agency.[32] Yet, while USADA was established as a private corporation, both Congress and the executive branch Office of National Drug Control Policy (ONDCP) had a significant role in creating USADA,[33] and Congress provides funding for USADA through public appropriations as part of other antidrug initiatives. Congress "designated" USADA as the "official" anti-doping agency of the U.S. Olympic and Paralympic Movement whose purpose is to ensure that athletes participating in Movement sport, particularly those who represent the United States in international competition, do not use banned, performance-enhancing substances or methods.[34] However, when the agency was formed, the ONDCP stated that, while USADA needed an elevated status in the U.S. Olympic and Paralympic Movement, the government wanted to "be very respectful of the notion of amateur sports and the independence of amateur sports from Federal intervention."[35] As with the USOPC, athlete disputes with USADA are largely kept out of court and instead must be brought to private binding arbitration.[36] Courts have also assumed that USADA, like the USOPC, is not a state actor subject to constitutional restraint.[37]

In 2017, Congress designated the U.S. Center for SafeSport (known as SafeSport), also a nonprofit private corporation, as the entity responsible for preventing all forms of athlete abuse in U.S. Olympic and Paralympic Movement sport, as well as investigating and resolving claims. As with USADA, matters arising under the SafeSport Code are sent to private arbitration, and SafeSport is largely immune from lawsuits.[38]

Intercollegiate and interscholastic sports programs also enjoy considerable freedom from government regulation, allowing voluntary associations such as the NCAA and the NFHS and their member institutions to largely set the agenda for structuring education-based sports programs and regulating the athlete experience.[39] The hands-off approach in this area has persisted for decades and through numerous calls for government action to address serious issues of athlete harm. In 1905 President Theodore Roosevelt responded to a crisis of violence and deaths in college football by convening a White House summit to urge colleges and universities to regulate themselves and make the game safer.[40] In 2009, in congressional hearings on the issue of concussions in football, several members made clear that the government could encourage discussion of the issue but should not regulate. As one U.S. representative warned, "We should also avoid the temptation to legislate in this area . . . we cannot legislate the elimination of injuries from the games without eliminating the games themselves."[41] In the same hearing, another representative condemned legislation that would "prohibit certain types of plays from taking place in high-school or college or major-league athletics" as a "kind of micromanagement of American athletics" that should be avoided. In 2014 hearings on college sports and the well-being of college athletes, one senator summed up the position of Congress when he said that "it is my hope that the NCAA, its member institutions . . . and other stakeholders will seek solutions . . . [that will] preserve amateurism in collegiate athletics. This is an area where . . . the solutions are most likely to come from [the NCAA]."[42]

Like Congress, courts also often take a hands-off approach to regulating sports by frequently upholding the decisions of sports sponsors. Athletes are highly regulated within sports. Sports are institutionalized, with rules establishing criteria for eligibility,[43] the rules of the game, the conduct of competitions,[44] and, in many contexts, the range of acceptable athlete behavior even when they are not participating.[45] In general, the legal basis for sports regulators' authority is consent, effectuated through private contracts so that athletes can take or leave the terms of play.[46] Courts therefore usually defer to sports sponsors to determine eligibility and the conditions of participation, and, as with the USOPC, athletes are generally limited to claims that the relevant sport regulator has failed to follow its own rules.[47] Likewise, the Supreme Court has held that the NCAA is not a state actor and, therefore, not subject to constitutional limits.[48]

Similarly, in cases involving athletes' civil rights, courts also often defer to sports sponsors. In *Knapp v. Northwestern University*, for instance, a college basketball player brought a claim under the Rehabilitation Act for discrimination on the basis of disability, challenging the school's determination that he was not eligible to participate because of a potentially fatal heart ailment.

Although the athlete and his parents were willing to assume the risk of harm, the federal court of appeals stated that "medical determinations of this sort are best left to team doctors and universities" and that "the university has the right to determine that an individual is not otherwise medically qualified to play."[49] Thus, while the court held that the Rehabilitation Act applied to Northwestern University, it found that the university did not violate the act, because the court deferred to the university's conclusion that Knapp was not an "otherwise qualified" athlete.[50] Other cases uphold the same ruling.[51]

Like the court in *Knapp*, the U.S. court of appeals in *Hollonbeck v. USOC* interpreted the Rehabilitation Act in a way that deferred to the USOPC's management of the Paralympic program. In *Hollonbeck*, Paralympic athletes alleged discrimination on the basis of their disabilities because the USOPC did not provide them with the same benefits it provided to Olympic athletes. The court held that it was permissible to treat Paralympic athletes differently because they were not part of the same "program" as Olympic Movement athletes. "We sympathize with Plaintiffs' efforts to obtain benefits similar to those received by their Olympic counterparts," the court stated. "However, . . . Plaintiffs should seek a remedy with the legislative or executive branches, not the courts." The dissent, however, asserted that a "simple application of the plain language" of the relevant statute "forbids . . . exactly what has occurred and is occurring here."[52]

Finally, courts are careful in applying tort law in the context of sport. With respect to injuries to sports spectators, most courts adopt a "limited duty" rule, so that stadium operators have no duty to warn or protect fans from what courts deem to be the inherent risks of attending a sporting event, such as being hit with a flying ball or hockey puck. Some states have gone further and enacted statutes to limit the liability of stadium owners.[53]

Similarly, tort claims brought by athletes are also subject to a higher liability standard. The general rule for claims brought by an athlete against a coparticipant is that there can be no recovery unless the injured athlete can show the fellow participant intended to injure or acted recklessly.[54] Showing that a fellow player violated the particular sport's rules is not sufficient.[55] For instance, as the court stated in *Avila v. Citrus Community College District*, "for better or worse, being intentionally thrown at is a fundamental part and inherent risk of the sport of baseball."[56]

Claims brought by athletes against sport sponsors also face a higher standard, so that, in many instances, sport sponsors have no duty to protect an athlete from harm. As the California court stated in *Knight v. Jewett*, "Conditions or conduct that otherwise might be viewed as dangerous often are an integral part of the sport itself."[57] The general rule is that, under the doctrine of assumption of the risk, sport sponsors do not owe a duty to participants to protect them from the risks of injury inherent to the particular sport, as the purpose of the assumption of the risk doctrine is "to avoid imposing a duty which might chill vigorous participation in [sport] and thereby alter its fundamental nature."[58]

Courts also have hesitated to impose liability on sport regulators even when it appears the sport sponsor has sought to protect athletes from the harm at issue. The opinion in *McCants v. NCAA* is illustrative. In that case, athletes brought a class action suit against the NCAA for, among other things, negligence and breach of fiduciary duty. The students alleged that while athletes at the University of North Carolina they were steered to courses characterized as "academically unsound," in that the classes did not meet and had no faculty instruction. The athletes argued that the NCAA had a duty to ensure that they received adequate educational opportunities. Despite citing numerous NCAA statements about its commitment to athletes' educational success, the court held the students were unable to show the NCAA had a legal duty to ensure they were not the victims of academic fraud. The court noted that the athletes' complaint "raise[d] policy rather than legal issues."[59]

To be sure, the government's reflex to stay out of sport is not absolute. Although not the general trend, some plaintiffs bringing tort claims in the sports context are able to establish a duty of care and convince the court that the defendant breached it.[60] In addition, the Supreme Court in high-profile cases has rejected sports sponsors' claims for deference. For instance, in *PGA Tour v. Martin*, professional golfer Casey Martin sued the PGA Tour under the Americans with Disabilities Act (ADA), seeking the right to use a golf cart in competition due to a disability that affected his ability to walk the course. The Supreme Court interpreted the statute to encompass PGA Tour events and held that Martin was entitled to use the cart.[61] More recently, in *NCAA v. Alston*, a group of athletes challenged NCAA rules that limited the amount of education-related compensation and benefits that schools may provide to athletes. The Supreme Court unanimously held that the NCAA's rules violated antitrust law.[62]

While both *Martin* and *Alston* can be read as prominent exceptions to the government's hands-off approach, they also serve as examples of what this posture yields. In *Martin*, the PGA Tour argued that, although Congress did not provide an exemption for professional sports in the statute, it was not covered by the ADA. In this way, the PGA Tour was using the same legal strategy successfully employed by Major League Baseball (MLB) in arguing that its game was, in effect, above federal law. When the Supreme Court rejected that argument, the PGA Tour had little evidence to counter Martin's claim that his disability legally entitled him to use a cart. Moreover, while notable, the impact of the decision is limited to the unique facts of that case. Shaping private behavior through litigation is an indirect, and relatively light, form of regulation, and, indeed, the results in *Martin* have not meaningfully changed the operation of professional sport.

As with the argument made by the PGA Tour in *Martin*, the Supreme Court in *Alston* noted that the NCAA in effect sought "immunity from the normal operation of the antitrust laws." The NCAA's argument was grounded in decades of lower-court decisions providing exactly such de facto immunity by allowing the association to dictate the terms of athletes' experience without antitrust liability. Yet, here too, once the Court ruled that antitrust law in fact did apply, the NCAA had little convincing evidence that its restraint on athletes' education-related compensation was necessary for the operation of college sport—even under the more deferential, "rule of reason" antitrust standard that the courts applied.

While the impact of the *Alston* case was broader than *Martin* in that it invalidated an NCAA rule that applied to numerous athletes, it is still not as significant as what Congress could achieve if it directly regulated college sport—and is not even as significant as it might have been within the context of that case. In affirming the lower-court decisions in the case, the Supreme Court noted that "the district court extended the NCAA considerable leeway" and "left the NCAA considerable flexibility."[63] The Court specifically noted that the NCAA still had the authority to prohibit schools from providing athletes with compensation or benefits not linked to education. Both

Martin and *Alston*, therefore, demonstrate how entrenched the hands-off approach is. In both cases, what looked like significant interventions in the workings of sport was actually routine, limited application of federal law.

A similar phenomenon is evident in another recent example of an apparent break from the hands-off approach: state laws aimed at restoring athletes' rights to their name, image, and likeness (NIL). For decades, the NCAA had rules prohibiting college athletes from earning income in connection with their sports participation, including income related to the use of the athlete's NIL. In 2019 California enacted a statute permitting athletes to earn NIL income,[64] and numerous states soon followed suit. There are currently at least thirty-two states with statutes permitting intercollegiate athletes to earn income from their NIL.[65]

Yet, once again, while NCAA arguments have focused on these statutes as an unwelcome intrusion that threatens college sport, the statutes are akin to the *Martin* and *Alston* examples. NIL rights are created by state law, and all state citizens may claim them—they are not rights established by the NCAA. Therefore, state statutes that permit athletes to earn income from their NIL, like other, nonathlete students, are not regulating the NCAA as much as they are restoring rights that the NCAA forced students to relinquish as a condition of eligibility. The statutes also are not the final say on the matter. The NCAA currently is lobbying Congress for legislation that would limit athlete NIL activity and provide it with antitrust immunity.

Beyond these examples, however, Congress and the executive branch have recently shown a willingness to intervene more directly in sport to respond to scandal or crisis. For instance, Congress enacted two statutes in response to revelations of widespread sexual abuse of athletes across numerous Olympic and Paralympic sports, including that perpetrated by Larry Nassar, the USA Gymnastics team doctor who sexually abused hundreds of gymnasts under his care. The first was the Protecting Young Victims from Sexual Abuse and SafeSport Authorization Act of 2017. The statute requires an expansive list of covered adults to report any suspicions of child abuse to the relevant authorities. The statute also established SafeSport as an independent, private corporation with jurisdiction over the U.S. Olympic and Paralympic Movement with respect to protecting athletes from all forms of abuse, including sexual abuse, bullying, and hazing. The statute tasked SafeSport with developing training and policies and providing oversight in an effort to prevent abuse in the U.S. Olympic and Paralympic Movement and charged the corporation with investigating and resolving claims of abuse.

Congress followed the Protecting Young Victims Act with the Empowering Olympic, Paralympic, and Amateur Athletes Act of 2020. This statute mandates greater athlete representation on USOPC and NGB boards and requires the USOPC to submit annual reports to Congress and undergo annual financial audits. Congress also changed the USOPC's obligations to NGBs so that the USOPC no longer simply "recognize[s]" a single NGB for a sport, but "certif[ies]" each NGB every four years to ensure these governing entities meet their obligations under the Ted Stevens Act. The statute grants Congress the authority to dissolve the USOPC's board of directors and terminate its recognition of an NGB. To combat athlete abuse in the Olympic and Paralympic Movement, the act requires the USOPC to provide $20 million per year to help fund SafeSport. Congress also required SafeSport to conduct annual audits of the USOPC and each NGB to ensure compliance with SafeSport policies, as well as to provide an annual report to Congress.[66] With these statutes Congress added two additional purposes to the USOPC's mission: "to promote a safe environment in sports that is free from abuse"[67] and "to effectively oversee the national governing bodies."[68]

Finally, Congress enacted the Equal Pay for Team USA Act in 2022 in response to the widely publicized suit brought by members of the women's U.S. National Soccer team alleging sex discrimination because their pay, travel accommodations, and other benefits were far less generous than those provided to their male counterparts. The statute requires the USOPC and sport NGBs to provide male and female athletes representing the United States in international competition in the same sport "equivalent and nondiscriminatory" pay, medical care, and other benefits.

The ultimate effect of these reforms is not yet clear. Critics have pointed out problems with SafeSport's operations that have undercut its efficacy, and previous attempts to restructure the USOPC board, for instance, have not had the hoped-for impact. Moreover, the difference between U.S. Soccer's national team model and the approach used in other sports could make the Equal Pay for Team USA Act's influence more symbolic than transformative. At a minimum, however, these statutes show the federal government's continued willingness to respond to crises in U.S. Olympic and Paralympic Movement sport. Yet that response reinforces the approach taken in the 1970s with the original Ted Stevens Act, in that the recent reforms preserve the existing privatized sport structure, with few new rights for athletes and little systematic oversight of the USOPC, USADA, or SafeSport.

Another apparent example of the government not taking the reflexive, hands-off approach is the National Labor Relations Board (NLRB) General Counsel's decision in 2021 to treat certain college athletes as employees under the National Labor Relations Act (NLRA), which protects workers' rights to unionize and engage in collective bargaining with employers. In 2015, the NLRB responded to college football players' attempt to unionize with the traditional hands-off approach.[69] While a regional director determined that Northwestern University's scholarship football players were "employees" within the meaning of the NLRA, the NLRB rejected the unionization effort, stating that, "even if the scholarship players were statutory employees, . . . we have concluded that it will not effectuate the policies of the Act to assert jurisdiction in this case." The NLRB cited the unique nature of league sports, the NCAA's oversight of college sports, and the reforms the NCAA had undertaken to address the needs of scholarship football players, so that asserting jurisdiction "would not promote stability in labor relations."[70]

In 2021, however, the NLRB General Counsel clarified in a memorandum that some college athletes should be considered employees under the NLRA. In keeping with this position, the NLRB General Counsel brought unfair-labor practice charges against the NCAA and a handful of universities and conferences.[71] While the NLRB General Counsel's recent position is important and noteworthy, ultimately it may not be sustained. The NCAA is lobbying for an explicit exemption from the NLRA, and the political composition of the NLRB means that this current position may be rescinded with a change in presidential administrations.

Thus, despite these notable exceptions, the government's hands-off reflex remains a powerful presumption in sport today. It is perhaps also not surprising that the hands-off approach is most often supported by those who control the games and determine an athlete's eligibility to play. Sport sponsors assert several reasons why they should be insulated from government regulation. First, with respect to sports programs in schools, sponsors argue that courts and legislatures should not interfere with the "educational process."[72] Second, sports sponsors often predict that regulation will make sports administration too costly, thereby limiting participation opportunities.[73] Finally, sponsors argue that greater legal regulation could make sport too difficult to administer and will thereby threaten its very existence.[74]

The argument that legislative or court intervention in sport could threaten the games as we know them was vividly articulated by Justice Antonin Scalia in his dissenting opinion in *PGA Tour v. Martin*. In objecting to the majority view that the ADA applied to the PGA Tour and that Martin carried his legal burden of demonstrating he had a right to use a cart, Justice Scalia envisioned a bleak future for sport. He foresaw the Court's opinion spawning numerous cases of athletes seeking special accommodations, to the point that "one can envision the parents of a Little League player with attention deficit disorder trying to convince a judge that their son's disability makes it 25% more difficult to hit a pitched ball" so that a court could grant the child four strikes instead of the usual three.[75] The Court's ruling would mean that sport would be fundamentally changed, Scalia argued, to the point that "everyone gets to play by individualized rules" so that no participant's "lack of ability" will make a difference.[76] While these arguments are frequently advanced, there is little evidence that greater regulation would reduce sports opportunities or significantly impede sport sponsors' ability to implement their programs. Little League baseball remains, as ever, a three-strike game.

Significantly, cases like *Martin* and *Alston* show that the hands-off argument generally is not one advanced by sport participants, as it is not a position that usually results in more rights or produces greater protections for athletes. As with the law of the family and child, the government's purportedly neutral, noninterventionist approach to sport does not necessarily make *all* parties better off; instead, it operates to perpetuate existing power structures and understandings of the way sport should be.

LAW IN SERVICE OF SPORT

There are, of course, other examples that might appear to be exceptions to the government's hands-off approach, situations where law is specifically directed to sport or law is applied by courts to sports leagues or regulators' actions. However, a closer look shows that this use of law is usually aimed at facilitating the growth of sports leagues and programs and enhancing their commercial legitimacy—and generally is welcomed by sports sponsors.[77]

Law was used in several early instances to promote the professional sports industry. As previously mentioned, the Supreme Court interpreted antitrust law to give MLB a sweeping exemption from the law.[78] Similarly, federal statutes allowing for pooling of broadcasting rights and the merger of the National Football League (NFL) and American Football League (AFL) were meant to facilitate the growth and protect the integrity of professional sports, as are statutes that prohibit sports bribery.[79] Congress and individual states have also enacted laws to aid NCAA member institutions through the Sports Agent Responsibility and Trust Act and the Uniform Athlete Agent Act.[80] State and local governments often provide public funding for the development of professional sports facilities and sports programs that operate in schools.

Congress and state legislatures have also enacted laws that regulate specific sports, such as boxing, mixed martial arts, and horse racing,[81] as well as those that ban use of performance-enhancing drugs. While these initiatives in some sense protect the health and safety of participants, an additional and important motivation is to make the games safer in order to enhance their commercial legitimacy[82] and to preserve the commercial viability of sport as a forum for "fair" competition.

Moreover, the efforts to combat doping and athlete abuse in Olympic and Paralympic Movement sport can also be viewed as the use of law in the service of sport and, in this way, are not as much of an exception to the hands-off approach as they might appear. First, USADA's jurisdiction is limited to athletes in the Olympic and Paralympic Movement and does not include professional, intercollegiate, or high school sports.[83] Further, while a reason for creating USADA may have been to protect athletes, the establishment of an anti-doping program was crucial to legitimizing the United States' participation in international sport.[84] Notably, the primary burden of anti-doping regulation is carried not by sport regulators but by athletes.

Like USADA, SafeSport has a jurisdiction limited to the U.S. Olympic and Paralympic Movement. While not insignificant, SafeSport's policies do not reach the many sport organizations that are unaffiliated with a sport NGB, such as NCAA member institutions, high schools, or non-NGB-affiliated youth sport providers. Also like USADA, SafeSport has the important effect of shoring up the legitimacy of U.S. Olympic and Paralympic Movement sport, which was badly damaged after the Larry Nassar-USA Gymnastics scandal and numerous other reports of athlete abuse that long plagued the USOPC and NGBs. Accordingly, much law that might in one sense be viewed as regulating sport often has the more substantial effect of advancing the goals of sport sponsors and enhancing the legitimacy of current systems.

The federal Curt Flood Act, enacted in 1998, illustrates this well. As previously discussed, when the Supreme Court created, and continued in subsequent cases to uphold, an antitrust exemption for MLB, its impact on players was enormous. The facts of Curt Flood's Supreme Court case detail the stakes. In *Flood v. Kuhn,* Flood challenged under federal antitrust law what was known as baseball's reserve clause, which meant players were legally bound to the team that first signed them; there was no possibility of free agency that would permit players to make a deal with a new team for a better salary and working conditions. After being assigned to a new team in a trade about which he was not consulted, and with no ability to seek other offers, Flood had to choose between playing for the new team or not at all. He sued MLB, arguing that the reserve clause violated numerous federal and state statutes and the Thirteenth Amendment's prohibition on involuntary servitude. In denying his claim, the Supreme Court stated that the remedy was with Congress.

Notably, the dissent in *Flood* asserted that the majority had possibly become so "enamored of athletics" that it had lost sight of the real issue, which was that it was the Court's actions in continuing to exempt MLB owners from antitrust law, even when legally it was unwarranted, that rendered the players politically isolated and "impotent."[85] The hands-off view adopted by the majority, the dissent argued, was in this way hardly neutral. Although baseball's reserve clause was later discontinued and players now have the benefit of a union, MLB's antitrust exemption continues, except to the extent Congress changed it through the Curt Flood Act.

Characterized as a win for players and strongly supported by MLB, the act grants major league players the same rights under antitrust law that any other professional athletes have. It does so by amending the relevant antitrust statute to make clear that issues related to players' employment at the MLB level "are subject to the antitrust laws to the same extent" as other professional players.[86] While this language supplants, to some extent, the Supreme Court's *Flood v. Kuhn* holding, its legal effect in practice is limited. In the years since the Court's decision in *Flood*, another antitrust exemption developed through case law—referred to as the nonstatutory labor exemption—which prevents athletes who are part of a labor union from bringing an antitrust claim. The exemption reflects a policy preference for protecting the collective bargaining process and the agreements over workplace issues that result, instead of allowing parties to resort to antitrust law remedies not so well suited to that end.

In reality, then, unionized MLB players are still prevented from bringing suit under antitrust law, so that MLB will likely face no new liability as a result of the Curt Flood Act. Perhaps most important, the bulk of the Curt Flood Act is dedicated to reaffirming MLB's existing exemption from antitrust law for every issue other than major league player employment, including those involving minor league players, umpires, and franchise relocation. While not without some positives for some players, the statute is, therefore, another example of law in service of a sports league.

Even where law directed at sport is not clearly advancing the interests of sport sponsors, it still evidences a high degree of deference to sport regulators. Perhaps the highest-profile example of law directed at sport is Title IX. Although the statute itself does not mention sports,[87] the regulations and policy clarifications that constitute the legal substance of Title IX all cover education-based sports programs. Title IX's central purpose is to require institutions to provide "equal athletic opportunities" for male and female students,[88] and its impact on education-based sports programs is undeniable.[89] However, even Title IX, which is considered one of the most important government initiatives ever aimed at U.S. sport, does not regulate the actual content of sports programs themselves. Instead, the law requires that programs meet the regulatory definition of "equal athletic opportunity" for men and women. Title IX does not require covered educational programs to give preferential treatment to women[90] or have the same sports teams for men and women, or require institutions to spend equally on men and women's sports. It requires only that where a school has separate programs for men and women those opportunities must meet the regulatory definition of equitable.[91] Accordingly, while the equality mandate itself has been defined through case law and Title IX's implementing regulations and policy clarifications, the content of that mandate is left to be defined by the institutions themselves.[92] And, of course, the full impact of Title IX has never been realized, because of lack of compliance and robust enforcement.

The foregoing explanation of the government's hands-off approach is not meant to suggest, however, that it is wholly without any benefit or justification. Government involvement in sport at its extreme brings to mind Soviet-era sportive nationalism, whereby Eastern Bloc governments invested heavily in sports as a means of cultivating international influence and prestige, regardless of the costs to athletes.[93] In addition, a case can certainly be made that voluntary associations and private governing bodies generally do an adequate job prescribing rules for competition, hosting sporting events, and enforcing rules of eligibility and play. Thus, the USOPC's private dispute resolution procedures may provide a faster and cheaper resolution process than a federal or state court claim. It is also not hard to see that a heightened standard for recovery in tort claims involving sport can, in some cases, be important in accounting for the physical nature of participation.

The hands-off approach may also have additional justifications depending on the level of sport. For instance, the values underlying participation in professional sports are consistent with their mission: an emphasis on winning, fan appeal, and discrimination in favor of the most talented athletes. These values support the commercial interests of the professional sports enterprise, and a professional league is not likely to succeed without emphasizing them. Because professional sport is a business, leagues and teams should be treated like firms in other industries. In addition, concerns over the conditions under which athletes perform can be addressed through the collective bargaining process and existing legal remedies for employees, such as workers' compensation laws.[94] As the Supreme Court stated in *Brown v. Pro Football, Inc.*, collective bargaining is important to workplace "harmony," so that taking a hands-off approach by disallowing athletes' antitrust claims can empower the parties to work together to find the best solutions.[95] Thus, while there are arguments for additional regulation at the professional level regarding specific issues, such as MLB's monopoly power, because of their commercial nature and the legal protections available to the athlete-employees, a strong argument can be made that the hands-off approach to professional sport makes for sound policy.

The hands-off law and policy approach should not, however, be so readily applied to other sports settings. As the context shifts from professional sport to Olympic and Paralympic, intercollegiate, interscholastic, and grassroots youth levels, the deference to private sports regulators and commercial impulses warrants greater scrutiny, as such deference can facilitate the professionalization of sport outside the professional context and a "money and medals" attitude that neglects other important values. A more nuanced approach is, therefore, warranted.

As the following chapter explains, a nuanced approach is not what we take in connection with the law and policy of youth sport. The traditional rosy, romanticized view of sport, and the resulting hands-off regulatory reflex, leads to the same pattern identified in sport generally: protecting the games as currently constructed, privileging sport sponsors, and promoting the view that sport in all its forms is inherently good.

CHAPTER FOUR

The Law and Policy Approach to Youth Sport

> A primary justification for limiting liability in the sports context is to avoid fundamentally altering, or discouraging participation in, the sport at issue.
>
> *Karas v. Strevell*, 884 N.E.2d 122 (Ill. 2008)

Youth sport operates at the crossroads of the law of the child and family and the law of sport. As the previous chapters explain, these two areas are shaped by formidable assumptions that impact children's sport experience. The law assumes that sport sponsors are entitled to deference because they are the stewards of what makes the games special. Moreover, while the law assumes parents act in the best interests of their children, as explained below, the law also assumes that the interests of children are advanced by and aligned with the interests of sport sponsors. With these understandings, we can appreciate the final piece of the law and policy that greenlight our current approach. This is the preference for encouraging participation in, but generally not funding or regulating, grassroots youth sport.

To begin, as chapter 1 explains, no single entity has jurisdiction over youth sport. Therefore, just as it is difficult even to define youth sport, it is also challenging to map in full the legal and policy terrain. It is perhaps most useful to start with what, from a law and policy standpoint, grassroots youth sport is not. Broadly speaking, law and policy aimed at grassroots youth sport may target two areas: providing opportunities to participate and regulating the experience. Federal and state governments, by and large, do little of either.

Without a sports ministry or similar government agency overseeing U.S. sport, there is no federal entity charged with funding, regulating, or setting a uniform standard for youth sport.[1] Indeed, researchers have noted that the U.S. federal government has had little interest in funding or regulating the safety of children's sport or otherwise ensuring the availability of youth sport opportunities.[2] Moreover, while states regulate in a host of areas involving children, they too generally have no overall policy or strategy to ensure widespread, safe, developmentally appropriate grassroots youth sport participation.

This is not due to lack of power. The federal government has ample authority to regulate grassroots youth sport through, for instance, its powers under the Constitution's Commerce Clause, which permits Congress to regulate matters that affect interstate commerce, as much of youth sport does. Indeed, with this power Congress has enacted statutes instructing federal agencies to regulate a host of products aimed at children, such as toys and other children's items, television programming, and the internet.[3] Congress could further shape sports participation in schools by also using its spending power, as it did with prohibitions on sex discrimination through Title IX, race discrimination through Title VI, and discrimination against individuals with disabilities under the Rehabilitation Act. Through this power, Congress could condition receipt of federal financial assistance on meeting minimum safety or participation goals. The federal government instead chooses to limit its youth sport efforts to collecting data, promoting participation "through public figures," and providing some grant funding.[4]

States also may regulate youth sport through their general police and parens patrie powers (explained in chapter 2). In addition, both the federal government and states certainly have the authority to fund grassroots youth sports expansively (and, in the case of sport occurring in public schools, states do). As with other areas where federal and state law regulates children's experiences and products, legislatures would have strong policy justifications for setting at least some standards for the youth sport experience. As explained below, however, the presumptive hands-off policy approach to sport generally has been applied to youth sport, revealing that, in the eyes of the law, the activity is more sport than youth.

OUR YOUTH SPORT POLICY

While there is no public entity setting policy for youth sport, there is no shortage of government enthusiasm for the activity. As explained in chapter 1, high-profile federal government promotion of youth sport began in 1953, when President Dwight Eisenhower created the President's Council on Youth Fitness in response to reports of the poor state of youth physical fitness in the United States.[5] The council was to be a "catalytic agent" focused on creating public awareness of the benefits of youth physical fitness. President Lyndon Johnson continued this effort, changing the name to the President's Council on Physical Fitness and Sports to encourage greater youth fitness through participation in sports. Subsequent administrations established the "Presidential Sports Award" to spur children's participation in physical activity, issued executive orders seeking to encourage participation in youth sport, and provided grant funding for the National Youth Sports Program.[6] More recent presidential administrations have continued to promote awareness and involvement in youth sport to enhance physical fitness,[7] and in 2002 President George W. Bush issued an executive order directing the Department of Health and Human Services (HHS) to "develop and coordinate" a national program to stimulate sports participation and physical fitness as well as good nutrition.[8] The goals of the President's Council have largely been limited to promoting awareness and generating interest in sports participation.[9] The council does not have the authority to create a youth sports structure that would ensure greater access or regulate the opportunities that are currently provided.[10]

In addition to the work of the President's Council, other executive branch initiatives promote the benefits of youth sport. For instance, the Council of Economic Advisers issued a report in 2018 encouraging youth sport participation because of the potential it could foster for long-term positive "labor market outcomes."[11] More recently, the HHS Office of Disease Prevention and Health Promotion, through its Healthy People 2030 program, set a national objective to "increase the proportion of children and adolescents who play sports."[12] The report sets a target participation rate of 63.3%, which it states will generate health benefits and increase children's academic, social, and long-term economic prospects. The National Youth Sports Strategy (NYSS), released by the HHS in 2019, states that the government's goal is to increase "youth engagement" with areas of sport showing lower rates of participation and otherwise support "U.S. youth sports culture" so that, ultimately, all children "have the opportunity" and "motivation" to participate.[13]

In addition to these executive branch efforts, members of Congress have introduced countless bills and resolutions to encourage youth sport participation. There exists a "Congressional Caucus on Youth Sports," and members of Congress have introduced numerous resolutions to endorse the benefits of youth sport.[14] Legislation has provided grant funding for youth sport programs as part of, for instance, the war on drugs[15] and as a strategy to assist "low income youth."[16] Congress has recognized "National Youth Sports Week," "Youth Sports Safety Month," and the contributions of adults who are involved in youth sport.[17] Members of Congress have also introduced bills to provide tax incentives to enroll children in sport.[18] In addition, Congress has supported youth sport through initiatives such as incorporating Little League baseball[19] and granting liability protections for volunteers who serve in nonprofit and other associations, including youth sport organizations.[20] Youth sport is even promoted through the tax code. The Internal Revenue Code grants tax-exempt status to "amateur sports organizations."[21] Most recently, members of Congress introduced the PLAYS in Youth Sports Act, which would direct the HHS to establish a $75 million annual grant program to support and encourage youth sport participation.[22]

States also strongly encourage participation in grassroots youth sport. As discussed more fully in chapter 7, this encouragement often comes in the form of promoting youth sport tourism. Reflecting this trend, the Illinois legislature enacted the Commission on Amateur Sports Act, establishing a state commission to ensure the "promotion, development, expansion, hosting, and fostering of amateur sports . . . events and tournaments." The commission is charged with creating "business opportunities" and "economic development" relating to "amateur sports" and, to meet this goal, is tasked with holding "workshops, training, and conferences" to "increase youth participation in [sport]" and "support[ing] and encourag[ing] the development of sports tourism."[23] Similarly, the Maryland legislature created the "Youth and Amateur Sports Grants Program," which offers state funding to help offset the costs of bringing "new youth and amateur sporting events to the state," as well as to "attract sports fans, participants, and tourists."[24] Other states, such as Indiana and Florida, have also invested heavily in supporting youth sport tourism,[25] while some encourage participation through mentoring or other programs meant to draw children into sport.[26]

A PRIVATIZED SYSTEM

The government's policy to encourage children to participate in sport has long been accompanied by a heavy reliance on the private sector to provide the opportunity, and youth sport participation has grown steadily over the past several decades. This growth has led to greater privatization,[27] so that today, as previously explained, most youth sport programs are operated by private, not government, entities through a "pay-to-play model."[28]

Congress endorsed a privatized approach to youth sport in 1978 through the Ted Stevens Act. Policy discussions around the statute demonstrate that sport advocates and policy makers thought of widespread grassroots youth sport participation as a key way to ensure U.S. international sporting success. At the time, the vision was to develop Olympic talent through a pyramid structure of sports settings,[29] with the base being grassroots youth sport, so as to bring large numbers of children into the system and help the most talented to emerge and ascend.

The executive director of the USOPC lobbied Congress for federal funding, arguing that it was necessary to the development of a "successful amateur sports program" that could "provide broad-scale . . . opportunities for a maximum number of individuals at all ages and all levels of ability" and that such a program would be a "deterrent to many of our current social problems" and would help develop "the individual" and "society."[30] However, while grassroots youth sport participation was viewed as necessary for U.S. Olympic success, Congress rejected the recommendation to fund widespread sport participation, choosing to allow the existing youth sport system—with a host of private and some public providers, including schools—to continue.

Congress instead made a gesture toward at least some coordination of grassroots youth sport and development of youth sport participation opportunities by including it in the USOPC's purposes. The statute lists among the USOPC's purposes that it must "establish national goals for amateur athletic activities," "promote and encourage physical fitness and public participation" in sports, and "assist . . . in the development of amateur athletic programs" and "foster the development of amateur athletic facilities."[31] To achieve its objectives, the Ted Stevens Act provided that the USOPC would recognize private NGBs for each Olympic sport, and charged these entities to develop grassroots youth participation.[32]

The legislative history of the Ted Stevens Act, both at the time Congress originally enacted it and through subsequent hearings and revisions, reinforces the notion that Congress intended the USOPC to have significant responsibility for developing grassroots youth sport.[33] However, Congress did not provide the USOPC with the power and funding to enable it to carry out that responsibility. Although the act granted the USOPC "exclusive jurisdiction" over U.S. participation in the Olympic, Paralympic, Pan-American, and Parapan-American Games, it did not give the USOPC similar power over grassroots youth sport. Thus, youth sport that occurs outside the NGB structure, through private groups such as the AAU, are not within the USOPC's purview, and the USOPC has no authority to regulate their activities. Similarly, the USOPC does not have authority over school sports, which are left to state high school athletic associations and their member institutions. Rather, Congress tasked the USOPC with simply encouraging youth sport participation.

Accordingly, without clear direction or government funding, the USOPC has, over time, effectively limited its mission to developing elite Olympic (and later Paralympic) talent and has done relatively little to support grassroots youth sport.[34] Congress acquiesced to this approach by not acting on numerous pleas to provide the USOPC with adequate funding to support the effort. For example, in 1995 congressional hearings on issues in the U.S. Olympic and Paralympic Movement, then USOPC president LeRoy T. Walker testified: "The other major issue . . . which has become critical in the years since the passage of the Amateur Sports Act of 1978, is the grassroots programs and opportunities for youth across this nation. The [USOPC] has never shirked this responsibility, nor have we ignored this mandate. . . . The fact remains, however, that we cannot be all things to all people with a limit to our financial resources."[35]

Walker went on to say that no other nation's Olympic committee faced the task of also supporting grassroots youth sport.[36] At the same hearing,

Tom McMillen, cochair of what was then known as the President's Council on Physical Fitness and Sports, pointedly testified to the way law and policy shaped the current state of grassroots youth sport and challenged the notion that the government, in fact, took a hands-off approach to sport:

> As a nation, we have done little more than pay lip service to grassroots sports opportunities. . . . Our government policies have helped develop and maintain an elite sports structure of significant support for the Olympic Games, professional sports monopolies, tax breaks for mega-stadiums, and antitrust exemptions for pro teams. In contrast, our government is doing next to nothing for the masses. . . . Some argue that the government should have no role in sports. . . . In fact, . . . our government has *created* our upside down priorities that are skewed to elite athletes.[37]

Little has changed since McMillen's testimony. While the federal and state governments urge children to participate in sports, policy makers have largely refrained from using public authority to build a system that would ensure such a result.

LITTLE REGULATION

In addition to a largely privatized system for furnishing youth sport participation opportunities, the federal and state governments have allowed for a heavily privatized system of youth sport regulation. This approach amounts to courts and policy makers taking the somewhat curious position that, because sport for children is so important, we cannot take significant law and policy steps to ensure the well-being of children who engage in it.

Like athletes in other settings, children who participate in sport are highly regulated. Their eligibility and other terms of participation are determined by the particular sport provider, such as Little League baseball and Pop Warner football. Yet, whereas athletes are regulated within sport, youth sport providers are subject to relatively little external government oversight or regulation. The choice to rely primarily on the private sector to provide youth sport opportunities has, therefore, resulted in a law and policy approach that purportedly seeks to incentivize private providers to sponsor the activity by promising limited government regulation and, in many cases, at least some measure of tort immunity. Thus, the law emphasizes the supply side of youth sport: creating conditions believed necessary for youth sport sponsors to provide opportunities. The law and policy of sport is less focused on creating favorable conditions for children to participate.

To be sure, numerous state statutes address issues at the margins of youth sport or support youth sport providers. For instance, at least seventeen states have immunity statutes that insulate volunteer coaches and youth sport programs from tort liability except for cases of willful or wanton conduct.[38] More than half of all states provide immunity for the handling of sport concussions.[39] Some states have statutes encouraging youth sport providers to obtain criminal background checks on coaches,[40] establishing athletic codes of conduct for spectators at youth sporting events,[41] or exempting children from labor laws so they may work as youth sport officials.[42] Some state statutes promote awareness of certain adverse health conditions (such as sudden cardiac arrest or heat stroke) that may occur during youth sports,[43] and, as chapter 2 explains, all states have statutes that address youth sport concussions. Most recently, some states have enacted laws related to sports betting that forbid gambling on youth sports,[44] while others have enacted statutes to limit the participation of transgender girls in school sports.[45] Notably, the California legislature enacted a statute prescribing the number, duration, and timing of full-contact youth football practices.[46] Overall, however, state initiatives aimed at youth sport demonstrate that states do give grassroots youth sport legislative attention, just not in a way that would impose significant regulation on the experience.

Likewise, grassroots youth sport is subject to little regulation through the operation of tort law. The law of tort provides a potential source of regulation in that successful recovery by an injured party will theoretically encourage rational youth sport providers to change their behavior to avoid future liability.[47] Here too the notion that sport is good and to be encouraged has significantly affected our approach, limiting potential recovery and any subsequent regulatory effects. To begin, many states permit parents to waive tort liability on behalf of their child. Courts often uphold such waivers, stating that it is necessary as a policy matter to ensure that youth sport opportunities will be provided, as courts believe that "negligence claims pose grave risks to the viability of youth sports."[48] A concurring opinion in the case of *Woodman v. Kera* illustrates the thinking where it predicts that failing to enforce a parental waiver of tort liability on behalf of a child would cause youth sports opportunities to "dwindle out of a reasonable fear of tort liability."[49]

In cases where parents have not waived a child's right to bring a claim, the liability analysis incorporates a policy preference in favor of the current construction of sport, with little regard to whether the participant is a child.[50] For instance, the analysis of whether a party has a legal duty to act with care toward another—and the standard of care that measures whether there was a breach of any such duty—relies on the same policy considerations that are used for adults in sport. As a result, courts frequently recognize the assumption of the risk defense to deny claims. As the court stated in *Campagna-McGuffin v. Diva Gymnastics Academy*, "Primary assumption of the risk is a defense of extraordinary strength because it essentially means 'that no duty was owed by the defendant to protect the plaintiff from that specific risk.'"[51] The assumption of the risk defense "has fallen into disfavor" in tort law generally but remains important to the law of sport, including in the youth sport setting. The purpose, according to courts, is to ensure litigation does not change "the nature of sport."[52] Thus, the California court in *Kahn v. East Side Union High School* explained that the purpose of the assumption of the risk doctrine "is to avoid recognizing a duty of care when to do so would tend to alter the nature of an active sport or chill vigorous participation in the activity."[53]

Moreover, if a court finds a child injured while participating in sport was owed a legal duty, the standard to show that the duty was not met is, as with sport cases generally, higher than in the usual nonsport tort case. Accordingly, courts usually hold that a child asserting a claim must demonstrate that the defendant engaged in intentional or reckless conduct or was grossly negligent, a higher standard than just negligence. The purpose behind this rule was articulated by the Illinois Appellate Court in *Nabozny v. Barnhill* where it asserted its belief "that the law should not place unreasonable burdens on the free and vigorous participation in sports by our youth."[54] While the *Nabozny* court seemed to focus on limiting liability to benefit children, the Illinois court in *Karas v. Strevell* articulated what are often viewed as the real stakes of imposing tort liability in youth sports. "If a negligence standard were imposed on participants," the court states, "contact sports would be fundamentally altered or, perhaps, eliminated altogether."[55] Other courts have expressed similar policy concerns: the Indiana Supreme Court, in *Megenity v. Dunn*, declared that "since athletic activity is to be encouraged . . . a sports participant commits no breach by engaging in conduct" that is within the norm for the sport,[56] while the New Mexico court in *Kabella v. Bouschelle* stated that "vigorous and active participation in sporting events should not be chilled by the threat of litigation."[57]

Notably, these doctrines are not adjusted for children participating in youth sport even when an injury results from "extreme misconduct."[58] Indeed, in some sports, dangerous conduct is considered part of the game. As the court stated in *Karas v. Strevell*, "In full-contact sports such as tackle football and ice hockey where bodychecking is permitted, a conscious disregard for the safety of the opposing player is an inherent part of the game." Similarly, in *Borella v. Renfro*, the Massachusetts Appeals Court refused to impose liability for conduct that rendered the minor athlete unconscious and with permanent injuries. The dissent pointed out that, while the majority opinion was meant to ensure sport opportunities continued to be provided for children, the decision had significant costs, as it served to deprive "children who play competitive sports of the protections against reckless violence to which they are entitled."[59] The majority ruling, it contended, could lead not only to more serious injuries in youth sport but also to parents not allowing their children to play.

There is some recent evidence of change, at least in one state, to the usual application of tort law. For instance, in *Doe v. U.S. Youth Soccer Association*, a twelve-year-old brought suit against the U.S. Youth Soccer Association after the girl was sexually abused by her coach. The California court held the organization had a duty to conduct a criminal background check on adults, such as coaches, who would be involved with children in its programs. The court found significant the fact that U.S. Youth Soccer had long-standing knowledge that sexual predators were attracted to their programs and that it had established policies for hiring coaches.[60] Similarly, a California court in *Brown v. U.S.A. Taekwondo* held that the NGB, but not the USOPC, had a duty to protect children from "foreseeable sexual abuse" perpetrated by a coach. In that case, the plaintiffs alleged that there was a clear history of sexual abuse of young athletes by USA Taekwondo coaches, including rape, and that the NGB had "regularly" received complaints of such abuse.[61]

A federal circuit court in *Mayall v. U.S.A. Water Polo* held that the sport's NGB had a duty of care to an athlete who was harmed after being permitted to return to play following an apparent concussion. The court rejected USA Water Polo's assumption of the risk argument, distinguishing between the first head injury, which the court said plainly is inherent to the sport, and the secondary injury, caused by returning the athlete to play. The court found pivotal the fact that USA Water Polo had detailed return-to-play guidelines for its national team athletes so that managing concussions would not fundamentally alter the sport. Failure to have such rules at the youth level—and, indeed, including language for youth concussion management that was vague and not mandatory—led the court to conclude that USA Water Polo did not meet its duty of care.[62]

While important for the individual claimants and, perhaps, significant in their break from the usual approach, these cases are likely limited in what they might ultimately mean for youth sport. First, the cases reflect the law of only one state, California, and are, therefore, not binding (though they may be persuasive) elsewhere. Thus, their full deterrent effect is not clear, and other states may respond to these developments by further protecting youth sport providers. In addition, while tort suits like those in *Doe*, *Brown*, and *Mayall* may spur changes by at least some youth sport providers, those changes will likely extend only to the point that the sport sponsor can claim to have acted with the care requisite to avoid liability. Meeting a standard that can avoid liability, however, still leaves the child with a substantial risk of harm. In the language of law and economics, the "optimal liability rule" in youth sport will still be set to promote sport, not protect children. Indeed, many courts still dismiss claims by finding that the sport sponsor did not have a duty to protect the child.[63] Finally, while tort recoveries may alter some future behavior in a way that may benefit children participating in sport, it does nothing to set broader policy goals around grassroots participation or provide uniform standards. For now, tort law remains an uneven, unpredictable, and inefficient means of regulating youth sport.

FEW RIGHTS FOR CHILD ATHLETES

Lack of meaningful, uniform regulation in youth sport is significant because, unlike athletes participating in other sports settings, children participating in grassroots youth sport often do not have the same legal rights and remedies available to protect their interests. For one thing, grassroots youth sport is not, like professional sport leagues, unionized. Children in this context, therefore, do not have the benefit of an advocate with a legal duty to protect their interests or the benefit of rights and protections secured through collective bargaining. While children who are athletes may have access to private dispute resolution procedures and rights, such as those provided by SafeSport and guaranteed under the Ted Stevens Act (if they participate through a sport NGB), they must rely on parents or guardians to advance such claims. Accordingly, because of their age and the relative lack of regulation, children participating in grassroots youth sport must rely on adults, such as their parents or coaches, to ensure their interests are protected. In this way, as Silbaugh has noted in the context of youth sport concussions, the law's assumption that parents act in the best interests of their children does the heavy lifting of ensuring the well-being of a child enrolled in youth sport.

Thus, with little external regulation and few rights of their own, children who participate in sport are subject to the particular rules of the sport provider. This means children in sport in general are provided only with the rights granted by sports sponsors and regulators, some of which—the USOPC or a state high school athletic association, for instance—have exclusive authority over sport within their jurisdiction. As with other levels of sport, the dominant legal theory is one based on contract and consent, so that a participant may either accept the terms or not participate. Parents, again, are the key to this transaction. Children may also claim any applicable civil or constitutional rights provided by federal law and state equivalents.

NGB-Affiliated Youth Sport
Youth sport operating through a sport national governing body recognized by the USOPC is connected to the overall private international sport framework. The USOPC is part of the international Olympic Movement "pyramid."[64] At the top of the pyramid are the IOC and IPC, which have exclusive jurisdiction over matters relating to the Olympic and Paralympic Games, respectively, and private sport international federations (IFs), which set the rules for their respective events. Each NGB administers its sport in the

United States according to the rules promulgated by that sport's IF. Thus, a child who participates in gymnastics in the United States likely participates through a club affiliated with USA Gymnastics, the NGB for the sport in the United States. USA Gymnastics enforces rules for the sport established by the International Gymnastics Federation (or Fédération Internationale de Gymnastique; FIG), the IF for the sport. Through a series of contracts, the child who participates accepts the various rules and procedures promulgated by the private entities that control the sport.

In the Olympic and Paralympic Movement context, in addition to state tort law and any applicable general federal statutes, such as the Americans with Disabilities Act, a child is subject to all the rights, obligations, and protections that flow from the Ted Stevens Act, such as the right to file a complaint with SafeSport and the obligation to follow the World Anti-Doping Code as administered by USADA. Because the USOPC and sport NGBs are private entities, children participating in Olympic and Paralympic Movement sport do not have constitutional rights. Moreover, because they are not educational programs and the federal government generally does not provide the USOPC or NGBs with federal funding, Title IX, the Rehabilitation Act, and Title VI do not apply.

Sport in Schools
State high school athletic associations, some of which are public entities while others are private, comprise public and private schools that create and enforce the rules governing high school athletics in the state.[65] In addition to state athletic associations, institutions have authority, as they do for all students, to regulate athlete conduct. Rules set standards for athlete eligibility, such as eligibility for students who are homeschooled, rules governing transfer, and age limits for participation.

When a sports program is embedded in school, however, children who participate may have rights that do not exist in private programs, rights protected most notably by the Constitution (for programs that occur in public schools) and by civil rights statutes, such as Title IX, Title VI, and the Rehabilitation Act, which apply to educational institutions that receive federal financial assistance. Moreover, just as children participating in the Olympic and Paralympic Movement have the benefits of any rights provided by the

USOPC and their sport's NGB, children participating in school sports have the rights provided by the relevant state interscholastic athletic association and their school.

For instance, students who participate in public school sports programs may bring a claim that their constitutional right to due process of law was violated.[66] However, while they may claim such protection, courts usually deny children's claims, routinely holding that participating in high school sports is a privilege and not a right.[67]

Similarly, in *Vernonia School District v. Acton*, the Supreme Court recognized that children participating in public school-based sports programs are entitled to at least some Fourth Amendment protection against unreasonable searches. However, while the Court asserted that drug testing high school athletes constituted a search subject to the Fourth Amendment, it held that the school's drug-testing policy was permissible.[68] In *Vernonia*, a child's status as an athlete worked to diminish their level of constitutional protection, as athletes, the Court reasoned, have a lesser expectation of privacy because they "suit up" in locker rooms that afford no individual privacy and because joining a sports team means athletes "voluntarily subject themselves" to a higher "degree of regulation" than nonathlete students. Also important to the Court was that athletes, in its view, are school "role model[s]."[69] The Court stated that students who participate in sports "have reason to expect intrusions upon normal rights and privileges, including privacy."[70]

The Supreme Court's decision in *Mahanoy Area School District v. B. L.*, however, is an exception. In that case, the Court held that a high school cheerleader had a First Amendment right to post "vulgar" criticism of the program on social media, outside school hours. The opinion rested heavily on the notion that during after-school hours, regarding off-campus speech, the authority of parents is more important than that of schools. Notably, the Court suggested that the outcome might have been different if the speech had impacted "team morale" or "cohesion."[71]

However, while the Supreme Court decided *Mahanoy* in favor of the child-athlete, courts more frequently hold that important sport interests outweigh children's First Amendment claims.[72] *Menora v. Illinois High School Association* is instructive. There, the Seventh Circuit Court of Appeals rejected a free-exercise challenge to the state high school athletic association's ban on headwear during games brought by an Orthodox Jewish high school basketball player. The court held that the player had "no constitutional right to wear yarmulkes insecurely fastened by bobby pins" during basketball games and therefore that the athletic association's rules, purportedly for safety, should prevail.[73]

Further, athletes' free-speech claims frequently fail because courts highlight the need for the coach to maintain team discipline. For example, the federal circuit court in *Wildman v. Marshalltown School District* rejected the First Amendment claim brought by a high school basketball player, citing coaches' "reasonable" need for "respect."[74] A different federal circuit court used similar reasoning in *Lowery v. Euverard*, in which it rejected an athlete's First Amendment challenge to dismissal from the football team for speaking out against the coach. "There is a difference," the court averred, "between the way a school relates to the student body at large, and to students who voluntarily 'go out' for athletic teams. . . . [R]estrictions that would be inappropriate for the student body at large may be appropriate in the context of voluntary athletic programs" because, among other things, the "conflict between a player and the coach can shake 'the very foundation of team chemistry.'"[75]

Although constitutional claims frequently fail, civil rights statutes can be an important source of rights for youth athletes. Title IX, of course, had a transformative effect on sport embedded in schools by requiring institutions to provide sports participation opportunities for girls.[76] More recently, Title IX has been invoked to protect the rights of transgender children to participate in school sports programs.[77] However, while the statute is unquestionably important, as advocates have long documented, Title IX's mandates have not been fully enforced, especially at the high school level.[78]

Similarly, the Rehabilitation Act prohibits discrimination on the basis of disability in education-based sports programs.[79] Here too, however, courts often defer to institutions and sport regulators. For instance, in *Holzmueller v. Illinois High School Association*, a high school student with significant physical disabilities who participated on his school's track and field team petitioned the state high school athletic association to create a separate division with different state qualifying times for para-ambulatory athletes like himself. While on the track team and fully able to participate, his disability and the association's qualifying times meant he had no chance to qualify for the state championships because he had to race against able-bodied competitors. The federal circuit court stated that, although the proposed accommodation of a separate category and qualifying times for those with a similar disability would not affect the standards for able-bodied athletes, the accommodation would, in the opinion of the court and the governing body, lower standards overall. The court reasoned:

> The essential nature of a track and field race is to run a designated distance in the shortest time possible. The [high school athletic association's] time standards, which govern which runners can qualify for the State championship, underscore the essence of the sport: one must run as fast as possible to achieve the predetermined times. According to the IHSA, the qualifying time standards ensure a certain level of competition and maintain a necessary scarcity of opportunity. To lower the qualifying times for State by creating a new division of runners would fundamentally alter the essential nature of the . . . State track and field meet.[80]

The requested accommodation was, therefore, deemed "unreasonable as a matter of law." Similarly, in *McFadden v. Grasmick*, a high school student who used a wheelchair challenged a state high school athletic association's decision that permitted her to race at the state meet but not earn points for her team. The federal district court upheld the athletic association's decision, stating that, although inclusivity served the public interest, that interest was also served "when responsible educational officials, faced with a clash of interests among students," are permitted to determine how to best run their sports programs.[81]

Moreover, while athletes who participate in high school sports may have greater legal rights than children who participate in other settings, recovery in a lawsuit can be further complicated by the fact that educational institutions and their employees may enjoy sovereign and other immunities. Indeed, with respect to tort claims, at least one court has held that schools should not face greater liability in tort than private youth sport providers. As a result, the Massachusetts court in *Sharon v. City of Newton* stated that failing to uphold a parental waiver of liability in the school sport context would "create the anomaly" that a child participating in a private youth sport program would be unable to state a claim, whereas a child engaging in the same sport in school would. The court therefore held the liability waiver was enforceable and cited the familiar concerns that subjecting school sports programs to tort lawsuits would "inevitably lead to the reduction of those programs" and is therefore "contrary to the public interest."[82]

Finally, while school sport participation may provide children with rights that do not apply in other settings, accessing those benefits often requires children already to be athletes with at least some athletic skill. Coakley acknowledges the problems with high school programs that emphasize "winning" and "excellence," leading high school programs often to seek the most skilled performers.[83] Sport researchers, therefore, describe interscholastic sport as "selective" and "highly competitive."[84] Accordingly, although publicly supported opportunities exist in most high schools, and high school participation may come with some rights, the competitive nature of those programs means that adolescents who hope to make the team in high school often must start in private grassroots youth sport programs as children.

Private Unaffiliated Youth Sport

Private youth sport programs that are unaffiliated with a sport NGB are not legally obligated to provide children who participate with the rights that flow from the Ted Stevens Act. In addition, private programs that occur outside any school are not subject to the rules promulgated by state high school athletic associations. Moreover, because these youth sport providers are private entities, children who participate through their programs do not have constitutional rights. With little regulation aimed at sport, child participants in these programs may avail themselves of any applicable rights granted by Congress or state legislatures. In this regard, the statute that has, perhaps, had the greatest impact on private youth sport programs is the Americans with Disabilities Act. For instance, the U.S. Department of Justice has taken action against private youth sport providers that fail to accommodate children who are deaf and hard of hearing.[85]

In whatever setting grassroots youth sport occurs, then, no overall policy strategy or funding ensures opportunities are provided, and no consistent standard of regulation guarantees the quality of the experience. Courts and legislatures instead grant youth sport sponsors significant deference to manage their programs. The legal and policy response to youth sport concussions (explained in chapter 2) warrants additional discussion because it may be viewed as an exception.

The states' response to the problem of youth sport concussions has drawn significant critiques. The first is Katharine Silbaugh's argument that youth sport concussion statutes use the cloak of parental authority to grant liability protection for sport providers. In addition, critics discount youth sport concussion statutes as at best ineffective and at worst an example of "regulatory capture."[86] These views encompass several important points.

First, critics point out that the content of the statutes was heavily influenced by the NFL's and NCAA's lobbying, so that the legislative outcomes reflect the goal of protecting the commercial interests in the game of football more than the goal of protecting children.[87] Thus, the NFL advanced the proposition that the problem to be solved was reducing the harmful consequences of concussions, not actually reducing the incidence of the initial head injury. This idea ensured that legislative outcomes did not "directly regulat[e] the content, rules, or procedures of football itself." The statutes do not, for example, ban certain high-risk sports or limit children's sport activity that might produce concussions (such as football tackles, soccer "headers," or ice hockey bodychecking).[88]

A second critique of concussion statutes is that, regardless of the motivation behind the reforms, because they do not actively limit the incidence of concussions in youth sports, they are simply ineffective. The statutes do not mandate any changes to the games themselves except to the extent that a player suspected of having a concussion be removed from play.[89] Concussion statutes and other concussion management guidelines might, then, provide a false sense of security to parents and athletes by giving the appearance that the games as currently played can be made safer. Moreover, because youth sport concussion statutes focus on managing concussions that occur, taking as a given that they will, the laws may reinforce the notion that the traditional games, played in traditional ways, are the only authentic sport experiences.[90]

Concussion statutes have been criticized as ineffective not only from a public health perspective but also from a legal perspective. Legal scholars have asserted that, because the statutes have no enforcement mechanism and many include immunity provisions for coaches and health professionals, there is little accountability for failing to manage youth concussions as the statutes require. The claims available to potential plaintiffs and immunities available to potential defendants vary from state to state depending on the language of the legislation. However, youth sport concussion statutes generally do not create any new cause of action.[91]

Thus, the legislative response to youth sport concussions can easily be viewed as consistent with our overall approach to sport generally, wherein government power is usually deployed to benefit and protect the legitimacy of the sports industry. Moreover, because the statutes regulate only at the margins of the concussion issue, they may encourage continued participation by restoring public confidence in the games as currently played and are, in this way, consistent with the government's approach to youth sport, which is to encourage participation, not regulate.

Yet, even with these critiques, youth sport concussion statutes may still be viewed as a change from the usual approach. The statutes contemplate a role for the law to protect children who participate in sport. They do so by declaring that a certain category of participants—those suspected of suffering a concussion—are ineligible to continue playing and may not return until medically cleared. This goes to the heart of "field of play,"[92] and determinations of who may and may not take the field have traditionally been an internal sport issue. In this way, state youth sport concussion statutes might serve as at least a tentative step in a new direction, where children's well-being is not premised on simply participating in sport but in participating in sport experiences constructed for that purpose.

However, even viewed in this way, youth sport concussion statutes and other law and policy applied to youth sport still do not reflect a robust concern for the well-being of children who participate and for the children who would like to participate but cannot access the opportunity. Instead, accessing sport is considered a private matter, and protecting children who do participate too often is still viewed as coming at the price of sport, not being consistent with it. The lower court's opinion in *Mayall* reflects the sentiment. The court opened its opinion dismissing the child's tort claim:

> From Ancient Greece and before to the twenty-first century, sports enrich our society. For spectators, sports bring people from all walks of life together. . . . For athletes, sports promote the lifelong values of team work, good health, athletic excellence, fair play, and robust competition. For young athletes, sports may be the ticket to college. This case raises a significant question facing society about how best to maintain those values, while also ensuring the safety of athletes. . . . The Court reaches this decision sensitive to the continued pain and suffering of [the child] and recognizing the conflicting interests of not discouraging athletes from going "faster, higher, stronger."[93]

Thus, the law and policy of youth sport continues to rest heavily on the assumption, dating back at least to the Progressive era, that merely participating in sport contributes to children's well-being, so that the legal and policy environment must be constructed to encourage youth sport sponsors to provide the opportunity. Yet, in contrast to other Progressive-era initiatives aimed at children, there has been little rethinking of our approach to youth sport. Moreover, while the law of the child has evolved (though not as much as some scholars argue it should) to understanding children as persons with their own important interests—and an entitlement to at least some rights as a result—these views have not translated to the youth sport setting.

For now, then, what law and policy we aim at youth sport sends a mixed message at best, at once encouraging widespread participation and touting sport participation as a beneficial experience but providing little government funding or regulation to ensure that such is the case. In this system, grassroots youth sport participation is left as a private family matter, not an issue for public policy. The following chapter explains the politics behind that approach, and the results.

CHAPTER FIVE

The Politics of Youth Sport

> Largely because of the changes which have taken place in the world and the new problems these changes have created, sport has evolved considerably and has spread . . . in all countries. . . . Sport is becoming an indispensable element required to compensate against the strain of modern living . . . [and] it offers an exceptional means of shaping the young.
>
> International Council on Sport and Physical Education and UNESCO, Declaration on Sport (October 1964)

The previous chapters explain how the law of the family and child and the law of sport together create a territory for youth sport that both places it on law and policy agendas and keeps it off. The government strongly encourages youth sport participation, but the content of the experience is often considered beyond the reach of courts and policy makers. Reflecting the government's traditional preference to stay out of the operation of both families and sport, our prevailing law and policy approach provides a powerful green light to parents and the private sector to determine the goals for and the means of engaging children in sport. This result is not a necessary feature of youth sport; rather, as this chapter explains, it is a political choice.

It is a choice that has long endured. The lightly regulated, largely pay-to-play, professionalized model for youth sport has prompted substantial critiques for decades. High-profile issues, such as youth sport concussions, athlete abuse, and bad parental behavior, have drawn widespread public attention, and the barriers to participation and lack of access for many children are well known. As currently operating, our approach to youth sport likely cannot and will not achieve the federal government's ambitious goal that a majority of children engage in sport and stick with it. Yet all of these conditions and critiques of youth sport thus far have, for the most part, not amounted to a problem that the federal or state governments have attempted to solve. To better understand why, we must consider the politics of sport and its effects on law and policy outcomes. Critical theorists and policy scholars offer useful tools to this end.

SPORT IS POLITICAL

To appreciate this perspective, we must set aside the commonly held view that sport occupies a realm separate from politics and that "sport and politics should not mix."[1] This view was articulated as part of a lower-court opinion rejecting Curt Flood's antitrust claim against Major League Baseball. "The game is on higher ground," the district court stated; "it behooves everyone to keep it there."[2] This belief is not just a thing of the past. A recent popular media article echoed the sentiment when the reporter wrote that sport brings individuals from all walks of life together in "a spiritual experience, an endeavor with almost mystical properties" that exists as a "magic circle" separate from day-to-day reality. The author noted that, for many, bringing politics into that elevated sphere through, for instance, professional leagues using initiatives such as "Pride Night" to demonstrate support for gay rights or showing support for other social justice causes can "spoil" the experience.[3]

Scholars have challenged this view by explaining that much of our thinking about sport is based on what Jay Coakley calls the "Great Sport Myth," which is the assumption that sport is inherently "pure" and "good" and that these values "are necessarily passed on to all who engage" with it.[4] The belief in the power of sport to do good seems universal, and it connects to the system of international sport through the frequent narrative of sport as an instrument to promote peace and understanding. Indeed, as Barbara Keys explains, society is "saturated" with the claim that international sport can do everything from reducing poverty and discrimination to advancing human rights. However, as Keys observes, while "the claims are plentiful and pervasive," the actual support for them is "sparse and weak."[5]

The government's hands-off approach to sport incorporates this thinking. Whether through consequentialist arguments that sport makes society better off overall, or through arguments that sport is an important part of human flourishing, courts and legislatures see their role as protecting sport, not regulating it. The goodness of sport is, in this way, taken as an objective truth. This view, of course, obscures the fact that sport as it exists today was constructed from a particular perspective, and so it acts to "preserv[e] and . . . legitimate[e]" the current social order.[6] Accordingly, despite wishful thinking to the contrary, sport at all levels was not somehow received by us in a hypothetical pure form but is "already political."[7]

Thus, in debates over the meaning of sport, philosophers explain sport as "mirror[ing], reflect[ing], or reinforc[ing] the values found in the wider society,"[8] and there are countless examples of the ways professional, Olympic, Paralympic, and intercollegiate sport reflects these connections. Prominent ones include political battles over Title IX, the 1980 Olympic boycott, and President Donald Trump's response to NFL player Colin Kaepernick taking a knee during the national anthem to protest systemic racism and police brutality directed at Black citizens.[9] The late Senator John McCain and former senator Jeff Flake even issued a report on the Department of Defense's use of "paid patriotism," whereby the agency paid more than $53 million between 2012 and 2015 to sports leagues and teams to honor servicemembers at games.

Because of its entwinement with politics, sport is frequently called "paradoxical,"[10] in that it simultaneously can be an individual experience while also intersecting with larger political and cultural forces.[11] For this reason, sport historians argue, our knowledge of sport should be understood in the broader context of these forces, rather than simply accepted as the way things must be.[12] Thus, while the predominant discourse encourages participation in the current model for grassroots youth sport and stresses its importance to individual health and a good childhood,[13] it is important to explore how these understandings fit within the overall political landscape.

FEATURES OF YOUTH SPORT

While the politics of professional, Olympic and Paralympic, and other elite levels of sport might readily be apparent, the politics of youth sport are perhaps not so obvious. The prevailing discourse characterizes youth sport as an indisputable and universal benefit and as promoting an activity for children that seemingly advances their health and well-being; thus it hardly appears political. Further, unlike professional sport, where players and teams, for instance, engage with current political issues, or Olympic and Paralympic sport, which necessarily involves the politics of international affairs, youth sport seemingly has no such dimension. Yet, just as the politics of college sport was not so visible because of the cover of the educational setting and the belief that amateurism was a great American tradition, the politics of youth sport also hide in plain sight. Occurring within the private family sphere and with the benefit of decades of presumptions about its inherent value, youth sport's political dimension is in some ways even more potent.

Perhaps the most obvious manifestation of the politics of youth sport is that Congress intended to make a political statement when, through the Ted Stevens Act, it established the privatized structure of U.S. Olympic and Paralympic Movement sport. Congress rejected federal funding for grassroots youth sport and expressed a strong preference for private sector athlete development through the USOPC, NGBs, and other sport providers. Privatization was in keeping with the preference of the President's Council on Youth Fitness's goal to promote an American style of youth fitness built on the individual's "freedom and liberty" to choose programs that fit their goals, in contrast to Soviet-era nationalized fitness programs.[14]

Cold War politics shaped not only the structure of our youth sport system but its goals as well. As Matthew Bowers and Thomas Hunt explain, during the Kennedy administration the President's Council on Youth Fitness moved from promoting play-based fitness programs to those based on "measurable physical fitness standards." During the Nixon and Ford presidencies, federal sport policy again evolved, this time from an emphasis on broad-scale physical fitness to an emphasis on producing elite athletes.[15] Researchers with the Centre for Sport and Human Rights state that sports development systems that emphasized talent identification, early specialization, and competition emerged during this period as part of the "arms race" of international sport. Professionalization of youth sport continued even after the Cold War era, this research shows, because success in international sport remained an important domestic political goal in many nations at the same time that sport in general was growing commercially.[16]

Our approach to youth sport takes on a political dimension not only because of its connection to international sport success but through policy makers' claims as to the many ways youth sport benefits American society. Children's sport participation has been cited as a solution to numerous perceived societal problems, such as juvenile delinquency and lack of fitness for military duty.[17] Congress previously funded a "Youth Sports Program" aimed at children in "public and Indian housing projects" with the goal of providing these children a way out of the "drug environment" in their communities.[18] Presidents often cite the benefits of youth sport programs to produce other positive societal outcomes. For instance, President Bill Clinton described the long-held belief of the benefits of youth sport programs aimed at "economically disadvantaged children" when he said that sport provides "opportunities to earn and learn self-respect. . . . By utilizing competitive sports as a means of expression, it has allowed these children to express their pain and deal with their difficult living conditions in a positive way, rather than in a self-destructive manner."[19] A Council of Economic Advisers report lists youth sport among "interventions" that can help children develop into productive labor market participants. Youth sport, of course, also has long been upheld as an experience that helps "build character" and that teaches other socially useful values.[20] Policy makers regularly highlight additional societal benefits of youth sport participation, among them combating childhood obesity, overcoming social divisions, building social capital, and empowering girls.[21]

While policy makers emphasize these potentially positive and, they assume, universally desired outcomes of youth sport participation, critical theorists explain the way sport operates to reproduce existing power structures in society. For instance, scholars emphasize sport's use in the "performance and production" of patriarchy and masculinity, so that the professionalization of sport, including for children and adolescents, is a means of solidifying male privilege and "masculine identity."[22] As Kathleen Bachynski observes, "The history of debates over the safety of youth football is, in part, a history of beliefs about how to raise boys to meet particular ideals of manhood."[23] Other scholars assert that an emphasis on sport participation is part of societal discourses that construct our views of the body and health.[24] One of the most forceful critiques of youth sport is that it reflects and contributes to broader societal manifestations of neoliberalism.[25]

Critical theorists who argue that neoliberal political values explain the privatized, professionalized operation of U.S. youth sport point out that by the mid-twentieth century, sport, including youth sport, was swept up in capitalist expansion.[26] Public programs declined, while private opportunities proliferated.[27] These trends have affected publicly available resources for youth sport, as the decline in public programs and increase in private sport providers has meant that local governments are now just "brokers" of public property for private sector youth sport sponsors.[28] Today, youth sport is a target for investment by private equity firms.

Moreover, critical theorists emphasize that sport in capitalist society operates as a powerful "cultural expression of agonism" that exalts winning and promotes the belief that competition produces ideal, just, legitimate outcomes.[29] This thinking pervades grassroots organized youth sport, as programs manifest "an orientation toward competitive results rather than physical activity promotion or personal growth."[30] In this regard, sport is particularly effective in teaching children the values of agonism, because, as one scholar puts it, sport "is a *major* institution" tied to, among other things, notions of a good upbringing.[31] Thus, for sport in the United States and many Western, capitalist societies, "the social and moral aspects of play" are deemphasized, while the elements of talent development, skill, and competing to win are amplified.[32]

Politics also influences what is considered the prevailing knowledge of youth sport, including our interpretation of the evidence used to support the current approach. Donnelly and Atkinson cite the oft-repeated view that participation in sport as a child leads to long-term career success. The research showing such an outcome, they point out, actually supports the conclusion that youth sport helps reproduce social inequality, in that most corporate leaders and professionals were raised in a socioeconomic status that strongly correlates with high levels of sport participation and attaining "the highest levels of occupational prestige." As the authors write, "The road to the boardroom may lead through the locker room, but that does not necessarily democratize access to the boardroom." Research purportedly demonstrating that youth sport delivers the long list of benefits frequently cited to encourage participation is, in reality, "often equivocal and inconclusive."[33]

Indeed, the politics of our knowledge production around youth sport is reflected in the evolution of pediatricians' views on competitive youth sport, particularly tackle football. After World War II, Bachynski explains, pediatricians were "wary" of highly competitive youth sport programs aimed at preteens and were "foremost among the medical professionals who challenged the extension of highly competitive sports to young children in the 1950s."[34] But, as youth sport programs continued to proliferate and become an ever more important part of American childhood, the AAP position changed. Bachynski highlights in particular the AAP's stance on tackle football, noting that "although the AAP had formally recommended against body contact sports for boys and girls under twelve in the 1950s, by the twenty-first century, the AAP advised no limits."[35] Instead, the Academy focused on individual family decision making about the risks and closer medical monitoring through sports medicine physicians and athletic trainers.

The political aspects of grassroots youth sport are, therefore, obscured by the law and policy presumption, fueled by the Great Sport Myth, that youth sport is an important part of a healthy childhood. The politics is also obscured by the fact that it largely circulates through private transactions between parents and sport providers. Operating in this way, the laudable goals of grassroots youth sport participation may be stymied, and calls for reform ineffective, not because the individuals who operate youth sport programs or support youth sport participation have purely self-interested or even nefarious motives, but because of the "cunning of history."[36]

Philosopher and critical theorist Nancy Fraser's work provides insight. Fraser has mapped the way second-wave feminism intersected with the rise of neoliberalism, with the result that "women's emancipation was harnessed to the engine of" capitalism. During this period, the notion of gender equality became highly popular culturally, yet feminism did not fully change "institutions." Feminists failed to account for this wider historical perspective, Fraser argues, so that feminism's cultural successes acted to "legitimate" neoliberal transformations that, in fact, undermined the feminist notion of a "just society."[37] Feminism was, in this way, hoodwinked by the forces of history.

Similarly, organized youth sport's expansion and solidification as an important feature of childhood occurred, as did second-wave feminism, during the period of neoliberal ideology's proliferation. Indeed, it was the efforts of second-wave feminists to open sport up to women and girls that helped fuel the expansion of youth sport programs, as the fight for equal access included (and still does) arguments about the many benefits that sport participation provides. It is, therefore, important to explore how the seemingly laudable goals of grassroots youth sport participation might be undermined by failing to account for the way political forces operate to amplify and legitimate a particular approach to the activity to the exclusion of others.

WHY THE CURRENT APPROACH TO YOUTH SPORT PERSISTS

Understanding that sport, including grassroots youth sport, reflects the politics of the moment, we can then move to consider our prevailing youth sport discourse and the hands-off policy approach in a new light, through the power that shapes it. One way to better understand this power is to explore how problems with youth sport are articulated and how the prevailing narrative around youth sport may preference certain approaches while keeping others, such as greater regulation, off state and federal policy agendas.

Despite the known harms and critiques of today's youth sport experience, the prevailing description of the problem, particularly as articulated by the federal and state governments, is that not enough children participate and that most of those who do fail to stick with it. This conception of the problem has strong intuitive appeal, as our prevailing approach presents many barriers to sport participation for a significant number of children. If we assume that children benefit from participation, then a description of the problem that highlights those who are left out of youth sport is consistent with liberal notions of treating citizens equally and invokes a strong utilitarian justification that everyone will be better off if more children engage in sport. Moreover, characterizing the problem as insufficient participation connects to arguments about the way societal structures work to discriminate against traditionally marginalized groups such as girls, children of color, youth with disabilities, and those who are socioeconomically disadvantaged. Removing barriers so that these children may participate is certainly a worthwhile goal. Policy theory, however, supplies a deeper answer by explaining that controlling the definition of political problems is an important source of social power.

Legal realists and critical legal theorists long ago established the connection between politics and law.[38] To explain how the political content of law takes shape, public policy scholars use the theory of "problem definition," which focuses on "what we choose to identify as public issues," the resulting characterization of such issues in the political process, and the impact of those choices on policy making[39] Specifically, problem definition is important for agenda setting—moving an issue to the forefront of the political agenda or keeping it off.[40]

Accordingly, before legislatures enact law, social conditions must be defined as public "problems" that reach the government's policy agenda;[41] and "conditions become defined as problems when we believe we should do something about them."[42] This process involves interpretation, and interest groups, government actors, and other stakeholders "deliberately and consciously fashion portrayals" of problems that advance their preferred solution.[43] This is fundamentally a political act,[44] Deborah Stone and other scholars argue, because problem definition is always "strategic" in the sense that social problems are articulated in ways that "accomplish political goals," so that "there is no such thing as an apolitical problem definition."[45]

The issue of child labor (discussed in chapter 2) reflects the power of problem definition. Before policy makers contemplate enacting law that subjects a particular form of child labor to regulation, the activity must be defined as work and widely accepted to be, in fact, a problem.[46] Progressive-era reformers were highly successful at convincing policy makers of the problems of oppressive child labor and that children belonged in school, not mines or factories, arguing that putting children to work was "the worst evil of the nation since slavery."[47] However, conceptualizing child labor as something that is "bad" or "evil" left many activities outside the scope of regulation,[48] including agricultural work and work children perform within the family under the direction of their parents.

Problem definition is at work in the law and policy of sport, as well. For instance, in the case of baseball's antitrust exemption, the problem for decades was defined as the unique needs of the game and those who sponsor it. When Curt Flood challenged this view through his antitrust claim, he offered a starkly different presentation of the issue, as one of the fundamental right of players to participate in a free market for their services—a problem, he argued, that the Court had the power to solve (and the Court agreed to this extent) under existing legal doctrine. Instead, however, the Court adopted the conception of the problem advanced by MLB, that the needs of the game were so important and complex, the issue should be left to Congress.

The power of problem definition in sport is also illustrated by the notion of amateurism. Amateurism grew out of the movement to define it as a problem for Olympic and Paralympic Movement and intercollegiate sport—indeed an existential threat—if athletes earned any income related to their participation. With this conception of the problem, the USOPC, AAU, NCAA, and other sport sponsors adopted and enforced the "solution" of eligibility rules that prohibited athletes from accepting any form of compensation for their efforts. Deferring to sports regulators, courts and legislatures accepted this narrative and allowed it to structure the legal relationship between sports sponsors and athletes that continues in many respects today.

With these examples in mind, we can put the current conception of the problem with youth sport—that not enough children participate and continue—in context. To begin, it has the weight of history behind it. As explained in the previous chapters, from at least the Progressive era, the solution to what were believed to be a range of children's issues, from juvenile delinquency to learning how to be a man and an American citizen, was youth sport participation. Matthew Bowers and Thomas Hunt note that in 1955 children's fitness became a Cold War-era federal policy problem when *Sports Illustrated* reported on a study of American children's level of fitness. The research found American children "alarmingly unfit," which, it was believed, had serious implications for our military readiness. As chapter 4 explains, the results of the study spurred President Eisenhower to create the President's Council on Youth Fitness. The federal government's solution at the time, Bowers and Hunt show, was to promote "play-based" physical activity, including sport, in a way that was consistent with "American freedom."[49]

Yet, while the early solution to the problem of children's fitness was to encourage children's physical play "without excessive adult oversight," this approach gave way to another, Bowers and Hunt explain. By the 1960s and 1970s, the policy problem was the need for Americans not only to be fit for military duty but to win in Olympic and other international sport competition. Youth sport participation was once again the solution, but during this time the philosophy of engaging children in physical activity moved from encouraging "play-centered" activities to producing elite athletes.[50] Moreover, with youth sport offered as the remedy for numerous perceived social issues, it has long been considered a problem that not enough children participate and remain engaged with it.

In addition, viewing the problem as how best to stimulate participation in sport and ensure children continue achieves at least two things. First, it is consistent with the privatized, hands-off approach. This formulation of the problem assumes the issue of sport participation is one for individuals and families to address, through choices made in the private family sphere, and not a public policy issue. This narrative centers families choosing to enroll children in sport programs, and (with the urging of their parents) children choosing not to quit, rather than sport providers changing their programs or the government providing the opportunity. In this way, the participate-and-stick-with-it messages are not unlike the conception of the problem implicit in youth sport concussion statutes. That formulation kept the solution largely within the private family realm through educating parents and generating awareness of the risks of concussion. Moreover, the participation formulation of the problem that emphasizes the benefits of sport harkens back to concepts of amateurism and the goodness and magic of sport. It keeps the terms of participation itself from being scrutinized.

Similarly, the participation formulation of the problem sidesteps more nuanced thinking about the goals for youth sport and whether our current approach meets them. Since at least the time Congress enacted the original Ted Stevens Act, we have assumed that grassroots youth sport participation is part and parcel of our Olympic (and later Paralympic) program and elite development pipeline. Developing talent and creating an opportunity for truly talented children to advance to the highest levels of sport certainly can be an important policy goal. But it is not clear that all children should be put into the same professionalized system to meet such a goal. The approach we have currently conflates talent development with other general health and well-being outcomes, in that we promote sport participation to meet one goal and deliver it using a system suited for another.

The participation conception of the problem also helps preserve the games as currently played. The youth sport concussion issue is an example. As previously explained, the state statutes addressing sport concussions take the games as currently played as a given and thus focus on preventing the harm of a second head injury, not avoiding the first. The pervasiveness of this approach to the problem can be seen with what Bachynski describes as the evolution of the medical community's advice regarding preteen participation in competitive contact sports. Despite decades-long concerns over physical harm to children in contact sports such as football, the AAP position on the issue evolved to incorporate the NFL's conception of the problem, which emphasized rule enforcement and medical intervention for injuries as a way to reduce harm.[51] Thus, the AAP's most recent policy recommendations, featured on the NFL's website, steers clear of changing the game and focus instead on rule enforcement and medical management, particularly through wider use of athletic trainers: "Removing tackling from football altogether would likely lead to a decrease in the incidence of overall injuries, severe injuries, catastrophic injuries, and concussions. The [AAP] recognizes, however, that the removal of tackling from football would lead to a fundamental change in the way the game is played."[52]

Finally, the politics of the message to participate can be seen in recent legislation introduced in Congress to encourage children to get involved in sport.[53] The bill would provide $75 million in annual funding for grants that would support children's access to sport. The bill is endorsed by the PLAY Sports Coalition, a group that includes numerous local, state, and national youth sport providers as well as the NFL, NBA, National Hockey League (NHL), and youth sport industry trade groups.

The widely accepted children-quitting formulation of the problem also requires scrutiny. The Aspen Institute's Project Play puts this conception of the problem in stark commercial, business terms by highlighting the "churn rate" in youth sports, based on data from the Sports and Fitness Industry Association: "The more participants a sport loses, the greater need for the sport to recruit new children."[54] Leaving aside the problem of youth sport providers losing customers, there is no research consensus on how long a child should participate in sport to reap the hoped-for physical and developmental benefits. Indeed, medical research suggests the opposite: that prolonged intense sport participation can lead to overuse injuries and other harms. The time commitment and pressure of the professionalized model suggest that quitting sport as a child enters high school is, in fact, a rational choice given other time demands and developmental needs. From this perspective, it is not clear why a child's choice to stop participating in the professionalized model for youth sport is a problem at all—at least for children.

In addition, the children-quitting formulation of the problem most commonly is positioned as a matter of private choice for children and their families, with campaigns and documents like the NYSS focused on urging children and their families to stick with youth sport. In this sense, privatizing the problems with youth sport and conceptualizing them as a matter of personal preference avoids what could be important public policy questions about the operation of youth sport programs and the resulting high attrition rate.

We can also see the politics behind the participate-and-stick-with-it formulation of the problem when we consider that, despite all the ways public law and policy could be applied to grassroots youth sport, proposals have never ascended to the political agenda. For instance, Congress certainly would be justified in taking action to require the USOPC and sport NGBs to do more for grassroots youth sport. Congress could require the USOPC to invest more in community sports programs as a condition of retaining its exclusive rights to the Olympic and Paralympic trademarks and tax-exempt status.[55] Congress could set targets for underserved populations of children who are less likely to be involved in sports. It could also grant the USOPC funding to develop a more comprehensive grassroots youth sport system to increase recreational opportunities. Or it could set aside the notion of the USOPC having anything to do with grassroots youth sport in the United States, assign the USOPC only the responsibility for elite, Olympic and Paralympic athletics, and create a second organization, with suitable funding, to address children's entry-level athletic opportunities.[56] Indeed, these were among the recommendations offered in a report issued by Congress's bipartisan, independent commission tasked with studying broader reforms to governance of the U.S. Olympic and Paralympic Movement, of which this author served as a cochair.[57] Notwithstanding this and other efforts, however, the social condition that the USOPC cannot or will not do more to support grassroots youth sport has, for decades, not successfully been translated into a problem for the government to solve.

Similarly, while private sector grassroots youth sports programs might justifiably enjoy some freedom from government regulation, given the law's assumption that parents can, in the first place, best protect their child's interests and make informed choices about programs that suit their child's needs and the family budget, there is certainly policy space to respect parental authority while still providing for greater access to sport and promoting the well-being of those who participate. Much has been written about the tendency of many parents to encourage children's unhealthy engagement in sports and the incidence of overuse injuries and harms of overtraining.[58] The government would, therefore, be well justified in setting uniform, national safety standards. Moreover, with limited public recreational programs available and the market full of pay-to-play options, the government would be justified in giving parents more choices through greater public funding of sport and better regulation of the experience.

Another policy argument favors limiting or otherwise regulating how certain sports are played to ensure that children are better protected from harm. As explained in chapter 4, tort law principles applied to cases involving children who are injured in sports, especially tackle football and ice hockey, are the same standards applied to adults. The central animating policy in these decisions is not fundamentally to alter the games as currently played. As the court stated in *Karas v. Strevell*, "If liability could be established every time a body check or tackle resulted in injury—because that conduct demonstrates a conscious disregard for the safety of the opposing player—the games of ice hockey and football as we know them would not be played."[59] Defining the policy problem as what imposing liability would do to *sport*, rather than on what sport, or at least certain sports, might be doing to children, reflects the politics underlying our current system. Indeed, a different definition of the problem in youth sport could lead us to ask why the sponsors of these games, played in these ways, are so often insulated from liability, or why these sports are available to children at all.

Finally, a strong policy argument can be made for subjecting grassroots youth sport occurring in schools to the greatest amount of regulation, though here, too, prevailing conceptions of the issue keep proposals off the political agenda. School-based sports programs are touted as an extension of the educational process and, therefore, should not necessarily be grounded in the same commercial, elite sport norms and values that understandably animate professional, Olympic, and Paralympic sport. Policymakers would therefore be justified in considering ways interscholastic sports programs could be used in the public interest. Indeed, through Title IX, Title VI, and the Rehabilitation Act, the government has taken a step toward doing so. Yet the issue of the broader goals and content of school-based sports programs has never ascended policy agendas.

For instance, the federal and state governments could incentivize schools to experiment with new sport options that could boost grassroots youth sport participation and the creation of sport opportunities that provide less risk of harm to participants and appeal to a variety of abilities. Federal and state governments could use sports in schools as a way to expand the definitions of sport and reshape the view of who is an athlete, so that the benefits of participation outlined in the NYSS and other government reports can be more widely shared. The federal and state governments, in this way, could more directly support participation among a wider range of children. Once again, however, although experts and advocates have made these and other compelling policy arguments for decades, the state of sport for children in schools has not successfully been redefined as an issue for the government to address. Even with Title IX and the Rehabilitation Act, policy makers have not fully ensured the laws' enforcement, despite decades of data showing that the promise of both statutes has not been fulfilled.

The prevailing conception of the problem with U.S. grassroots youth sport also stands in contrast to approaches to and policy discussions around youth sport outside the United States. As Coakley notes, the U.S. approach is "exceptional" in that even countries that stress the skills-and-excellence model for youth sport provide uniform standards and at least some oversight.[60] Thus, while policy makers here largely have not targeted youth sport for regulation,[61] outside the United States, grassroots youth sport reform is often seen as part of the broader children's rights movement stemming from the U.N. Convention on the Rights of the Child (UNCRC).[62] The United States is the only country in the world not to ratify the UNCRC, because of the concern, among others, that it would undermine parents' rights.[63] The Convention provides that children have the right "to engage in play and recreational activities appropriate to the age of the child."[64] This right has been affirmed by the United Nations Children's Fund (UNICEF), which endorsed children's rights to participate in sport and to do so free from harm.[65] UNICEF also published a set of UNCRC-based sports "principles" intended to reaffirm that while "play is a child's right," sport for children must be conducted in a way that does no harm.[66] Based on these rights and principles, there is a significant discussion outside the United States regarding the structure and conduct of youth sport programs that has had little policy impact here.[67]

Outside the United States, a nuanced discussion, also based on the UNCRC, highlights the ways that youth sport participation may turn into harmful child labor. At the 2022 Global Conference on the Elimination of Child Labour, the Centre for Sport and Human Rights reported that children working in high-performance and professional sport settings experience conditions and effects that are analogous to the harms of child labor. The report explains that high-performance and professional sport is now a "global industry" that relies on a continuous stream of children who participate in or are "on the pathway to" the elite level of sport. The report warns that, in many circumstances, the "work" children in this pipeline do, whether they are professional athletes or not, violates the UNCRC and child labor conventions. The Centre recommends that parties to these measures "should recognise that some situations of children's participation in sport are analogous to child labour and take the necessary measures to ensure the respect and protection of the rights of children in such situations." Moreover, the report recommends that nations should "consider taking a child rights-based approach" to youth sport.[68] Assumptions about child labor, children's rights, and parental authority mean that these conversations have not ascended on U.S. political agendas.

Further, Norway's approach to youth sport provides a well-known example of a starkly different system that has not captured significant political attention in the United States. The Norwegian model limits the very things the U.S. youth sport approach emphasizes.[69] Norway's system is led by the government's Ministry of Culture and is based on the mission of cultivating an environment promoting "health and regular exercise," not competition. Drawing on the UNCRC, Norway adopted a set of principles to govern youth sport.⁷⁰ The principles are centered on children's needs and grant children the right to choose how much they train and compete and provide activities that correspond with their age and level of development. Safety is the number one priority, as Norway provides that children have the right to participate in sports activities "without any inappropriate pressure or exploitation."⁷¹ Norway specifies by children's age a plan for development, and competition and travel teams are limited before age twelve. Sports opportunities must be open to all, and youth sport clubs must designate an individual who is responsible for protecting the participants' rights.⁷² With generous government funding, nearly every child is able to participate.⁷³ This model has not diminished (and, indeed, some consider it a reason for) the country's success in international sports competition, as Norway regularly tops the medal count at the Winter Olympics.⁷⁴

Seen in its fuller political context, then, the professionalization of grassroots youth sport and the government's hands-off approach are plainly not an objective necessity.⁷⁵ Just as the law's conception of the family as a private sphere worked to reinforce existing power relations between men and women, the government's reflexive hands-off approach to regulating sport benefits some groups more than others. These understandings allow us to move beyond the common assumptions, fueled by the Great Sport Myth, that the particular U.S. youth sport approach necessarily benefits children and that conducting sport in this way is in any sense required.⁷⁶ Instead, the prevailing messages about U.S. youth sport—that it is a positive experience all children should take part in and stick with—blurs the reality that our society demands athletic supply. With this in mind, we can best appreciate the full range of distributional effects our current approach to youth sport produces.

PART III

Distributive Consequences of Our Current Approach to Youth Sport

CHAPTER SIX

The Youth Sport Surplus

> Today, the Council of Economic Advisers released a report outlining how children's lives may be positively affected by participation in youth sports.
>
> The White House, Office of Communications, May 30, 2018

In addition to being called "dysfunctional," youth sport in the United States is sometimes described as the "Wild West,"[1] a term that implies an environment of few rules, organization, or government intervention. It is true, as previously explained, that there is relatively little regulation of youth sport, and the epidemic level of injury and efforts to curb bad parental behavior,[2] among other signs, suggest youth sport is an environment that needs taming. However, U.S. youth sport may not be as wild as it appears. As part 2 explains, our approach to the activity is no accident but is, in fact, the result of law and policy choices.

With that in mind, this section of the book moves to the final steps necessary to make greater sense of American youth sport. Sport philosophers have observed that "games are made by us and for us."[3] A critical part of understanding U.S. youth sport, then, is determining what, and whom, the experience is for. By exploring the issue in this way, we can move beyond our idealized assumptions to view U.S. youth sport through a distributive lens, so that we may better understand the current approach by accounting for the benefits and costs it produces.

Under the traditional narrative, of course, asking what and whom American youth sport is for is unnecessary. The usual account is that youth sport is for the children who participate. Yet, while not necessarily untrue, this answer is incomplete. Children participating in sport certainly might be acquiring athletic skills, developing friendships, building character, learning life lessons, or staying out of trouble. They are undoubtedly getting exercise, and we often say they are having fun. But under today's professionalized, pay-to-play approach, there is much more to it.

To appreciate the fuller picture and, ultimately, better understand whom youth sport is for, we first must consider an alternate account of what children in youth sport are doing. This chapter contributes to that end by asserting that, in addition to producing benefits for themselves, what children are doing in our prevailing model of youth sport is generating a surplus, subject to appropriation by others, through activity that is much more than play.

YOUTH SPORT AS HIDDEN LABOR

To understand how children's participation in sport today generates a surplus, we must acknowledge the labor that is the core of the enterprise. To be sure, likely everyone understands that children participating in the professionalized youth sport model are providing considerable effort, and not simply playing in the sense of idling away their time on a trivial activity. Parents, coaches, and others often take youth sport very seriously and expect the children who participate to do the same.

Yet, like homework and household chores, youth sport is most often viewed as part of the work of growing up, not the kind of activity that produces benefits for others. Moreover, the law's approach to child labor and our historical view of it as sweatshop exploitation and toiling in hazardous factories and mines put youth sport well outside the type of childhood experience commonly thought of as work.

To best appreciate what children are doing in youth sport, then, we must set aside our assumptions about family privacy and what counts as labor. Feminist legal theorists provide substantial insight into this issue, as they have long established that work performed within the home, usually by women, such as child raising, cooking, and cleaning, "was not conceived of as work."[4] Women's labor was instead considered private, domestic "altruism,"[5] and the law, therefore, did not conceptualize it as value-producing labor because of the "affectionate familial context" through which it was delivered.[6]

This thinking grew out of the traditional view of the family as a private realm in which the state should not interfere. As chapter 2 explains, however, critics of that logic demonstrated that the law in fact created this private sphere, so that courts and legislators staying out of it amounted to an endorsement of a husband's near-total power over his wife and children. Feminist theorists later advanced a similar critique of the law's view of what, within a family, should be valued as work. By denying the reality that cooking, cleaning, child raising, and other activity in service of the family was, in fact, labor, the law imposed costs on the women who engaged in it.[7] Failing to credit or compensate women for their domestic work, which was essential to maintaining the prevailing political order, was a defining feature of capitalism, scholars showed, and it concealed the fact that women were generating substantial "socially necessary production."[8] Accordingly, as Silbaugh explained, the law's treatment of housework as purely an exercise in altruism and not production had the effect of "turning labor into love."[9]

A similar analysis applies to youth sport. It may well be that parents enroll their children in sport and urge them to continue out of love and with the best of intentions. It may also be that children participating benefit from the experience and enjoy at least some aspects of it. That does not mean, however, that participating in the professionalized model for youth sport is not a kind of work.

Moreover, the belief that youth sport is a form of amateur athletics also has concealed the fact that it operates as a type of work. As discussed in chapter 1, the notion of amateur sport and the concept of the amateur athlete supported an ideology that, while purporting to be about practicing sport in its essential, pure form, operated instead as a labor relations tool that ensured sport sponsors reaped all of the rewards of athletes' participation.[10] In this sense, then, participating in amateur athletics was decidedly not work, because engaging in sport as a worker would engage in employment for pay was contrary to the very essence of a legitimate athletic experience. The court in *Berger v. NCAA* captured this view. In denying athletes' claims under the Fair Labor Standards Act (FLSA), the court stated that

> [the athletes] have not, and quite frankly cannot, allege that the activities they pursued as student athletes qualify as "work" sufficient to trigger the minimum wage requirements of the FLSA. . . . [T]he long tradition of amateurism in college sports, by definition, shows that student athletes—like all amateur athletes—participate in their sports for reasons wholly unrelated to

immediate compensation. Although we do not doubt that student athletes spend a tremendous amount of time playing for their respective schools, they do so—and have done so for over a hundred years under the NCAA—without any real expectation of earning an income. Simply put, student-athletic "play" is not "work," at least as the term is used in the FLSA.[11]

Through cases like *NCAA v. Alston*, courts are only now beginning to acknowledge how the concept of amateurism can be deployed to deny that what intercollegiate athletes are doing is a kind of work, both legally and normatively, and that the individuals who perform in sport may legitimately seek to claim some of the benefits they generate. However, we have not yet critically assessed the concept of amateurism as it relates to grassroots youth sport and still assume it to be, as the court stated in *Berger*, just play.

As a result, just as we often cling to the age-old conception of women's household labor, we usually view children's efforts in sport to be an activity that grows out of the love and altruism that characterize family relationships. And just as we have for decades with intercollegiate athletes, we also assume youth sport participation is nothing more than play. These characterizations, however, obscure the fact that children who participate in sport are, like women working within the home, a significant source of societally "necessary production."[12]

THE CONCEPT OF A SURPLUS

Understanding that youth sport's operation, within the family and under the umbrella of amateur sport, may conceal its full nature, we can now acknowledge the surplus the activity produces. Specifically, the concept of surplus can help us understand that what children are doing through their participation in the prevailing model of youth sport today is producing monetary and nonmonetary benefits for more than themselves.

The notion that athletes' participation in sport generates a surplus is a familiar one. At the professional level, the surplus is a subject of negotiation between leagues and unionized athletes as part of the collective bargaining process.[13] Working through advocates with a legal duty to protect their interests, professional athletes advance their claims to the sizable revenues generated by their work in sport. At the intercollegiate level, there is currently a movement to fully identify and potentially reallocate the considerable surplus generated in revenue sports that, in the name of amateurism, has been withheld for decades from athletes and distributed to schools, coaches, and administrators.[14]

But the concept of a surplus has not been as obvious in youth sport. The usual narrative, reflected in law and policy, is that the adults involved in youth sport, many of whom are volunteers, are providing a service to children. Indeed, the law rewards many youth sport providers with tort immunity and tax exemptions in recognition of the contributions they make, and policy makers regularly salute their efforts. In this view, sport providers, coaches, and parents are part of an important undertaking that does not use children to generate value but instead transfers considerable benefit to them.

The notion of a surplus value generated by youth sport also runs counter to classic liberal assumptions about the way children become involved in sport. Participation is assumed to be a matter of autonomy and individual choice, made by parents and children in the privacy of the family, and completed through rational market transactions. Indeed, the NYSS positions the "individual" at the very center of its "Framework for Understanding Youth Sports Participation" and states that getting more children to participate requires increasing children's and parents' "awareness" and "knowledge" of the benefits of sport.[15] Once informed, the thinking goes, children and parents will choose youth sport participation. Under this assumption, there is no surplus generation and appropriation: the benefits of sport are for the child and stay with the child. The youth sport transaction, then, is not only fair but benevolent.[16]

The traditional discourse, therefore, leaves little theoretical room for the idea that what children are doing when they participate in the prevailing youth sport model can be characterized as surplus value production. Fully appreciating what youth sport is requires us to acknowledge that nearly everyone—high schools, colleges and universities, the U.S. Olympic and Paralympic Movement, professional leagues, policy makers, state and local governments, and anyone who is a sports fan—has a stake in whether children take up sport.

This stake is not limited to generalized hopes for competitive Olympic or Paralympic teams or better overall societal health. Children's sport participation serves a continuing need—at the intercollegiate, professional, and

Olympic and Paralympic levels—for high-performing athletes. Even high school sport has become a local spectacle where winning, fans, and, for many programs, commercial appeal are the goals.[17] To be able to perform at the levels necessary to entertain and win, an athlete must necessarily begin training during childhood. Moreover, exposing children to youth sport helps develop a steady market of sports fans. By ensuring a future supply of talent for and interest in higher levels of sport, the current approach to youth sport serves as the foundation for all levels of U.S. sport.[18] The ostensibly private decision whether to participate in sport, therefore, affects not just the individual or family—it has societal consequences.[19]

Youth sport is also a site of production in that it generates numerous present economic benefits and acts to satisfy adults' emotional needs—primarily those of parents,[20] but also coaches, fans, and even policy makers. As a result, by training for society's sport future and satisfying adults' economic and emotional needs for sport performance in the here and now, children in today's U.S. youth sport model generate significant benefits for a range of stakeholders.[21] These benefits, in the language of economics, can be considered a kind of surplus value, so that to understand fully what youth sport is and whom it is for, we must appreciate the surplus the current model produces.[22]

In Marxist economics, generating surplus value is a defining feature of capitalism. In the simplest terms, workers under capitalism are paid a wage that is less than the market value of the goods they produce, resulting in both a profit for the owners of capital and the exploitation of labor.[23] The literature on surplus value generation is extensive,[24] and it is not necessary to review it all here. For purposes of understanding the "what" of youth sport, I use the concept of surplus value in a broader sense, to describe a system that generates both monetary and nonmonetary gains for more than the child who participates in sport.[25] With this conception in mind, I argue that the U.S. approach to youth sport generates surplus value through the training, skill development, travel, and competition that is over and above what would be necessary for children's benefit and enjoyment.[26]

I am not making the case that children's youth sport participation meets the legal definition of child labor or must be regulated as such, or that all children in sport are in all cases the equivalent of exploited workers. It is certainly true, however, as with certain intercollegiate athletes, and consistent with the Centre for Sport and Human Rights' 2022 report on child labor, that the experiences of at least some children participating in some sport environments may, in fact, meet the legal definition of an employee engaged in work, and that those children may be exploited as a result.[27] Instead, for purposes of this analysis, whatever the legal consequences, I am using the concept of surplus value more broadly to argue that children participating in the professionalized, pay-to-play system for youth sport, emphasizing skill development and performance, are generating benefits for more than themselves.

THE DIFFERENCE BETWEEN PLAY AND SPORT

With the foregoing conception of surplus value in mind, we are positioned to explore the way the U.S. youth sport experience produces a surplus. Key to this effort is describing the difference between *play* and *sport*. Philosophers have had much to say about the phenomenon of play,[28] and I do not intend here to capture it all. Instead, this discussion seeks to establish play and sport as different (though often related) experiences,[29] and to characterize sport, unlike play, as an activity that is not just for the enjoyment of the participant but one that also produces benefits for others.

Play and sport are ontologically distinct.[30] With play, the motivation to engage in it and the benefits of engaging in it remain with the individual. Social theorists define play as "a voluntary, expressive activity which is uncertain and unproductive; characterized by spontaneity . . . which focuses on process rather than product, and which can be initiated and terminated at will."[31] Philosophers have further explained that play's voluntary nature means that play on demand ceases to be play.[32] Play, then, is fundamentally "an autotelic activity . . . pursued for predominantly intrinsic reasons."[33] In addition, play contrasts with work in that play generates value or enjoyment only for the individual playing. Significantly, the value generated in play is consumed by the individual playing at the time of the activity so that no surplus is created.[34] Philosopher Johan Huizinga states that, in this way, play "is in fact freedom."[35]

Sport, including youth sport, certainly has aspects of play, as, for instance, when an athlete creatively executes an unexpected physical maneuver in the course of a game. However, the freedom of play that may exist in some aspects of sport is limited by the rules and framework within which organized sport takes place.[36] In play, the rules may be made up as the activity unfolds, whereas in sport the rules are carefully crafted and enforced so that sport, as commonly practiced, is not just play.[37] Thus, sport is conducted through "rules or customs and sometimes competition," while play is a physical activity experience that is "fun and participatory" and usually not structured or conducted under the supervision of adults.[38] Moreover, unlike play, the structure and regulation that accompany sport mean that sport can become a type of "commodity," as those who control the rule making and governance of what is deemed a sport can distribute it for consumption.[39]

Relatedly, sport also differs from play because it is often performed for fans and, in this transaction, becomes a "a site of social reproduction." This process takes place because, as Nathan Kalman-Lamb explains, the physical labor of athletes "has an *emotional* consequence" for those spectators with an interest in the game, so that an athlete's efforts satisfy not only the athlete's own goals but also fans' psychological "needs."[40] While most apparent with professional, Olympic and Paralympic, and revenue-generating intercollegiate sport, this effect is also present in youth sport, with children performing for adults, most notably parents, who are heavily invested in their child-athlete's success.[41]

Scholars have thus documented the way capitalism has shaped sport by commodifying it.[42] Sport is a "triple commodity" in that, first, the game itself can be sold as a product, so that participants pay fees to access the sanctioned versions of a game and access coaching to develop their skills.[43] Second, the sport product provides value to fans through the athletes' performances.[44] Third, there are the goods and services necessary to participate in and support the game.[45]

Yet sport's ability to produce benefits is not limited to the fact that it can be commodified. Lincoln Allison has called sport a "romantic good" in that sport "has a kind of meaning quite different from that of mere acts of consumption." In this way, Allison explains, a sports fan can derive a sense of community and meaning from life by dedicating oneself to a particular team or sport that positions the fan as "part . . . of a story."[46] Consequently, sport has the potential both to exploit the athletes who provide the labor for the enterprise and to provide the athlete with at least some individual pleasure in playing the game.[47]

Crucial to the romance and commodification of sport is employing a model that develops talent and gives rise to a desirable product for individuals to consume. This model emphasizes performance and winning—meeting externally imposed goals—which, sport philosophers note, help transform what would be play into sport. Games are infused with elements such as competition, performing for spectators, and keeping score.[48] Sport conducted in a way that emphasizes winning, therefore, takes an activity that could simply be play and turns it into a different experience, as playing to win requires skill, and skill requires training. Thus, it is the work of training to develop the skill to win (or at least compete well) that helps distinguish play from sport.[49]

Skill building, performing, and playing to win are, therefore, important to generating benefits—beyond those generated for the person engaging in sport—that flow to others with a stake in sport. This aspect of sport produces the surplus value for the variety of actors, including sport regulators, coaches, administrators, and spectators, who control and consume the games,[50] so that converting play from what economists call use value production that solely benefits players into sport results in the surplus value production that generates gains for others.[51] In short, then, whereas play results in creating enjoyment and benefit only for the individual who is playing, sport is an activity that also creates value for others, and this value increases the more an individual develops as an athlete.[52]

The distinction between sport and play is particularly relevant to understanding youth sport and the surplus the U.S. model for youth sport produces. Play is considered pivotal for child development,[53] and researchers have long recognized the value of play in children's lives. Play is thought to be critical to a child's "social, emotional, creative, and cognitive well-being."[54] Moreover, researchers have found that physical play, in particular, can provide children with numerous benefits.[55] UNICEF defines physical play as "any physical activity that is fun and participatory. It is often unstructured and free from adult direction."[56] As explained in chapter 5, play is considered so important that the UNCRC has deemed it one of children's fundamental rights. However, sociologists have explained that, due to changing notions of parenting and the purpose of childhood, "the culture of childhood play" in the United States has "nearly disappeared."[57]

Thus, most youth sport opportunities in the United States occur through "organized youth sport involvement" instead of "self-organized physical play." The result is that in organized youth sport, adults provide children not with the conditions of play but with "competitive sport opportunities" where the adults establish the "philosophy, goals, and structure" of the activity and make other key decisions, such as who will be permitted to participate and who does not make the cut.[58] Social theorists have described this organized youth sport as a kind of "adult-centered play" rather than a child-focused activity.[59] It has also been described as an experience that works as "an exchange" between the children who participate and the coaches, fans, parents, and others who are involved.[60] In the hands of adults, play has, in the words of critics, been "reengineer[ed]" into our current youth sport model,[61] with the consequence, as explained above, that U.S. youth sport is now "professionalized."[62] As one scholar stated with respect to youth sport: "There's the game of baseball and then there's the sport of baseball. Children play the game on their own initiative . . . no adults are required. . . . Organized sports, on the other hand, oblige youngsters to attend scheduled practices and competitive events under the supervision of adults. These activities incorporate formal rules and procedures. The competitive emphasis necessitates focused and protracted training directed by coaches."[63] In sum, as Stanley Eitzen has put it, in "adult-organized" youth sport "play is transformed into work."[64]

Conceptualizing the surplus generated through youth sport participation as the difference between play and sport is useful, therefore, because play is an experience that we know solely produces enjoyment and gains for the individual playing. We can, then, be certain that the benefits flowing from child's play accrue primarily to the child. Since youth sport purportedly is conducted for the benefit of children, play provides an important baseline for measuring the value generated by the effort children put into the enterprise.

In addition, using play as a baseline is helpful because youth sport frequently is considered play in the colloquial sense. It is thought to be different from revenue-generating, "big time" intercollegiate, Olympic and Paralympic, and professional sport, which produce measurable stakeholder benefits. Emphasizing the theoretical difference between play and sport, therefore, can help us home in on the value produced by children's participation in youth sport, value that is largely obscured by the traditional policy narrative and our long-held legal assumptions.

Accordingly, we can conceive of the surplus generated by youth sport participation as occurring across a continuum, with play on one end and professional sport on the other. Moving across the continuum, the amount of surplus generated grows as the amount of effort children dedicate to their sport participation moves further beyond play and deeper into the professionalized youth sport experience. In this conception, the additional training and competing required by our current professionalized approach at some point transforms an experience that would assuredly be for the sole benefit and enjoyment of the child to one that provides an increasing amount of benefit to others.

THE SURPLUS SOLIDIFIED

In addition to understanding the surplus generated through the way we engage children in sport, it is important to recognize the systems of power that propel the surplus value generation and give the current approach continued legitimacy. First and most important is the parent-child relationship. The law provides parents with ample authority to control their children's upbringing, and youth sport fits well within this power. That means parents may choose to put their children in sport and have the power, as much as one can control a child, to keep them there. From the hope of college admission and scholarships to the dream of future Olympic, Paralympic, and professional glory, parents are strongly incentivized to enroll children in youth sport and encourage them to stick with it. The traditional discourse and law and policy of sport heavily support this choice, as they send the message that good parents, in the language of the NYSS, "choose" youth sport.

The power of parents over their children is coupled with the power of sport sponsors over sport and those who participate in it. With little legal regulation, sport sponsors, many of whom have a monopoly over their sport context, serve as gatekeepers not only to the present youth sport experience but also to a child's future athletic aspirations. Few rights accorded to children, both as children and as athletes, mean children participating in youth sport have little choice but to adhere to the terms of the system as it is. The strong law and policy endorsement of youth sport participation, along with the general assumption that parents act in their children's best interests, also lends the current approach to youth sport substantial legitimacy. Parents and youth sport providers, therefore, work together to ensure that the current approach continues to generate surplus value. In this system, the primary power exercised by children is either to quit or refuse to participate at all.

As the following chapter explains, the propensity of our professionalized youth sport system to generate a surplus moves us to the final step of making greater sense of our current approach: identifying the stakeholders who lay claim to it.

CHAPTER SEVEN

Youth Sport's Beneficiaries

> The organization is formed to host high school sporting events around the country. . . . The contests take place in several cities across the country. . . . The purpose of the events . . . is to provide high school athletic programs . . . with an opportunity to further develop and demonstrate the educational aspects of sports through the competition of interstate interscholastic athletic competitions; exposure to world-class competition facilities; experience in team travel; . . . [and] the responsibility of citizenship and their community. . . . The revocation of your exempt status was made [because] a substantial amount of your organization's assets inured to the private benefit of your founder. Because a substantial amount of your charitable assets were used for private purposes, the organization is not operated for exempt purposes.
>
> IRS Private Letter Ruling, October 25, 2013

As preceding chapters demonstrate, the law, policy, and politics of U.S. youth sport both reflect and perpetuate the traditional discourse that youth sport participation is a nearly unqualified good in the lives of children. This view obscures not only the full picture of what the youth sport experience is but also the significant distributional consequences of the current approach that reveal whom, besides children, youth sport is for.[1] Having uncovered the current youth sport model's propensity to generate a surplus, we turn to the final step in making greater sense of the experience: outlining the benefits and burdens of the current approach to better understand why, despite the well-known, long-documented issues, the model resists change.

Youth sport exists within the broader social "struggle."[2] If we look at youth sport narrowly, as an individual choice and matter of concern primarily for children and their families, the possible distributional effects seem limited. However, understanding that grassroots youth sport is the foundation of the overall U.S. sport enterprise—high school, college, professional, as well as Olympic and Paralympic—it is clear that a wide range of actors, from the youth sport industry to parents, derive benefits from the way the United States engages children with sport. To understand and potentially reform our approach, we must therefore appreciate the full range of stakeholders that claim the benefits the current model generates and what they stand to lose under a different system.

To reveal the full distribution of the surplus generated by children's participation in the U.S. youth sport model, I describe in this chapter how the model benefits or burdens the relevant actors, and I suggest how each actor might fare if we were to adopt a different approach. To this end, I imagine a youth sport model that is positioned at the "play" end of the surplus continuum. This approach, which I call *play-based sport*, would incorporate the values of the pleasure and participation model and deemphasize the elements of our professionalized youth sport system. Play-based sport would instead be child-centered, not adult-centered, and would emphasize two things that we reliably know benefits children themselves: physical fitness and fun.[3]

While youth sport is often said to produce benefits for children beyond just fitness and fun, I am using these two as a baseline and calling it play-based sport because these are the values research suggests are preferred by children, and, more important, these values produce benefits that we know accrue primarily to the child. In addition, while other values, such as learning fair play and following rules, may be developed through sport, research to support these claims is mixed and highly dependent on how the youth sport provider delivers the experience. I imagine a change to such a hypothetical play-based model not so as to argue here that it should be adopted but in order to better illuminate the winners and losers under our current approach and reveal more fully whom the current approach to U.S. youth sport benefits.

YOUTH SPORT INDUSTRY

The costs and benefits of the current youth sport model are distributed widely, and the most obvious, immediate beneficiary of this arrangement is the youth sport industry. The current model generates an estimated $15–$19 billion in revenue to those investing in and sponsoring youth sport programs and providing affiliated services, such as travel teams and specialty coaching, as well as to the corporations that produce youth sport-related goods and services.[4] In addition to the industry as a whole, particular benefits of the current model certainly flow to individual actors—such as coaches, athletic trainers, and team doctors—who enjoy not only any financial rewards from their work in service of youth sport but also the emotional satisfaction and prestige that an affiliation with youth sport may provide.

All of this is not without any benefit to the children who participate. As noted above, research establishes that physical exercise provides "indisputable" health benefits.[5] Moreover, certainly anything children deem fun provides them with pleasure. Within the current model, children likely receive the benefit of exercise and some measure of enjoyment, at least initially.

However, as children continue in youth sport, they also likely move across the surplus continuum, becoming subject to increased professionalization. This is when early sport specialization, overtraining, and an emphasis on winning become more predominant. This is also when teams become more selective, narrowing opportunity and giving children the incentive to quit or perhaps leaving them no choice but to leave.[6] For the youth sport industry, a model that goes beyond play, then, is literally putting children's bodies to work for profit. In the language of liberal economic theory, this is a fair exchange, with parents and caregivers paying for what they understand to be the benefits of sport participation delivered to children as part of the transaction. This account is also consistent with the legal assumption that parents act in their child's best interests and have wide discretion to make choices about their child's upbringing.

Changing to a play-based sport model would have significant consequences for the youth sport industry. Such a model would put less emphasis on training, skill development, and competition; this kind of youth sport would undoubtedly generate less revenue. It might also generate less of an emotional and status benefit for coaches and individuals who assist with teams. On the other hand, a model that produces more enjoyment could mean that more children participate, and that more participate for a longer period of time. The question is whether the initial gatekeepers for children in sport, parents and caregivers, would pay for an experience that does not deliver the measurable results the current model provides. Retooling the current youth sport model would, therefore, be risky for the youth sport industry, while more of the same seems to amount to more revenue and more personal satisfaction for the adults who make the games happen.

SOCIETY AT LARGE

The distributional consequences of the current model go far beyond the youth sport industry. At the most abstract level, one can argue that society as a whole benefits greatly from the present approach. Nearly two-thirds of Americans identify themselves as "sports fans."[7] Society's sports fans consume sport performances at all levels, and elite Olympic and Paralympic Movement competition also delivers to fans and policy makers the added benefit of national prestige. Due to inevitable injuries, burnout, and other reasons for attrition, generating a large number of skilled athletes—more than the number of spots for higher-level opportunities—helps ensure a steady supply of talent. Children participating in the current youth sport model, therefore, create value for adults and society generally by filling the pipeline that supplies athletes for higher levels of sport.[8] Youth sport, in this way, is the ground-level factory producing the goods that facilitate sport consumption.[9] Thus, all sports fans reap a benefit from a youth sport model that is professionalized so that it develops and selects the most skilled and, thus, commercially successful athletes (and has those athletes performing for fans along the way). By producing a supply of talent for higher levels of sport, the current youth sport model is operating as intended.[10]

While the "more is more" analysis is arguably true for the youth sport industry and sports fans, the overall societal picture may not always be positive. Envisioning a change to a play-based sport model reveals the costs of the current model. First, in contrast to the current approach, a play-based model might attract and keep more participants. Assuming research on youth physical fitness is correct, there could be—as documents such as the NYSS assert—an aggregate benefit from greater participation in terms of short- and long-term societal health outcomes. In addition, a model that generates greater sport participation might mean that society would benefit from the emergence of a unique athletic talent who would otherwise not have been discovered. Consequently, both the current model's barriers to participation and the fact that so many children quit by adolescence support an argument that society is harmed by the present approach.

Second, the current system likely has significant opportunity costs that a play-based sport model might eliminate. In *The Winner-Take-All Society*, economists Robert Frank and Philip Cook explain that "perhaps the most important single task facing any economy is to assign each of its workers to the job in which his or her talents add the greatest value." With relatively few elite sport opportunities, there may actually be too many children participating in youth sport in the current, professionalized model; that is, many would be better off focusing on art, music, or some other hobby that could benefit themselves and society.[11] If youth sport, then, is viewed as part of the larger winner-take-all market for sport,[12] children *not* playing could produce a societal benefit. While the NYSS and similar discourses problematize children who do not participate,[13] too few elite athletic positions means that many of the children who devote time in the current youth sport model would do better focusing on something else. In this analysis, laboring in youth sport beyond the play-based level harms society because we lose the benefit of, say, another great pianist.

SCHOOL-BASED SPORTS PROGRAMS

The consequences of our current youth sport model can be further explored based on sports context. The United States relies heavily on developing athletes by embedding sports programs in schools—primarily high schools, colleges, and universities.[14] Both interscholastic and intercollegiate sport benefit from the professionalized U.S. youth sport model because it creates a buyers' market, enabling programs to be selective. Teams can be filled with skilled athletes who provide the greatest chance of winning (or at least producing a high-value athletic contest), and this generates fan interest, school and community pride, and for some programs, substantial revenue. Importantly, this analysis is not limited to revenue-generating sports (historically football and basketball, but increasingly other sports as well): even sports that do not attract television audiences or large numbers of fans are valued for being successful, so attracting skilled athletes is often a primary objective.

Yet, as with the analysis of society generally, in the school-based sports context the current professionalized youth sport model presents some potential costs, as more skilled athletes may not always be beneficial. Our current youth sport approach produces more talent than there are higher-level opportunities to support. Children compete for athletic scholarships and positions on high school and college teams and, if they are unsuccessful, must resign themselves to disappointment. However, if the NYSS goal were actually realized—that is, if instead of little more than half of all children playing sports, *all* did so and stuck with it—there would likely be a demand on the system that our education-based sports programs could not meet. Greater numbers of athletes who could credibly claim a place on a high school team, when there are already not enough opportunities, may lead to political pressure to recalibrate programs that have largely been left to administrators to construct. Public education-based sports programs are primarily state supported. Substantially larger numbers of disappointed children (and their parents) may prompt political pressure to reform education-based sports programs to increase opportunities for all individuals who have the ability to participate.

Again, considering a change to a play-based sport model reveals what's at stake. Such an approach would deemphasize early specialization and training and could very likely shrink the pool of players ready to perform at a highly skilled level on high school and maybe even college teams. It could also see many adults out of a job, at least in high school sports. High school sports are serious business, with complex rules and entities—such as state high school athletic associations—employing numerous administrators to implement them. A play-based youth sport model might generate pressure at the high school level for less competitive, more inclusive programs. Moreover, unlike the current approach, a play-based sport model that deemphasized competition in high school sports would almost certainly require fewer rules, in part to ensure "competitive balance," and less administrative infrastructure to make the games happen.

PROFESSIONAL SPORTS LEAGUES

Professional sports also benefit from the current youth sport model. As one team of scholars explain: "Children are at the centre of sustainability of professional sport. The future of sport as an industry is heavily dependent not only on the participation of children from a young age, but also on keeping the largest possible number of talented young athletes involved in sport, both as participants and as spectators. The children of today will be the stars and fans of tomorrow. Without [them] professional sport will collapse."[15] Baseball, basketball, hockey, and soccer are all sports with strong youth participation, and, while participation in youth football has somewhat declined, it too remains popular. Professional sports leagues certainly reap at least some of the benefits of the talent produced. Emerging professional sports, such as lacrosse, benefit as well. For these entities, the current youth sport model is delivering the necessary talent.

On the other hand, established professional sports are already highly popular and lucrative. While a wider pool of participants in youth sport might yield a few more superstar talents, there are now enough of them to satisfy consumer demand so that more participation might not yield any additional marginal benefit in terms of player talent. Moreover, the current model has the potential to harm professional sports if it serves to turn children off as sports *fans*. Thus, if children's experience in sport is negative (and, as previously explained, research shows that for many it is), it might not serve to develop these children as future consumers of professional sport. This effect would pose a significant cost to professional leagues.

From this perspective, imagining a change to a play-based sport model reveals a downside to our current approach. A model that emphasizes enjoyment of sport might benefit professional sports leagues in the long term by instilling a childhood love for games that translates into increased adult consumption of professional sport. Moreover, while it is possible that a play-based sport model would produce fewer elite athletes, the Norway example demonstrates that this is not necessarily the case. Since there are already too few professional sport opportunities for the number of intercollegiate athletes who would claim them, the hypothetical play-based sport approach might produce greater gains for professional leagues in developing both athletic talent and future sports fans.

U.S. OLYMPIC MOVEMENT

Similarly, the U.S. Olympic Movement (the Paralympic Movement is addressed in the following section) also undoubtedly reaps benefits from the current grassroots youth sport model. Olympic sports, at least during the

Games, are a matter of national interest and pride. Scholars have called this phenomenon "sportive nationalism," whereby nations use international sports performance as a symbol of national prestige.[16] As evidenced by the President's Commission reports, U.S. policy makers and, presumably, the American public are committed to being at the top of Olympic medal counts, and the U.S. grassroots youth sport model is delivering results.

As previously explained, while Congress tasked the USOPC with cultivating grassroots youth sport as well as assembling strong teams for elite international athletic competition, the USOPC's portfolio of sports and responsibilities has become so expansive that it has left grassroots development largely to other private sector actors. The USOPC has reaped the benefits. Enough children are currently pursuing sport that the United States now routinely dominates, or is at least highly competitive in, many high-profile Olympic sports like swimming and track and field. In fact, the only sports in which the United States has not won any Olympic medals are badminton, table tennis, and team handball.[17] The United States also routinely tops overall medal counts at the Summer and Winter Olympic Games. While international sports performances of the 1970s prompted significant government concern, today's approach to youth sport feeds a high-performance pipeline that has brought substantial national prestige.

Here again, however, hypothesizing a change to a play-based sport model reveals additional costs to the current approach. First, while it may be risky to make such a switch, at least for medal counts, it need not be. The Norwegian example, again, provides support for the notion that a different model would have no negative effect on elite athletic performances. More important, however, a play-based sport approach might produce important benefits. There are at least fifty sport NGBs currently under the USOPC's umbrella. For many of these the talent well runs deep, while in others the United States is not highly competitive. From the perspective, then, of lesser-known Olympic sports, the market-based youth sport model, in some respects, fails to deliver much of any benefit. This model does not seek to grow interest in little-known sports but responds only to the demand for what is already popular. The cost of this approach goes beyond the struggle to field competitive elite teams in lesser-known sports. Society also incurs the cost of limiting children's options for a sport that best matches their interests and abilities. From this perspective, a different youth sport model that not only promotes wider participation but also offers a larger selection of sports could produce benefits greater than the current approach. On the other hand, many sport NGBs may rely on our youth sport system not to deliver athletes with specific skills but simply athletes. For instance, it is unlikely that a significant youth sport program in bobsled or skeleton will or could develop. But children who participated in other sports and developed overall athleticism may later be recruited into lesser-known sports without established youth pipelines. A play-based sport approach might, therefore, generate less athletic cream for these sports to skim—and, in that way, could burden our overall Olympic program.

U.S. PARALYMPIC MOVEMENT

The U.S. Paralympic Movement likely does not enjoy as many benefits as it could from the current youth sport model. Although our Paralympians post impressive competitive results, a general lack of sport programs for children with disabilities in both the private sector and schools makes for a Paralympic sport pipeline not as robust as it certainly could be.

However, the current youth sport model might, in some sense, be beneficial, at least to sport leaders. More potential Paralympians likely would, as the *Hollonbeck* case showed, advocate for greater resources and support for their efforts. A change to a play-based sport approach could, therefore, have a mixed result, bringing more children with disabilities into the Paralympic pipeline but likely putting pressure on existing resource allocation structures that still do not value Paralympians at the same level as their Olympic Movement peers.

FUTURE ELITE ATHLETES

As an extension of the benefits to sports sponsors and regulators, future elite athletes—whether intercollegiate, Olympic and Paralympic, or professional—also benefit from the current youth sport model. Determining athletic excellence requires "comparison."[18] To find the best athlete, there must be others to compete against, and the others must prove "worthy" competition.[19] Thus, a Michael Phelps or Simone Biles does not emerge as a talent standing alone. It is the elite athlete's talent as distinguished from that of others that makes an athlete truly impressive and able to rise in the hierarchy of sport. From this perspective, the aggregate surplus generated by the pipeline benefits not only those who sponsor higher levels of sport but also those who *seek* higher levels of sport.

The benefits for future elite athletes are clear when we imagine a change from the current youth sport model to a play-based sport approach. The Norway example shows that, even when competition and travel elements that are part of the professionalized youth sport model are delayed, Olympic winners still emerge. However, if the play-based sport model, because of its lower cost and inclusiveness, resulted in a larger pool of talented athletes, such a model may be less desirable for future elite athletes than the current system. While Michael Phelps and Simone Biles might, in fact, be unique talents who would emerge no matter how many others they competed against, for most athletes, the talent difference is small. For an athlete seeking to win a college scholarship or make a national or Olympic or Paralympic team, the most desirable pool of competitors would provide "worthy" competition, so that an athlete can claim the prestige of accomplishment—but not one athlete more. In this respect, the current model with barriers to fuller participation is working.

STATE AND LOCAL GOVERNMENTS

Less obvious but significant beneficiaries of the current U.S. youth sport model are the state and local governments that have captured part of the revenue the model generates. Emphasizing competition and winning inevitably leads youth sport teams to venture beyond their own neighborhoods, and travel is one of the costliest features of our professionalized youth sport model. Not surprisingly, this delivers benefits to cities and towns that host competitions and tournaments.

What scholars call "youth sports tourism"—travel related to children's sport—is "an emerging market" representing "at least 10 percent of the national leisure travel market."[20] States have capitalized on this trend by enacting statutes aimed at attracting such travel[21] by, for instance, building large tax-supported stadiums and undertaking other facilities development projects designed to host youth sport tournaments and competitions.[22] Youth sport tourism has grown over the past ten years, and communities have responded by investing in it.[23] The city of Vicksburg, Mississippi, well illustrates the payoff. In 2019, the city was "expected to host 1,845 tournament teams and attract 175,000 visitors. The impact on hotel rentals was estimated at 25,000 room nights, and the total economic impact was expected to be $24 million."[24] Market researchers analyze travel tournaments and competitions in soccer, volleyball, softball, baseball, lacrosse, and other sports to gain insights into "youth sport consumers" and the optimal "service marketing mix."[25]

Litigation over these projects also highlights the benefits for a locality. In *Long v. Napolitano*, the Arizona court rejected a challenge to the state's Tourism and Sports Authority, which directed public revenue to sports facilities, including those for youth sport. The court stated that "construction and improvement of youth and amateur sports facilities in Maricopa County, with its international airport, and numerous hotels and restaurants, would enable it to compete with similarly populated communities for large-scale youth sports tournaments that draw thousands of visitors."[26] Similarly, the Louisiana court in *Town of Sterlington v. East Ouachita Recreation District* rejected a challenge, brought by parents whose children played in a local Louisiana recreation league, to a sports tourism initiative that would use tax revenue to support development aimed at attracting sports tournaments, particularly in youth baseball and softball.[27] The parents were concerned that hosting "travel ball" tournaments would displace the recreation league's use of the facilities. The court reviewed the "tremendous" economic benefits from sports tourism, including the fact that "a single large tournament will generate at least $500,000 for Northeast Louisiana," and held that using tax revenue to improve facilities and host travel league tournaments was sufficiently within the state's power under the relevant statute.[28]

In addition to the financial benefits flowing to state and local governments through the current youth sport model, there is, one could argue, a social benefit as well. Researchers state that the current approach can promote "social cohesion" by bringing communities together for "cooperative and competitive social bonding activities."[29] While this may certainly be true, it may also be that the U.S. youth sport model does at least as much social harm as good. Litigation over sports tourism demonstrates that, while attracting youth sport to a community for tournaments can increase revenue, it may also displace local, recreational sports programs. Moreover, while social "bonding" might take place during youth sport tournaments, there are also countless reports of harmful behavior, including violence, among those in attendance.[30] In addition, while sport may bring communities together, it is often not building relationships among different socioeconomic groups; at least one research team finds that "many sports leagues and teams . . . continue to act as informal segregating institutions."[31]

Imagining a shift to a play-based sport approach illuminates what is at stake for the communities seeking to generate revenue from the current youth sport model. Deemphasizing performance and competition would undoubtedly mean that there would be many fewer families traveling for the purpose of their children's sport and many fewer spectators arriving to watch competitions. Sport tourism and the revenue it generates would be significantly reduced. Yet, despite the obvious losses, envisioning a change to a play-based sport model reveals more hidden costs to the current approach. Promoting travel for youth sport takes people (and their recreational spending) out of their communities. A change to a model that deemphasizes competition and relies on local resources might, therefore, strengthen community ties and shift political efforts toward building better local recreational spaces, not to attract large numbers of out-of-state visitors but to serve residents every day.

SPORTS MEDICINE PHYSICIANS

Although youth sport did not drive the development of sports medicine, the emergence of sports medicine as a field coincided with the growth of organized, competitive youth sport. During this time, as previously explained, the medical community shifted its stance on sports like youth football to focusing on "medical supervision" instead of encouraging the development of other forms of athletic activity for children. It is clear, then, that the professionalized model for youth sport, producing an epidemic level of injuries and a substantial risk of injury due to overtraining, delivers benefits to, if not a reason for, the expansive community of professionals who claim to practice sports medicine. Indeed, youth sport concussion statutes codify the benefits by requiring medical clearance before a child suspected of having a concussion is permitted to return to play. Shifting to a play-based sport approach emphasizing less training and, perhaps, less risky sports would, therefore, have a significant impact on sports medicine physicians, athletic trainers, and the many others who provide medical services that support the current model.

PARENTS

The surplus generated by the U.S. youth sport model also benefits parents, though the picture is more complex than for other actors. Research on what the psychological community calls "sport parenting" shows that it is a "nuanced phenomenon" and "an intricate and dynamic social experience" with a wide range of "factors and variables."[32] Parents are central to their children's participation in sport;[33] at the most basic level, then, one might argue that when parents put their children into sport they must believe that they and their child will benefit. Indeed, research shows that the vast majority of all parents believe that youth sport participation is good for children.[34] The benefits to parents of youth sport participation could range from the emotional satisfaction of believing they are "good" parents to the relief of knowing their children are supervised.[35] These benefits may be particularly enhanced for fathers, as youth sport is, researchers conclude, "an important context for men to do the 'identity work' of being involved with, and emotionally connected to, their children."[36]

Yet, at this most basic level, parents also shoulder numerous burdens. Youth sport is costly and can significantly impact family life by requiring driving to practices, travel to games, and overall disruption of normal schedules and routines. There is at least some evidence that these burdens are shouldered most frequently by mothers, who often take primary responsibility for transporting children to practices and providing other logistical support—cleaning uniforms, furnishing food, and coordinating schedules—required to keep a child in sport. As one scholar has observed, the "lives of middle-class mothers revolve around their children's sports commitments."[37] Fathers, too, may experience youth sport as a burden because of cost and, given that the majority of youth sports coaches are men (often fathers), an expectation that they provide time and energy to shepherd a team.

Beyond this logistical level, however, youth sport participation also provides many benefits for families as a whole. Youth sport can facilitate a connection between parents and their children, both through time spent together and in sharing healthy levels of pride and pleasure in the child's participation. Through these experiences, parents can develop deeper bonds with their children and within their communities by making new and enhancing existing social connections. In addition, research shows that middle-class parents use youth sport "to acquire 'competitive kid capital'" that they believe will privilege their children in the future.[38] Some African American parents believe that sport can provide an important "way out" and path to a better life for their sons.[39] We might conclude, therefore, that the surplus generated by children's participation in youth sport is kept in-house and shared mutually throughout the family.

For parents acting within the normal range of investment in their children's sport participation, then, the benefits and burdens might be considered roughly equal. The positive shared experiences and joy for the child's accomplishments are balanced against the burdens of cost, time, and family disruption.

Under the current professionalized youth sport model, however, the potential for children's participation to become surplus appropriated by parents is great. Because of their authority over their children, parents have considerable influence over the extent of children's engagement with sport. If a surplus is generated when children's play becomes work, parents are complicit in this exchange. This surplus occurs when parents enjoy a payoff from their children's participation that goes beyond sharing the child's successes and spending time together.

Research shows that investment in a child's success as an athlete is not uncommon for parents, and they often exert pressure on their child related to sports participation and performance.[40] A key feature of the current youth sport model is competition, and it very often entails children "perform[ing]" for spectators, including their parents. Psychologists, policy makers, sports scholars, and even casual observers understand that at youth sport events "the adults in the audience lose their sense of distance" and become so involved in the game that they often, and often problematically, "share in its action and outcome vicariously."[41] There is, then, a kind of conflict of interest presented for families with a child participating in the current youth sport model: "In a culture that values achievement, organized sports offer an indicator of children's accomplishments while play doesn't."[42]

The psychiatric community has studied this phenomenon and the use of children to fulfill parents' goals. There is of course the "normal pride" that all parents experience when their children participate in activities like youth sport, and parents may enter their children in sport with healthy levels of detachment.[43] But some parents may become emotionally "socialized within youth sport," so that their normal level of detachment can quite easily slip into what is known as "achievement by proxy," whereby a child is placed in a situation that gratifies an adult's own "needs or ambitions."[44] The adult or parent is, therefore, motivated not just by the benefit to the child but by the (often unconscious) drive to secure for themselves the "collateral benefits" to be gained by the child's participation.[45] This motivation occurs on a spectrum, ranging from benign parental pride and loving sacrifice to situations where parents "construct conditions" that serve to exert pressure and communicate to the child that he or she must "perform." Children often do not resist but "collude with their parents' and coaches' goals." Accordingly, children can become easily "objectified," in that parents lose the ability to distinguish their own needs and goals from those of their child.[46] At its most extreme, this objectification can even become outright abuse and exploitation if the child becomes "an adult's meal ticket."[47]

In such circumstances, research shows, the conflict of interest between parents and their children who participate in sport is exacerbated in that most parents believe they are acting within normal levels of parental engagement, but their own emotional needs lead them to rationalize problematic emotional involvement tied to their child's participation.[48] For instance, sports medicine physician James R. Andrews describes parents bringing their athletic children to him seeking treatment to facilitate continued play, though it is apparent the child needs rest or to discontinue sport completely. "Parents markedly underestimate their child's risks for playing a specific sport," he notes. "They have no idea that there could be the possibility of a catastrophic injury."[49] Research also shows that parents' and children's experiences of youth sport often do not align. For instance, while children may feel pressure, fatigue, or disinterest in traveling to compete in youth sport tournaments, parents often "treat these trips as family vacations."[50] Family conflict may occur when parents' and children's perceptions of the child's ability do not match.[51] Sport participation can go from being in a child's interest to limiting his or her development, as with children who are homeschooled to support their sports training.[52]

The foregoing account suggests that parents could be one of the biggest losers if the current youth sport model shifted to become more play than sport. While parents would enjoy gains in that participation would likely be less costly and time-consuming, there would be an almost certain emotional loss. A play-based sport model would include far fewer competitions and performances for adults, and travel for sport would be greatly reduced. For parents who derive emotional satisfaction from watching their children play and who build their own social capital through the process, a model deemphasizing performance and competition would not deliver the same payoff. While parents may adjust to such a loss, finding that their happier children produce a kind of satisfaction as well, there remains the question posed by critical theorists about the role youth sport plays in satiating adults' emotional "need for meaning and rejuvenation."[53] If adults do not get their "rejuvenation" from youth sport, there presumably would be an unmet need that would have to find satisfaction elsewhere.

CHILDREN

Perhaps the most difficult question is, What part of our current approach to grassroots youth sport is, in the language of economists, retained by the child as pleasure or *use value*? This analysis is, without doubt, highly individualized and depends on the particular child and sports program in which the child participates. For the relatively small number of children destined to be elite athletes, it can be argued that the surplus the child's participation creates was not appropriated at all. The child who grows into an elite athlete gets to keep the satisfaction, acclaim, medals, endorsements, and prestige that this level of accomplishment brings.

In addition, for at least some children, the surplus generated by the current model is, in a sense, gambled for a bigger reward—usually the hope of a college scholarship or at least college admission. For these children, the surplus can come with a significant upside. The additional training hours, injuries, and pressure can result in an educational investment, elevated status, and the experiences of being a college athlete, and athletes who earn a full or partial scholarship have reduced education debt or no debt at all. For about

180,000, or 2% of all high school athletes, this is the case.[54] About 500,000 total will have the opportunity to play college sports, and playing a sport can help with college admission.[55]

However, reports of abuse of athletes in the U.S. Olympic and Paralympic Movement, including elite gymnasts, swimmers, and volleyball players,[56] undercut the notion that the child-turned-elite athlete reaps only benefits from participation. Moreover, the children whose investment in youth sport was successfully bet on a future in college sport still may not get the full value of the surplus they continue to create. A considerable amount of legal literature details the appropriation of the value produced by college athletes, particularly in revenue-generating sports like football and basketball.[57] Nevertheless, for the children of the pipeline who emerge athletically talented, there is at least a credible claim that the benefits primarily stay with the child and that they outweigh the burdens.

For the millions of children who participate in youth sport and do not emerge as the next great talent, assessing the benefits and burdens is perhaps even more complex. These children certainly reap at least some gains from participation, even though they do not reach elite status. While the current youth sport model is not necessary to produce such benefits, it may, in many cases, be sufficient to confer exercise, increased physical literacy, enhanced social connection, and the other benefits cited in the research in support of sport participation.[58] Children exchange their athletic labor for the medals and trophies that can be a form of "payment" for their efforts and a source of the self-satisfaction that comes with learning new skills. Thus, Messner and Musto have stated that "*playing sports* can be a very good thing."[59]

In contrast, being a "highly involved *athlete*," Messner and Musto note, may have considerable costs.[60] Research has well documented the consequences of the current youth sport model. As previously explained, most children quit by adolescence because it is no longer fun. There is a youth sport injury "epidemic," including entirely preventable "overuse" injuries that are the result of overtraining. Children experience pressure from their parents and coaches that can be so intense they want doctors to prohibit them from playing.[61] The youth sport culture can, in some cases, contribute to and normalize forms of athlete abuse.[62] Time spent laboring in youth sport can also impact a child's education, or at least the hours spent focusing on education.[63] For most children, all that is necessary to provide the benefits of sport "is that they be given the opportunity to play in recreational or competitive leagues when they show an interest in doing so." In the case of children who are not gifted athletes, then, early participation in competitive sports "runs the risk of *narrowing* their future options."[64]

Not surprisingly, the current model also imposes unique burdens based on race, gender, and class. The surplus appropriation at the intercollegiate level particularly impacts Black male athletes.[65] Regarding the impact on Black male children participating in youth sport, research consistently demonstrates that participation in sport is influenced by socioeconomic factors, and the pay-to-play model often means that socioeconomically disadvantaged children of color have fewer sport options than more privileged children.[66] This pattern, combined with the fact that Black families often see sport participation as a pathway to a better life, means that Black boys disproportionately participate in sports such as basketball and football. Disproportionate representation in football imposes a particular burden on Black males because Black male bodies serving predominantly white audiences' desire to consume the product of intercollegiate and professional football risk concussions and other physical trauma of the game.[67] Moreover, scholars assert, the belief that sport can lead to a better life for Black males is largely a "myth," and some argue that sport particularly harms Black males because it perpetuates narratives that "reinforce racism."[68]

Children of color and economically disadvantaged children are also uniquely harmed by the current youth sport model because not only are they often excluded from participation but they are also burdened by the prevailing narrative that views them as needing to be saved through sport. Sport is promoted as a solution to get them "off the streets."[69] Researchers find that, for socioeconomically disadvantaged children, youth sport can take the form of "deficit reduction" or "social control" aimed at fixing those who are deemed "at risk."[70]

Lack of access to sport in the current model can be a burden for girls, especially girls of color. While Title IX has transformed school-based sports programs and societal norms around women's and girls' participation in sports, the lack of robust Title IX enforcement means that girls who want to continue in sport do not get the full measure of opportunity that boys enjoy.[71] Further, although the landscape is changing, the relative lack of established and lucrative professional opportunities means that a girl's participation in sport can generate many benefits for others today while leaving her with less of a payoff down the line. While opportunities in elite Olympic and Paralympic Movement sport are generally more equal, girls and women have suffered more of the abuse that such training environments in some cases fosters.[72]

Children with disabilities also are significantly burdened by the current youth sport model. Medical researchers have long known that children with disabilities, like their nondisabled peers, benefit from "physical activity."[73] Despite programs such as the Paralympic Movement and the Special Olympics, however, opportunities for children with disabilities to participate in sport are in short supply.[74] Children with disabilities are a diverse group—including those with physical, cognitive, and behavioral impairments—and opportunities for participation are limited for them all in terms of both the paucity of suitable programs and lack of access to those that exist.[75] Children with disabilities are also discouraged from participating by programs that emphasize competing to win rather than "participation for the sake of fun, enjoyment, and inclusion."[76]

Finally, burdens are also imposed on children who do not participate, for whatever reason, in youth sport. The first is the burden identified by the prevailing discourse that lack of access to sport is a type of harm. For many children who wish to play and cannot access a sports program due to socioeconomic circumstances, this is certainly true. But the prevailing discourse *itself* has the potential to produce more harm than does lack of access, because it makes children the center of a societal "problem." As nearly everyone is steeped in the sport-is-good discourse, children who do not play, documents such as the NYSS suggest, present, at best, an issue to be addressed or, at worst, are "failure[s]."[77]

For many, if not all, children, then, a change to a play-based sport model could confer substantial benefits. Less emphasis on training and competition would leave children who participate in sport with more time for other activities and would certainly take less of a toll on their bodies. Children also would not experience the same psychological pressures—from parents, coaches, and others—to perform and excel in sport. Moreover, without the excess costs associated with the current model, more children could participate. Similarly, without a focus on traditional sports that have elite or professional opportunities, a change to a play-based model could more readily include children, such as those with disabilities and those who are not currently interested in the standard sports,[78] and give them the benefits of participation. A child-centered focus on fun, rather than "saving" children or social control, also suggests that a different approach could produce benefits in that children would not be problematized through the discourse of sport.

Ultimately, however, it is difficult to account fully for the range of benefits and burdens that result from the current youth sport model because of the relative lack of research. As previously stated, sport scholars have noted that entrenched assumptions about sport's inherent "goodness" contribute to a lack of and resistance to critical sports research.[79] As Messner and Musto advise, "We need strong and reliable scholarly research, rather than unfounded assumptions or ideology."[80] Thus, the assumption that sport is beneficial for children, among other factors, has meant that we have little research aimed at youth sport when viewed in the context of the millions of children who participate. We also have little research on children's *present* experiences in sport (beyond that they quit because of burnout, injury, or that it is no longer fun).[81] The limited research, particularly critical research, means the prevailing youth-sport-is-good narrative continues to define our reality, so that fully understanding the benefits and burdens of the model is necessarily contingent and incomplete. It also limits the possibilities for meaningful change. It is, one might argue, a manifestation of what scholars call the ongoing "struggle to convert children from a status as objects to a status as subjects."[82]

Conclusion

In its 2021 memorandum clarifying that at least some college athletes met the NLRA's definition of an employee, the NLRB General Counsel noted that the agency would no longer use the term *student-athlete*. Instead, it would refer to a college athlete as a "player."[1] *Student-athlete* is, of course, a decades-old term widely used to describe college and high school students who participate in school-based sport, and it is a key part of the narrative around the uniquely American model of embedding sports in schools. Most courts, policy makers, commentators, and fans likely have given the term little thought beyond the image of the scholar-sport hero who is fortunate to represent their school and reap the many benefits of participation.

The General Counsel's memorandum, however, took a different view. It stated what has long been known to sport scholars: that the term *student-athlete* was created in the 1950s by the NCAA for legal reasons, with the intent to ensure that college athletes would not be considered employees subject to the protection of state workers' compensation statutes. As such, the General Counsel explained, it is not a benign term with positive, patriotic connotations but a label designed to "deprive" college athletes of employee protections provided by law.[2]

While the full extent of the NLRB General Counsel's legal and policy position may not survive future presidential administrations or congressional action, the statement nevertheless provides a powerful insight that goes far beyond how we refer to and legally categorize college athletes under the law. The General Counsel's new approach reflects the fact that, as our knowledge of sport has developed—particularly as we have made greater sense of the athlete experience—our discourse around it has changed. When the discourse changes, policy problems may be identified in new ways, so that today's revered traditions become tomorrow's *Alston*.

Moreover, the collective consciousness-raising around the sport experience that includes and values the perspective of athletes—as well as those of sport sponsors, administrators, and fans—makes courts' and legislatures' traditional deferential approach more difficult to maintain. Thus, it is perhaps not a coincidence that, as sports law has developed as a field and researchers have generated scholarship exploring the implications of the hands-off approach, legal and policy institutions have begun to respond. With the analysis in this book, I take a step in that direction with respect to our understanding of youth sport, where the participants are not simply athletes: they are, to state the obvious, children.

I have described the long-standing narrative in the United States that youth sport is an integral part of a good childhood. Citing a long list of benefits, the government and adults, including parents, urge participation in a professionalized, pay-to-play youth sport model that, while undoubtedly delivering some positives, also imposes significant burdens on the children who do, and do not, participate.

Exploring these distributional consequences helps us understand youth sport beyond the romanticized version of our usual discourse and reveals the reality that our current approach is structured and promoted by those with a significant stake in the system. This is a conflict of interest with consequence. While often thought of as play or just another character-building childhood experience, a closer look at our current approach to youth sport shows that it is a system that puts children's bodies to work generating surplus value that is appropriated by a host of stakeholders—far beyond what would be necessary for most children's benefit. Because of the power imbalance, supported by law, between parents and children and between sports regulators and athletes, the U.S. youth sport model operates to ensure that this surplus continues to be generated and its appropriation solidified.

If we view in this way the message to participate in and stick with the current U.S. youth sport model, we can better appreciate how it creates a kind of epistemic injustice that perpetuates the interests and power of a range of adult and institutional actors.[3] It is a message that prevents a full understanding of what U.S. youth sport is and whom it is for and, therefore, limits the prospects for meaningful reform. It does not have to be this way.

Our traditional, hands-off law and policy reflex concerning sport, including youth sport, is hardly necessary to preserve what is special about the experience. Like the government's one-time policy choice to stay out of what was considered the private family sphere and, through that choice, effectively to endorse a husband's near-total control over his wife and children, the hands-off approach only serves existing power structures in sport; it is not necessary for preserving the essence of sport itself. Thus, as we develop greater knowledge of sport, and as sports law has developed as a field, we have started to take law and policy steps in a new, more nuanced direction, and this lights a way for reform in youth sport.

One sports philosopher has commented that "the erosion of the play spirit in contemporary win-at-all-costs sport could be regarded as moral regress."[4] A deeper understanding of U.S. youth sport, with its full range of burdens and benefits, does not inevitably lead to the conclusion that sport participation for children is wrong, in all instances results in harm, or should be avoided. It also does not require a rejection of the vibrant U.S. sport culture. To the contrary: raising our collective consciousness by making greater sense of youth sport provides a vital foundation for consequential future reform to ensure that the real promise of youth sport may finally be realized. In this way, our grassroots youth sport system can be built on more than adults' romanticized images and the political interests that drive our current law and policy assumptions. It can instead be constructed primarily for children's present well-being, informed by the notion that play—and the benefits it provides children—is enough.

NOTES

INTRODUCTION

1. Campagna-McGuffin v. Diva Gymnastics Academy, Inc., 199 N.E.3d 1034 (Ohio Ct. App. 2022).

2. Lawrence J. Hatab, "The Drama of Agonistic Embodiment: Nietzschean Reflections on the Meaning of Sports," *International Studies in Philosophy* 30, no. 3 (1998): 98–99.

3. Stephen H. Hardy, "Entrepreneurs, Organizations, and the Sports Marketplace," in *The New American Sport History: Recent Approaches and Perspectives*, ed. S. W. Pope (Urbana: University of Illinois Press, 1997), 344.

4. Ben Carrington and David L. Andrews, "Part I: Sporting Structures and Historical Formations," in *A Companion to Sport*, ed. Andrews and Carrington (Malden, MA: Wiley Blackwell, 2013), 19. Sport scholars have explained that sport has no required "universal elements" or content but is instead "wholly relational."

5. Ben Carrington and David L. Andrews, "Introduction: Sport as Escape, Struggle, and Art," in *A Companion to Sport*, 7–8.

6. On Olympic and Paralympic sport, see, for example, Protecting Young Victims from Sexual Abuse and Safe Sport Authorization Act, Pub. L. No. 115-126, 132 Stat. 318 (2018); Empowering Olympic, Paralympic, and Amateur Athletes Act, Pub. L. No. 116-189, 134 Stat. 943 (2020). On intercollegiate sport, see, for example, National Collegiate Athletic Association v. Alston, 141 S. Ct. 2141 (2021), holding that the NCAA's "amateurism" model violates antitrust law to the extent it limits the amount of education-related benefits schools can provide athletes; and Memorandum from NLRB General Counsel Jennifer A. Abruzzo to All Regional Directors, Officers-in-Charge, and Resident Officers, "Statutory Rights of Players at Academic Institutions (Student Athletes) under the National Labor

Relations Act," No. GC 21-08 (September 29, 2021), advising that certain athletes at some colleges and universities will be considered "employees" under the National Labor Relations Act and that "misclassifying" these persons as "student-athletes" to mislead them about their rights will be considered a violation of the act.

7. Johnson v. National Collegiate Athletic Association, 556 F. Supp. 3d 491 (E.D. Pa. 2021), affirmed in part in Johnson v. National Collegiate Athletic Association, 108 F. 4th 163 (3rd Cir. 2024).

8. James R. Andrews, "Why Are There So Many Injuries to Our Young Athletes? Professionalization and Specialization in Youth Sport," *University of Baltimore Law Review* 40, no. 4 (Summer 2011): 577. At least one scholar has referred to this as an "adult-induced dropout rate." Douglas E. Abrams, "The Challenge Facing Parents and Coaches in Youth Sports: Assuring Children Fun and Equal Opportunity," *Villanova Sports and Entertainment Law Journal* 8, no. 2 (January 2002): 255.

9. D. Stanley Eitzen, *Fair and Foul: Beyond the Myths and Paradoxes of Sport*, 6th ed. (Lanham, MD: Rowman and Littlefield, 2016), 114.

10. Jay Coakley, *Sport in Society: Issues and Controversies*, 13th ed. (New York: McGraw-Hill, 2021), 88.

11. Andrews, "Why Are There So Many Injuries," 577.

12. "Youth Sports Facts: Challenges," Aspen Institute Project Play, accessed March 11, 2022, https://projectplay.org/youth-sports/facts/challenges, explaining that the cost of youth sport is a barrier to initial and continuing participation, especially for specific demographic groups; U.S. Department of Health and Human Services, *National Youth Sports Strategy* (Washington, DC, September 2019); N. Jeremi Duru, "It's Not Child's Play: A Regulatory Approach to Reforming American Youth Sports," *Virginia Sports and Entertainment Law Journal* 20, no. 1 (Spring 2021): 41, citing "socioeconomic stratification" as a problem in youth sport.

13. Exceptions in the legal literature include Abrams, "Challenge Facing Parents," 255; Duru, *It's Not Child's Play*, 25; and scholarship that addresses youth sport concussions, for example, Katharine Silbaugh, "The Legal Design for Parenting Concussion Risk," *UC Davis Law Review* 53, no. 1 (November 2019); Sydney Diekmann, Christine Egan, Carly Rasmussen, and Francis X. Shen, "The Failure of Youth Sports Concussion Laws and the Limits of Legislating Health Education," *Yale Journal of Health Policy, Law, and Ethics* 19, no. 1 (2019); and Vivian E. Hamilton, "Play Now, Pay Later? Youth and Adolescent Collision Sports," *Hastings Law Journal* 71, no. 1 (2020).

14. Matthew J. Mitten, Timothy Davis, N. Jeremi Duru, and Barbara Osborne, *Sports Law and Regulation: Cases, Materials, and Problems*, 5th ed. (Frederick, MD: Aspen, 2020), 4.

15. National Collegiate Athletic Association v. Board of Regents of the University of Oklahoma, 468 U.S. 85 (1984).

16. *Board of Regents*, 468 U.S. at 120.

17. See, for example, Taylor Branch, "The Shame of College Sports," *The Atlantic*, October 2011; Marc Edelman, "A Prelude to *Jenkins v. NCAA*: Amateurism, Antitrust Law, and the Role of Consumer Demand in a Proper Rule of Reason Analysis," *Louisiana Law Review* 78, no. 1 (Fall 2017); Marc Edelman, "A Short Treatise on Amateurism and Antitrust Law: Why the NCAA's No Pay Rules Violate Section 1 of the Sherman Act," *Case Western Reserve Law Review* 64, no. 1 (2013); James Landry and Thomas A. Baker III, "Change or Be Changed: A Proposal for the NCAA to Combat Corruption and Unfairness by Proactively Reforming Its Regulation of Athlete Publicity Rights," *New York University Journal of Intellectual Property and Entertainment Law* 9, no. 1 (February 2020); and Michael H. LeRoy, "Courts and the Future of 'Athletic Labor' in College Sports," *Arizona Law Review* 57, no. 2 (2015).

18. *Alston*, 141 S. Ct. at 2169 (Kavanaugh, J., concurring).

19. On consciousness raising, see Catharine A. MacKinnon, "Feminism, Marxism, Method, and the State: An Agenda for Theory," *Signs* 7, no. 3 (Spring 1982): 519, explaining "consciousness raising." See also Miranda Fricker, *Epistemic Injustice: Power and the Ethics of Knowing* (Oxford: Oxford University Press, 2007), 6, explaining what she terms "hermeneutical injustice" as a type of "epistemic injustice" that arises from a "gap in our shared tools of social interpretation."

20. Miranda Fricker, "Powerlessness and Social Interpretation," *Episteme: A Journal of Social Epistemology* 3, nos. 1–2 (2006): 96–108.

21. Travis E. Dorsch et al., "Toward an Integrated Understanding of the Youth Sport System," *Research Quarterly for Exercise and Sport* 93, no. 1 (March 2022).

1. DEFINITIONS, HISTORY, AND DATA

1. Ken Roberts, *Social Theory, Sport, Leisure* (London: Routledge, 2016), 129, explaining the influence of Foucault's theory of discourse in sport.

2. Douglas Booth, "Constructing Knowledge: Histories of Modern Sport," in *A Companion to Sport*, ed. David L. Andrews and Ben Carrington (Malden, MA: Wiley Blackwell, 2013), 31.

3. "The discourses of sport, often articulating assumptions about sport's inherent worthiness, permeate contemporary societies," Doune MacDonald and colleagues write, "such that it is nearly impossible to sit outside the circulation of these discourses." MacDonald et al., "The Will for Inclusion: Bothering the Inclusion/Exclusion Discourses of Sport," in *Inclusion and Exclusion through Youth Sport*, ed. Symeon Dagkas and Kathleen Armour (London: Routledge, 2012), 9.

4. U.S. Department of Health and Human Services, *National Youth Sports Strategy* (Washington, DC, September 2019); Andrew Bloodworth, Mike McNamee, and Richard Bailey, "Sport, Physical Activity, and Well-Being: An Objectivist Account," *Sport, Education, and Society* 17, no. 4 (August 2012). See also MacDonald et al., "Will for Inclusion," 9, stating that "worldwide, governments extol the virtues of sport for the benefit of the individual and society."

5. Proclamation No. 9870, 84 Fed. Reg. 19689 (April 30, 2019).

6. U.S. Department of Health and Human Services, *National Youth Sports Strategy*, 53; President's Council on Sports, Fitness, and Nutrition Science Board, "PCSFN Science Board Report on Youth Sports" (Washington, DC, September 17, 2020), 7.

7. MacDonald et al., "Will for Inclusion," 10.

8. Jay Coakley, *Sports in Society: Issues and Controversies*, 13th ed. (New York: McGraw-Hill, 2021), 6.

9. UNICEF Innocenti Research Centre, *Protecting Children from Violence in Sport: A Review with a Focus on Industrialized Countries* (Florence, Italy: UNICEF, July 2010), 3.

10. Matthew J. Mitten, Timothy Davis, N. Jeremi Duru, and Barbara Osborne, *Sports Law and Regulation: Cases, Materials, and Problems*, 5th ed. (Frederick, MD: Aspen, 2020), 6.

11. Coakley, *Sports in Society*, 6, 68.

12. Coakley, *Sports in Society*, 68–69.

13. B. David Ridpath, *Alternative Models of Sports Development in America: Solutions to a Crisis in Education and Public Health* (Athens: Ohio University Press, 2018), xvi.

14. Biedinger v. Quinnipiac University, 691 F.3d 85 (2nd Cir. 2012).

15. The U.S. Department of Health and Human Services (HHS), in its National Youth Sports Strategy (NYSS), states that "there is a distinct lack of a single, comprehensive data source. No single system, Federal or non-Federal, measures all aspects of sports participation" (12, 41). The NYSS also notes that "another limitation" on the available youth sport data "is that there is little distinction between sports and other physical activities" (43).

16. 410 Ill. Comp. Stat. Ann. § 145/5 (Westlaw through P.A. 103-586 of 2024 Reg. Sess.).

17. Ohio Rev. Code Ann. § 3707.51 (Westlaw through File 135th Gen. Assem. 2023-24).

18. Neb. Rev. Stat. § 77-2704.63 (Westlaw through April 2024 of 2nd Reg. Sess. 108th Legis.).

19. S.C. Code Ann. § 41-1-120 (Westlaw through 2024 Act No. 145).

20. Mont. Code Ann. § 20-7-1302 (Westlaw through 2024 Reg. Sess.).

21. Ore. Rev. Stat. § 418.691 (Westlaw through 2024 Reg. Sess.).

22. Iowa Code § 15E.321 (Westlaw through 2024 Reg. Sess.).

23. Ridpath, *Alternative Models*, xvi.

24. "Age of Majority," Legal Information Institute, Cornell Law School, updated November 2021, https://www.law.cornell.edu/wex/age_of_majority.

25. United Nations, "Convention on the Rights of the Child," *United Nations Treaty Series* 1577, no. 27531 (November 20, 1989): 46.

26. Kelsey Logan, Steven Cuff, and American Association of Pediatrics [AAP] Council on Sports Medicine and Fitness, "Organized Sports for Children, Preadolescents, and Adolescents," *Pediatrics* 143, no. 6 (June 2019).

27. Lincoln Allison, *Amateurism in Sport: An Analysis and Defense* (London: Routledge, 2001), 8-10.

28. Allison, *Amateurism in Sport*, 20, 3.

29. Joseph M. Turrini, *The End of Amateurism in American Track and Field* (Urbana: University of Illinois Press, 2010), 13-14.

30. Coakley, *Sports in Society*, 410.

31. Kenneth L. Shropshire, "Legislation for the Glory of Sport: Amateurism and Compensation," *Seton Hall Journal of Sport Law* 1, no. 1 (1991): 8-9.

32. Turrini, *End of Amateurism*, 2.

33. Ind. Code § 4-38-2-3 (Westlaw through 2024 Second Reg. Sess.).

34. S.D. Codified Laws § 10-46-74 (Westlaw through 2024 Reg. Sess.).

35. National Collegiate Athletic Association v. Alston, 141 S. Ct. 2141 at 2152 (2021).

36. Amateur Sports Act, 36 U.S.C. §§ 220501-220514 (1978).

37. Amateur Sports Act, §§ 220503, 220501(b)(3).

38. *Amateur Sports Act of 1978: Hearing Before the Senate Committee on Commerce, Science, and Transportation*, 95th Cong., 2nd sess. (March 21, 1978) (letter from F. Don Miller, Executive Director of the U.S. Olympic Committee, to Senator Ted Stevens), 12-13.

39. Logan, Cuff, and AAP Council on Sports Medicine and Fitness, "Organized Sports," 1.

40. Coakley, *Sports in Society*, 84.

41. David K. Wiggins, "A Worthwhile Effort? History of Organized Youth Sport in the United States," *Kinesiology Review* 2, no. 1 (February 2013): 65-75.

42. Coakley, *Sports in Society*, 85.

43. Wiggins, "A Worthwhile Effort?" 68.

44. Wiggins, "A Worthwhile Effort?" 65.

45. Wiggins, "A Worthwhile Effort?" 67.

46. John F. Kennedy, "The Vigor We Need," *Sports Illustrated*, July 16, 1962.

47. Matthew T. Bowers and Thomas M. Hunt, "The President's Council on Physical Fitness and the Systematisation of Children's Play in America," *International Journal of the History of Sport* 28, no. 11 (August 2011): 1496.

48. Dennis Gildea, "Youth Sports," in *The Routledge History of American Sport*, ed. Linda J. Borish, David K. Wiggins, and Gerald R. Gems (London: Routledge, 2017).

49. Wiggins, "A Worthwhile Effort?" 65–67.

50. Clare Huntington and Elizabeth S. Scott, "Conceptualizing Legal Childhood in the Twenty-First Century," *Michigan Law Review* 118, no. 7 (May 2020): 1373.

51. Coakley, *Sports in Society*, 85.

52. Kathleen Bachynski, *No Game for Boys to Play: The History of Youth Football and the Origins of a Public Health Crisis* (Chapel Hill: University of North Carolina Press, 2019), 81.

53. Jack W. Berryman and Roberta J. Park, eds., *Sport and Exercise Science: Essays in the History of Sports Medicine* (Champaign: University of Illinois Press, 1992), xii.

54. Bachynski, *No Game for Boys*, 73–94.

55. Berryman and Park, *Sport and Exercise Science*, xiii.

56. Coakley, *Sports in Society*, 87.

57. U.S. Department of Health and Human Services, *National Youth Sports Strategy*, 21.

58. Coakley, *Sports in Society*, 92.

59. Wiggins, "A Worthwhile Effort?" 69.

60. Ridpath, *Alternative Models*, xvi; U.S. Department of Health and Human Services, *National Youth Sports Strategy*, 12, stating that "there is no standard definition of youth sports used in national surveys."

61. Tess Britton, "Predictions vs. Reality: The Economic Impact of COVID-19 on Sports," *Michigan Journal of Economics*, March 31, 2021, https://sites.lsa.umich.edu/mje/2021/03/31/predictions-vs-reality-the-economic-impact-of-covid-19-on-sports/.

62. Richard K. Miller & Associates, *Sports Marketing 2023*, 21st ed. (Miramar, FL, 2023).

63. U.S. Department of Health and Human Services, *National Youth Sports Strategy*, 21; "Survey: Kids Quit Most Sports by Age 11," Aspen Institute Project Play, accessed April 2, 2022, https://projectplay.org/news/kids-quit-most-sports-by-age-11; Laura Newberry, "Kids Are Losing Interest in Organized Sports. Why That Matters," *Los Angeles Times*, December 6, 2021, calling youth sport a "$19 billion industry."

64. Richard K. Miller & Assoc., *Sports Marketing 2023*.

65. Coakley, *Sports in Society*, 383.

66. Richard K. Miller & Assoc., *Sports Marketing 2023*, 19.

67. Becky Gillette, "Youth Sports Tourism a Home Run When It Comes to Economic Impact," *Mississippi Business Journal*, July 12, 2019.

68. "2018-2019 High School Athletics Participation Survey," National Federation of State High School Associations, accessed April 2, 2022, https://www.nfhs.org/media/1020412/2018-19_participation_survey.pdf.

69. Mitten, Davis, Duru, and Osborne, *Sports Law and Regulation*, 711.

70. Women's Sports Foundation, *50 Years of Title IX: We're Not Done Yet* (New York, 2022), 24.

71. GLSEN Research Institute, *LGBTQ Students and School Sports Participation* (New York, 2021), 8.

72. Office of Special Education and Rehabilitative Services, Office of Special Education Programs, *Creating Equal Opportunities for Children and Youth with Disabilities to Participate in Physical Education and Extracurricular Athletics* (Washington, D.C.: U.S. Department of Education, 2011).

73. Benjamin J. Chun et al., "Concussion Epidemiology in Youth Sports: Sports Study of a Statewide High School Sports Program," *Sports Health* 13, no. 1 (January-February 2021): 18.

74. U.S. Department of Health and Human Services, *National Youth Sports Strategy*, 40.

75. "About Us," National Council for Youth Sports, accessed March 11, 2022, https://ncys.org/about-us/. The National Council for Youth Sports claims to be a fee-based membership association. Other organizations also rely on the 60 million figure. See, for example, "Intensive Participation in a Single Sport: Good or Bad for Kids?" Lerner Children's Pavilion, Hospital for Special Surgery, accessed April 2, 2022, https://www.hss.edu/pediatrics-intensive-participation-single-sport-good-bad-kids.asp.

76. Physical Activity Alliance, *2022 U.S. Report Card on Physical Activity for Children and Youth* (Washington, D.C., 2022), 10.

77. U.S. Department of Health and Human Services, *National Youth Sports Strategy*, 35.

78. Office of Disease Prevention and Health Promotion, "Increase the Proportion of Children and Adolescents Who Play Sports—PA-12," Healthy People 2030, accessed August 20, 2023, https://health.gov/healthypeople/objectives-and-data/browse-objectives/physical-activity/increase-proportion-children-and-adolescents-who-play-sports-pa-12.

79. U.S. Department of Health and Human Services, *National Youth Sports Strategy*, 35.

80. U.S. Department of Health and Human Services, *National Youth Sports Strategy*, 35, also explaining that "only 45 percent of youth from households with

less than a high school education participated, compared to 73 percent of youth from households with a college degree or higher."

81. "Survey: Kids Quit Most Sports by Age 11."

82. Coakley, *Sports in Society*, 90.

83. "Coaching Trends," in *State of Play 2023*, Aspen Institute Project Play, accessed May 24, 2024, https://projectplay.org/state-of-play-2023/coaching-trends; Coakley, *Sports in Society*, 94.

84. "Coaching Trends."

85. Jay Coakley, "Positive Youth Development through Sport: Myths, Beliefs, and Realities," in *Positive Youth Development through Sport*, ed. Nicholas L. Holt (London: Routledge, 2016), 27; Melanie Lang and Mike Hartill, eds., *Safeguarding, Child Protection, and Abuse in Sport: International Perspectives in Research, Policy, and Practice* (London: Routledge, 2015), 2.

86. Jean Côté, Colleen Coakley, and Mark Bruner, "Children's Talent Development in Sport: Effectiveness or Efficiency?" in *Inclusion and Exclusion through Youth Sport*, ed. Symeon Dagkas and Kathleen Armour (London: Routledge, 2012), 182–83.

87. Coakley, *Sports in Society*, 84.

88. Daniel Gould, "The Professionalization of Youth Sport: It's Time to Act!" *Clinical Journal of Sports Medicine* 19, no. 2 (March 2009); Martin Camiré and Fernando Santos, "Promoting Positive Youth Development and Life Skills in Youth Sport: Challenges and Opportunities amidst Increased Professionalization," *Journal of Sport Pedagogy and Research* 5, no. 1 (August 2019): 28; Charles A. Popkin, Ahmad F. Bayomy, and Christopher S. Ahmad, "Early Sport Specialization," *Journal of the American Academy of Orthopaedic Surgeons* 27, no. 22 (November 15, 2019).

89. U.S. Department of Health and Human Services, *National Youth Sports Strategy*, 54.

90. "Survey: Kids Quit Most Sports by Age 11." Other surveys report that nearly 70 percent of children quit by age 13. See Julianna W. Miner, "Why 70 Percent of Kids Quit Sports by Age 13," *Washington Post*, June 1, 2016.

91. D. Stanley Eitzen, *Fair and Foul: Beyond the Myths and Paradoxes of Sport*, 6th ed. (Lanham, MD: Rowman and Littlefield, 2016), 121 ("lack of fun"); U.S. Department of Health and Human Services, *National Youth Sports Strategy*, 55–56 (other factors).

92. U.S. Department of Health and Human Services, *National Youth Sports Strategy*, 22; Eitzen, *Fair and Foul*, 87–88; President's Council on Sports, Fitness, and Nutrition Science Board, *Benefits of Youth Sports* (Washington, D.C., September 17, 2020).

93. U.S. Department of Health and Human Services, *National Youth Sports Strategy*, 49–50.

94. President's Council, "PCSFN Science Board Report," 5.

95. "Active People, Healthy Nation," Centers for Disease Control and Prevention, accessed April 2, 2022, https://www.cdc.gov/physicalactivity/activepeoplehealthynation/index.html; U.S. Government Accountability Office, *K-12 Education: School-Based Physical Education and Sports Programs*, GAO-12-350 (Washington, D.C., February 2012), 4-5, https://www.gao.gov/assets/gao-12-350.pdf.

96. Toben F. Nelson, "Sport and the Childhood Obesity Epidemic," in *Child's Play: Sport in Kids' Worlds*, ed. Michael A. Messner and Michela Musto (New Brunswick, NJ: Rutgers University Press, 2016); U.S. Government Accountability Office, *K-12 Education: High School Sports Access and Participation*, GAO-17-754R (Washington, D.C., September 14, 2017), 1, https://www.gao.gov/assets/gao-17-754r.pdf. On preparing youth for the labor market, see Council of Economic Advisers, *Economic Report of the President and The Annual Report of the Council of Economic Advisers* (Washington, D.C., February 2018), 137-44.

97. Dionne L. Koller, "How the Expressive Power of Title IX Dilutes Its Promise," *Harvard Journal of Sports and Entertainment Law* 3, no. 1 (Winter 2012): 114.

98. Logan, Cuff, and AAP Council on Sports Medicine and Fitness, "Organized Sports," 4, 13.

99. Phoebe Friesen et al., "Overuse Injuries in Youth Sports: Legal and Social Responsibility," *Journal of Legal Aspects of Sport* 28, no. 2 (2018): 151; Eitzen, *Fair and Foul*, 90.

100. Friesen et al., "Overuse Injuries," 151. Medical groups such as the American Orthopaedic Society for Sports Medicine have adopted campaigns to generate awareness of overuse injuries in youth sport; "AOSSM and NCYS team up to STOP Sports Injuries," American Orthopaedic Society for Sports Medicine, accessed April 2, 2022, https://www.sportsmed.org/about-us/news/aossm-and-ncys-team-up-to-stop-sports-injuries.

101. Logan, Cuff, and AAP Council on Sports Medicine and Fitness, "Organized Sports," 13.

102. Logan, Cuff, and AAP Council on Sports Medicine and Fitness, "Organized Sports," 4.

103. Coakley, *Sports in Society*, 67.

104. Daniel Gould, "The Current Youth Sport Landscape: Identifying Critical Research Issues," *Kinesiology Review* 8, no. 3 (August 2019): 151.

105. Gould, "Current Youth Sport Landscape," 150.

106. Office of Special Education and Rehabilitative Services, *Creating Equal Opportunities*.

107. Peter Donnelly and Michael Atkinson, "Where History Meets Biography: Toward a Public Sociology of Sport," in *Playing for Change: The Continuing*

Struggle for Sport and Recreation, ed. Russell Field (Toronto: University of Toronto Press, 2015), 374, 375.

108. Michael A. Messner and Michela Musto, "Introduction: Kids and Sport," in *Child's Play: Sport in Kids' Worlds*, ed. Michael A. Messner and Michela Musto (New Brunswick, NJ: Rutgers University Press, 2016), 9, stating that the research "should not focus exclusively on access and attrition," as doing so "risks colluding with an ascendant popular health discourse that uncritically promotes sports participation as always good and healthy for kids."

109. Gould, "Current Youth Sport Landscape," 8.

110. Gould, "Current Youth Sport Landscape," 8.

111. See, for example, Tom Farrey et al., "Now Is the Time for Systemic Change to Youth Sports," *Medium*, September 25, 2021; "STOP Sports Injuries," National Council on Youth Sports, accessed April 10, 2022, https://ncys.org/safety/stop-sports-injuries/; "Project Play," Aspen Institute Project Play, accessed April 10, 2022, https://projectplay.org/.

112. "Call for Leadership," in *State of Play 2021*, Aspen Institute Project Play, accessed April 2, 2022, https://projectplay.org/state-of-play-2021/call-for-leadership.

113. President's Council, *PCSFN Science Board Report*, 11.

114. On "legal permissions," see David Kennedy, *A World of Struggle: How Power, Law, and Expertise Shape Global Political Economy* (Princeton, NJ: Princeton University Press, 2016), 70; Duncan Kennedy, "The Stakes of Law, or Hale and Foucault!" *Legal Studies Forum* 15, no. 4 (1991): 333.

2. THE LAW OF THE CHILD AND FAMILY

1. Bellotti v. Baird, 443 U.S. 622 (1979).

2. Samuel M. Davis, Elizabeth S. Scott, Lois A. Weithorn, and Walter Wadlington, eds., *Children in the Legal System*, 6th ed. (St. Paul: Foundation Press, 2020), 129.

3. Clare Huntington and Elizabeth S. Scott, "Conceptualizing Legal Childhood in the Twenty-First Century," *Michigan Law Review* 118, no. 7 (May 2020): 1371-1458.

4. Huntington and Scott, "Conceptualizing Legal Childhood," 1380.

5. Huntington and Scott, 1381-82.

6. Huntington and Scott.

7. Shanta Trivedi, "The Harm of Child Removal," *New York University Review of Law and Social Change* 43, no. 3 (2019): 523.

8. Davis et al., *Children in the Legal System*, 706.

9. Huntington and Scott, "Conceptualizing Legal Childhood," 1375.

10. Troxel v. Granville, 530 U.S. 57, 68-69 (2000); Anne C. Dailey and Laura A. Rosenbury, "The New Law of the Child," *Yale Law Journal* 127, no. 6 (April 2018): 1459-60.

11. Katharine Silbaugh, "The Legal Design for Parenting Concussion Risk," *UC Davis Law Review* 53, no. 1 (November 2019): 235-37.

12. Naomi R. Cahn, "Models of Family Privacy," *George Washington Law Review* 67, nos. 5-6 (June-August 1999): 1241.

13. Clare Huntington and Elizabeth S. Scott, "The Enduring Importance of Parental Rights," *Fordham Law Review* 90, no. 6 (2022): 2529.

14. Trivedi, "Harm of Child Removal."

15. Santosky v. Kramer, 455 U.S. 745 (1982).

16. Parham v. J. R., 442 U.S. 584, 621 (1979) (Stewart, J., concurring).

17. Anne C. Dailey and Laura A. Rosenbury, "The New Parental Rights," *Duke Law Journal* 71, no. 1 (October 2021): 75.

18. Dailey and Rosenbury, "New Parental Rights," 85.

19. Frances Olsen, "The Family and the Market: The Study of Ideology and Legal Reform," *Harvard Law Review* 96, no. 7 (May 1983): 1497.

20. Olsen, "Family and the Market."

21. Dailey and Rosenbury, "New Parental Rights," 107.

22. Meyer v. Nebraska, 262 U.S. 390 (1923); Pierce v. Society of Sisters, 268 U.S. 510 (1925); Prince v. Massachusetts, 321 U.S. 158 (1944); Wisconsin v. Yoder, 406 U.S. 205 (1972).

23. Emily Buss, "'Parental' Rights," *Virginia Law Review* 88, no. 3 (May 2002): 635.

24. Dailey and Rosenbury, "New Parental Rights."

25. *Troxel*, 530 U.S. at 65, 68, also stating that, given the extensive precedent, "it cannot now be doubted that the Due Process Clause of the Fourteenth Amendment protects the fundamental rights of parents to make decisions concerning the care, custody, and control of their children."

26. *Parham*, 442 U.S. at 602. The Court also explained that "our jurisprudence historically has reflected Western civilization concepts of the family as a unit with broad parental authority over minor children."

27. *Bellotti*, 443 U.S. 622.

28. Dailey and Rosenbury, "New Law of the Child," 1460.

29. Davis et al., *Children in the Legal System*, 1 ("broad"); Kristin Henning, "The Fourth Amendment Rights of Children at Home: When Parental Authority Goes Too Far," *William and Mary Law Review* 53, no. 1 (October 2011): 73.

30. On education, see *Meyer*, 262 U.S. at 390. On religion, see *Pierce*, 268 U.S. at 510; and *Yoder*, 406 U.S. at 205.

31. Elizabeth S. Scott, "Comment on Part 4 Essays: Goodwin and Dailey and Rosenbury." *University of Chicago Law Review* 91, no. 2 (2024): 633 (internet access); *Troxel*, 530 U.S. 57 (access to other family members); Dailey and Rosenbury, "New Parental Rights," 95-96 (discipline).

32. Dailey and Rosenbury, "New Parental Rights."

33. B. Jessie Hill, "Medical Decision Making by and on Behalf of Adolescents: Reconsidering First Principles," *Journal of Health Care Law and Policy* 15, no. 1 (January 2012): 37.

34. Dailey and Rosenbury, "New Parental Rights," 93.

35. Dailey and Rosenbury, 75.

36. Davis et al., *Children in the Legal System*, 19.

37. *Prince*, 321 U.S. 158.

38. Ginsberg v. New York, 390 U.S. 629 (1968).

39. Silbaugh, "Legal Design," 228.

40. *Parham*, 442 U.S. at 602.

41. *Parham*, 442 U.S. at 603.

42. Davis et al., *Children in the Legal System*, 129; *Bellotti*, 443 U.S. at 633, stating: "We have recognized three reasons justifying the conclusion that the constitutional rights of children cannot be equated with those of adults: the peculiar vulnerability of children; their inability to make critical decisions in an informed, mature manner; and the importance of the parental role in child rearing."

43. Schmidt v. Prince George's Hospital, 784 A.2d 1112 (Md. App. 2001).

44. Yale Diagnostic Radiology v. Estate of Harun Fountain, 267 Conn. 351 (Conn. 2004).

45. American Law Institute, *Restatement of the Law Third, Torts: Liability for Physical and Emotional Harm* (St. Paul, 2010), § 10.

46. Roper v. Simmons, 543 U.S. 551 (2005); Miller v. Alabama, 132 S. Ct. 2455 (2012).

47. Tennessee Secondary School Athletic Association v. Brentwood Academy, 551 U.S. 291, 298 (2007).

48. Brentwood Academy v. Tennessee Secondary School Athletic Association, 531 U.S. 288, 294 (2001).

49. *Brentwood Academy*, 531 U.S. at 296.

50. *Brentwood Academy*, 531 U.S. at 298-300.

51. Santa Fe Independent School District v. Doe, 530 U.S. 290 at 311 (2000).

52. Kennedy v. Bremerton School District, 142 S. Ct. 2407 (2022).

53. Va. Code Ann. § 54.1-2969(E) (2024); Cal. Fam. Code § 6925 (Deering 2024).

54. See, for example, United States v. Doe, 58 F.4th 1148 (10th Cir. 2023); Sharp v. Arkansas, 548 S.W.3d 846 (Ark. App. 2018); Ohio Rev. Code Ann. § 2152.12 (LexisNexis 2024).

55. For example, Fare v. Michael C., 442 U.S. 707 (1979).

56. Martha Minow, "What Ever Happened to Children's Rights?" *Minnesota Law Review* 80, no. 2 (December 1995): 278.

57. Dailey and Rosenbury, "New Law of the Child," 1460–61, stating that the persistence of the "authorities framework" meant that "by the mid-1990s, most scholars in the United States had abandoned their children's rights projects."

58. Pamela Laufer-Ukeles, "The Relational Rights of Children," *Connecticut Law Review* 48, no. 3 (February 2016): 741, 743.

59. Dailey and Rosenbury, "New Law of the Child," 1462.

60. Betsy Wood, *Upon the Altar of Work: Child Labor and the Rise of New American Sectionalism* (Urbana: University of Illinois Press, 2020).

61. Davis et al., *Children in the Legal System*, 18.

62. Seymour Moskowitz, "Save the Children: The Legal Abandonment of American Youth in the Workplace," *Akron Law Review* 43, no. 1 (2010): 107.

63. Moskowitz, "Save the Children," 141.

64. Wood, *Upon the Altar of Work*; Elizabeth Anderson, *Agents of Reform: Child Labor and the Origins of the Welfare State* (Princeton, NJ: Princeton University Press, 2021); Julie Novkov, "Historicizing the Figure of the Child in Legal Discourse: The Battle over the Regulation of Child Labor," *American Journal of Legal History* 44, no. 4 (October 2000): 369–404.

65. Hugh D. Hindman, *Child Labor: An American History* (London: Routledge, 2015), 295.

66. Moskowitz, "Save the Children," 132.

67. Fair Labor Standards Act, 29 U.S.C. § 203(l) (1938).

68. "Child Labor," Wage and Hour Division, U.S. Department of Labor, accessed August 24, 2023, https://www.dol.gov/agencies/whd/child-labor.

69. See "Child Labor"; 29 C.F.R. § 570.2.

70. "Child Labor."

71. Hindman, *Child Labor*, 295, 296–97.

72. Wood, *Upon the Altar of Work*, 152.

73. Moskowitz, "Save the Children," 107.

74. William Finnegan, "Child Labor Is on the Rise," *New Yorker*, June 4, 2023.

75. Hindman, *Child Labor*, 298–301.

76. Hindman, 303.

77. See, for example, Marina A. Masterson, "When Play Becomes Work: Child Labor Laws in the Era of 'Kidfluencers,'" *University of Pennsylvania Law Review* 169, no. 2 (2021): 583–84.

78. Fair Labor Standards Act, § 213(c)(3).

79. Novkov, "Historicizing the Figure of the Child," 378–79.

80. Masterson, "When Play Becomes Work."

81. See, for example, Masterson, "When Play Becomes Work"; Mikayla Minnich, "That's Just Show Business: Relying on Industrial Revolution Solutions for a 'Kidfluencer' Problem," *University of Louisville Law Review* 62, no. 2 (Spring 2024): 523–50; Holden C. Sinnard, "Family Time Is Money: Modernizing Iowa's Child Labor Laws," *Iowa Law Review* 109, no. 3 (March 2024): 1361–97.

82. Masterson, "When Play Becomes Work," 583–84.

83. Masterson, 591–93.

84. Masterson, 592–93.

85. Masterson, 592–96.

86. Cal. Health & Safety Code § 124241 (West 2021). At least one state's statutes explicitly recognizes parental authority over the decision to enter a child in football. The California Youth Football Act states: "The decision to play youth football ultimately rests with the parents, after their thoughtful consideration of the risks and benefits, as to whether participation in youth football is in their child's best interest."

87. Steven J. Overman, *The Youth Sports Crisis: Out-of-Control Adults, Helpless Kids* (Santa Barbara, CA: Praeger, 2014), 5.

88. Coakley, *Sports in Society*, 87.

89. Ben Carrington and David L. Andrews, "Introduction: Sport as Escape, Struggle, and Art," in *A Companion to Sport*, edited by David L. Andrews and Ben Carrington (Malden, MA: Wiley Blackwell, 2013), 9.

90. Charles A. Popkin, Ahmad F. Bayomy, and Christopher S. Ahmad, "Early Sport Specialization," *Journal of the American Academy of Orthopaedic Surgeons* 27, no. 22 (November 15, 2019): 996.

91. Sima Bernstein and Louis Z. Kern, "Parents Are Holding Kids Back in School to Make Them More Competitive Athletes," *Parents*, January 3, 2020.

92. Patrick Cohn, "The Advantages and Disadvantages of Homeschooling Young Athletes," *Kids' Sports Psychology* (blog), July 2, 2019, https://perma.cc/MCD3-G92J.

93. Alfred C. Yen and Matthew Gregas, "Liability Waivers and Participation Rates in Youth Sports: An Empirical Investigation, *Arizona State Sports and Entertainment Law Journal* 10, no. 1 (Fall 2020): 4, stating that "most states enforce sports liability waivers signed by adults."

94. Dailey and Rosenbury, "New Parental Rights," 98.

95. Sungwon Kim, Daniel Connaughton, John Spengler, and Joon Hoon Lee, "Legislative Efforts to Reduce Concussions in Youth Sports: An Analysis of State Concussion Statutes," *Journal of Legal Aspects of Sport* 27, no. 2 (August 2017): 162–86.

96. Kim et al., "Legislative Efforts," 163.

97. Dionne L. Koller, "Putting Public Law into Private Sport," *Pepperdine Law Review* 43, no. 3 (April 2016): 717-18; Diekmann et al., "Failure of Youth Sports Concussion Laws," 1, stating that "in less than 10 years, all 50 states adopted a youth sports concussion statute—and each law mandates concussion education for coaches and/or student-athletes. This expansive, expensive intervention was designed to reduce concussion incidence and improve concussion care. But based on a review of 54 peer-reviewed studies, we argue that concussion education has not, and likely will not, produce the desired public health outcomes."

98. Koller, "Putting Public Law into Private Sport," 717-18.

99. Koller, "Putting Public Law into Private Sport," 717-18.

100. Diekmann et al., "Failure of Youth Sports Concussion Laws," 1.

101. Hosea H. Harvey, "Refereeing the Public Health," *Yale Journal of Health Policy* 14, no. 1 (Winter 2014): 86.

102. Diekmann et al., "Failure of Youth Sports Concussion Laws," 1, stating that "each law mandates concussion education for coaches and/or student-athletes"; Cal. Health & Saf. Code § 124235(a)(3)(A) (Westlaw through 2024 Reg. Sess.); Utah Code Ann. § 26B-4-403(3)(b) (Westlaw through 2024 Gen. Sess.); Okla. Stat. tit. 70, § 24-155(C) (Westlaw through Ch. 359 2nd Reg. Sess. 59th Legis. 2024).

103. Harvey, "Refereeing the Public Health," 89-90.

104. Silbaugh, "Legal Design," 228.

105. Silbaugh, 228.

3. THE LAW AND POLICY APPROACH TO SPORT

1. Federal Baseball Club v. National League, 259 U.S. 200 (1922).

2. Flood v. Kuhn, 407 U.S. 258, 282 (1972).

3. Cohen v. Brown University, 991 F.2d 888, 891-92 (1st Cir. 1993).

4. Douglas E. Abrams, "References to Baseball in Judicial Opinions and Written Advocacy," *Journal of the Missouri Bar* 72, no. 5 (September-October 2016); Douglas E. Abrams, "References to Football in Judicial Opinions and Written Advocacy," *Journal of the Missouri Bar* 73, no. 1 (January-February 2017).

5. "John McCain Visits the Mancave to Share Stories, Talk Sports," hosted by Dan Patrick, featuring John McCain, *The Dan Patrick Show*, aired May 2, 2014, on NBCSN, http://www.danpatrick.com/2014/05/02/john-mccain/, cited in Dionne L. Koller, "Putting Public Law into Private Sport," *Pepperdine Law Review* 43, no. 3 (April 2016): 682.

6. Koller, "Putting Public Law into Private Sport," 688.

7. W. Burlette Carter, "Introduction: What Makes a Field a Field," *Virginia Journal of Sports and the Law* 1, no. 2 (Fall 1999): 244-45.

8. San Francisco Arts & Athletics v. U.S.O.C., 483 U.S. 522, 545 (1987).

9. Gray v. Ferris, 230 App. Div. 416 (N.Y. App. Div. 1930).

10. Brundage quoted in Jules Boykoff, *Power Games: A Political History of the Olympics* (New York: Verso Books, 2016), 86.

11. Santee v. Amateur Athletic Union, 153 N.Y.S.2d 465 (1956).

12. Joseph M. Turrini, *The End of Amateurism in American Track and Field* (Urbana: University of Illinois Press, 2010), 5.

13. Bloom v. National Collegiate Athletic Association, 93 P.3d 621 (Colo. App. 2004).

14. Berger v. National Collegiate Athletic Association, 843 F.3d 285 (7th Cir. 2016).

15. Dionne L. Koller, "Frozen in Time: The State Action Doctrine's Application to Amateur Sports," *St. John's Law Review* 82, no. 1 (Winter 2008): 196.

16. President's Commission on Olympic Sports, *First Report to the President* (Washington, DC: Government Printing Office, February 1976), xi, 2.

17. Dionne L. Koller, "Amateur Regulation and the Unmoored United States Olympic and Paralympic Committee," *Wake Forest Law Review Online* 9 (2019): 90.

18. Dionne L. Koller, "A Twenty-First-Century Olympic and Amateur Sports Act," *Vanderbilt Journal of Entertainment and Technology Law* 20, no. 4 (Summer 2018): 1046.

19. President's Commission on Olympic Sports, *The Final Report of the President's Commission on Olympic Sports* (Washington, DC: Government Printing Office, January 1977), 1, quoted in Koller, "Putting Public Law into Private Sport," 689.

20. President's Commission on Olympic Sports, *Final Report*, 79, quoted in Koller, "Twenty-First-Century Olympic and Amateur Sports Act," 1046.

21. Koller, "Amateur Regulation," 90–91.

22. The act gives the USOPC "exclusive jurisdiction" and authority over the participation and selection of athletes for Olympic Movement competition. Amateur Sports Act, 36 U.S.C. § 220503.

23. Ben Wilhelm, *The United States Olympic and Paralympic Committee: A Primer*, CRS Report R47850 (Washington, DC: Library of Congress, Congressional Research Service, 2023), 6.

24. B. David Ridpath, *Alternative Models of Sports Development in America: Solutions to a Crisis in Education and Public Health* (Athens: Ohio University Press, 2018), 27, describing the USOPC as "the only privately funded Olympic Committee in the world"; Wilhelm, *United States Olympic and Paralympic Committee*, 17.

25. Amateur Sports Act, 36 U.S.C. § 220506(a).

26. Tom Farrey, *Game On: How the Pressure to Win at All Costs Endangers Youth Sports and What Parents Can Do about It* (New York: ESPN Books, 2008), 184–90.

27. Behagen v. Amateur Basketball Association of the United States, 884 F.2d 524 (10th Cir. 1989) ("Amateur Athletes Bill of Rights"); Amateur Sports Act, 36 U.S.C. § 220505(b)(9), stating that "neither this paragraph nor any other provision of this chapter shall create a private right of action."

28. for example, Sanderson v. U.S. Center for SafeSport, 2021 WL 3206322 (D. Colo. July 29, 2021).

29. Ted Stevens Olympic and Amateur Sports Act, 36 U.S.C. Code §§ 220522, 220509 (1998).

30. Lindland v. U.S. Wrestling Association, 227 F.3d 1000 (7th Cir. 2000); Foschi v. United States Swimming, Inc., 916 F. Supp. 232, 239 (E.D.N.Y. 1996); Harding v. U.S. Figure Skating Association, 851 F. Supp. 1476, 1480 (D. Or. 1994), *vacated on other grounds* in Harding v. U.S. Figure Skating Association, 879 F. Supp. 1053 (D. Or. 1995).

31. *San Francisco Arts & Athletics,* 483 U.S. at 527.

32. Travis T. Tygart, "Winners Never Dope and Finally, Dopers Never Win: USADA Takes Over Drug Testing of United States Olympic Athletes," *DePaul Journal of Sports Law and Contemporary Problems* 1, no. 2 (Fall 2003): 127.

33. Dionne L. Koller, "How the United States Government Sacrifices Athletes' Constitutional Rights in the Pursuit of National Prestige," *Brigham Young University Law Review* 2008, no. 5 (2008): 1493, explaining that both ONDCP and Congress had "direct influence over how USADA would be structured and what its mission would be."

34. Office of National Drug Control Policy Reauthorization Act, Pub. L. No. 109-469, 120 Stat. 3502 (2006), § 701(b)(2).

35. *Effects of Performance Enhancing Drugs on the Health of Athletes and Athletic Competition: Hearing Before the Senate Committee on Commerce, Science, and Transportation,* 106th Cong. (October 20, 1999) (testimony of General Barry R. McCaffrey, Director, Office of National Drug Control Policy, Executive Office of the President).

36. U.S. Anti-Doping Agency, *Protocol for Olympic and Paralympic Movement Testing* (Colorado Springs, January 1, 2015).

37. Armstrong v. Tygart, 886 F. Supp. 2d 572, n.18 (W.D. Tex. 2012).

38. Gilbert v. U.S. Olympic Committee, Civil Action No. 18-cv-00981-CMA-MEH (D. Colo., May 6, 2019), stating that "SafeSport simply cannot effectively serve its purpose of protecting amateur athletes if it is subject to the threat of liability for every eligibility decision it makes."

39. Matthew J. Mitten, Timothy Davis, N. Jeremi Duru, and Barbara Osborne, *Sports Law and Regulation: Cases, Materials, and Problems,* 5th ed. (Frederick, MD: Aspen, 2020).

40. Dylan Oliver Malagrino and Christopher Davis Jr., "Hold Your Fire: The Injustice of NCAA Sanctions on Innocent Student Athletes," *Virginia Sports and Entertainment Law Journal* 11, no. 2 (Spring 2012): 439n21; Stephen R. Lowe, *The Kid on the Sandlot: Congress and Professional Sports, 1910-1992* (Bowling Green, OH: Popular Press, 1995): 5.

41. *Legal Issues Relating to Football Head Injuries (Part I and II): Hearing Before the House Committee on the Judiciary*, 111th Cong. (October 8, 2009, and January 4, 2010).

42. *Promoting the Well-Being and Academic Success of College Athletes: Hearing Before the Senate Committee on Commerce, Science, and Transportation*, 113th Cong. 1 (July 9, 2014) (statement of Senator John R. Thune).

43. See, for example, Oklahoma Secondary Schools Activities Association, *Rules Governing Interscholastic Activities in Secondary Schools, 2021-2022* (Oklahoma City, 2021), detailing eligibility rules; Massachusetts Interscholastic Athletics Association, *Handbook* (Franklin, MA, 2021), explaining eligibility rules; International Skating Union, *Constitution and General Regulations 2021* (Lausanne, Switzerland, June 2021), establishing, along with other "special regulations and technical rules," the eligibility rules for figure skating; National Collegiate Athletics Association, *NCAA Guide for the College-Bound Student-Athlete, 2021-22* (Indianapolis, 2021), explaining the eligibility rules for incoming students who seek to participate in sports.

44. See, for example, "Rules," Federation Internationale de Gymnastique, accessed April 2, 2022, https://www.gymnastics.sport/site/rules/, outlining, among other things, technical regulations and judges' rules for competition; "Football Rules Changes—2022," National Federation of State High School Associations, accessed April 2, 2022, https://www.nfhs.org/sports-resource-content/football-rules-changes-2022/, explaining high school football rules and updates.

45. See Frank D. LoMonte, "Fouling the First Amendment: Why Colleges Can't and Shouldn't Control Student Athletes' Speech on Social Media," *Business and Technology Law Journal* 9, no. 1 (January 2014): 1; International Olympic Committee, *Olympic Charter* (Lausanne, Switzerland: October 2023), Rule 50.2.

46. Lloyd Freeburn, *Regulating International Sport: Power Authority, and Legitimacy* (Leiden, Germany: Brill Nijhoff, 2018), 1.

47. See, for example, Tiffany v. Arizona Interscholastic Association, Inc., 726 P.2d 231 (Ariz. 1986); *Harding*, 851 F. Supp. 1476; *Bloom*, 93 P.3d 621.

48. National Collegiate Athletic Association v. Tarkanian, 488 U.S. 179 (1988).

49. Knapp v. Northwestern University, 101 F.3d 473, 484 (7th Cir. 1996).

50. *Knapp*, 101 F.3d at 485.

51. See Class v. Towson University, 806 F.3d 236 (4th Cir. 2015).

52. Hollonbeck v. U.S. Olympic Committee, 513 F.3d 1191 (10th Cir. 2008).

53. Mitten et al., *Sports Law and Regulation*, 883, 886.

54. Mitten et al., 898.

55. Karas v. Strevell, 884 N.E.2d 122 (Ill. 2008).

56. Avila v. Citrus Community College District, 131 P.3d 383 at 394 (Cal. 2006).

57. Knight v. Jewett, 3 Cal. 4th 296, 315 (Cal. 1992).

58. Mayall v. USA Water Polo, Inc., 174 F. Supp. 3d 1220 (C.D. Cal. 2016).

59. McCants v. National Collegiate Athletic Association, 201 F. Supp. 3d 732 (M.D.N.C. 2016).

60. See Mitten et al., *Sports Law and Regulation*, chapter 11 and cases cited therein.

61. PGA Tour, Inc. v. Martin, 121 S. Ct. 1879 (2001).

62. NCAA v. Alston, 141 S. Ct. 2141.

63. *Alston*, 141 S. Ct. 2141.

64. Cal. Educ. Code § 67456 (Deering 2023).

65. "NIL Legislation Tracker," Saul Ewing LLP, accessed May 25, 2024, https://www.saul.com/nil-legislation-tracker.

66. Empowering Olympic, Paralympic, and Amateur Athletes Act, Pub. L. No. 116-189 (2020).

67. Protecting Young Victims from Sexual Abuse and Safe Sport Authorization Act, Pub. L. No. 115-126 (2018); 36 U.S.C. § 220503 (15) ("safe environment").

68. Empowering Olympic, Paralympic, and Amateur Athletes Act, 36 U.S.C. § 22050 (16) ("oversee the national governing bodies").

69. See Northwestern University and College Athletes Players Association, Case 13-RC-121359, 362 NLRB 1350 (August 17, 2015); Ben Strauss, "In a First, Northwestern Players Seek Unionization," *New York Times*, January 28, 2014.

70. Northwestern University and College Athletes Players Association, 362 NLRB 1350.

71. See, for example, University of California Los Angeles, Pac-12 Conference, and the National Collegiate Athletics Association, as joint employers, Case 31-CA-290328, NLRB (February 8, 2022).

72. Dionne L. Koller, "The Obese and the Elite: Using the Law to Reclaim School Sports," *Oklahoma Law Review* 67, no. 3 (Spring 2015): 430.

73. See *Brentwood Academy*, 531 U.S. at 935; Woodman v. Kera LLC, 785 N.W.2d 1 (Mich. 2010).

74. See *Big Labor on College Campuses: Examining the Consequences of Unionizing Student Athletes: Hearing Before the House Committee on Education and the Workforce*, 113th Cong. (2014) (testimony of Kenneth W. Starr, President and Chancellor,

Baylor University); 160 Cong. Rec. S2362–S2366 (daily ed. April 10, 2014) (statement of Senator Alexander on student athletes); "IHSA Responds to Concussion Lawsuit," Illinois High School Association, updated December 3, 2014, https://www.ihsa.org/News-Media/Announcements/ihsa-responds-to-concussion-lawsuit, stating that "potential repercussions" of a concussion lawsuit would "threaten the future of all high school sports for the millions of students around the country who annually benefit from their participation experiences."

75. *Martin*, 121 S. Ct. at 1904.

76. *Martin*, 121 S. Ct. at 1905.

77. See Mark S. Rosentraub, *Major League Losers: The Real Cost of Sports and Who's Paying for It*, rev. ed. (New York: Basic Books, 1999), stating that "owners, not consumers, with the help of court decisions and the U.S. Congress, have established cartels" for the four major sports leagues, and that "legislation to create a free and open market for professional sports has never been passed by Congress; in fact, when Congress has acted, it has been to extend protections to the sports leagues"; Lowe, *Kid on the Sandlot*, 81; *Amateur Sports Act: Hearing Before the Subcommittee on Consumer Affairs, Foreign Commerce, and Tourism of the Senate Committee on Commerce, Science, and Transportation*, 104th Cong. (October 18, 1995) (testimony of Tom McMillen, Co-chair, President's Council on Physical Fitness and Sports).

78. *Federal Baseball Club*, 259 U.S. 200; Toolson v. New York Yankees, 346 U.S. 356 (1953); *Flood*, 407 U.S. 258; Lowe, *Kid on the Sandlot*, 17–24.

79. Sports Broadcasting Act, 15 U.S.C. § 1291 (1961); Sports Bribery Act, 18 U.S.C. § 224 (1994).

80. Sports Agent Responsibility and Trust Act, 15 U.S.C. §§ 7801–7807 (2003); Marc Edelman, "Disarming the Trojan Horse of the UAAA and SPARTA: How America Should Reform Its Sports Agent Laws to Conform with True Agency Principles," *Harvard Journal of Sports and Entertainment Law* 4, no. 2 (Spring 2013). Critics have explained that the effect of both the UAAA and SPARTA is to provide NCAA member institutions with a cause of action against athlete agents who contact players in a way that jeopardizes their amateur status and NCAA eligibility.

81. On boxing, see Professional Boxing Safety Act, 15 U.S.C. § 6302 (1996); on mixed martial arts, see, for example, W.Va. Code § 29-5A-3a (Westlaw through 2024 session); on horse racing, see Kan. Stat. Ann. § 74-8843 (Westlaw through 2024 Reg. Sess.).

82. See Lowe, *Kid on the Sandlot*, 81.

83. Michael Straubel, "The International Convention against Doping in Sport: Is It the Missing Link to USADA Being a State Actor and WADC Coverage of U.S. Pro Athletes?" *Marquette Sports Law Review* 19, no. 1 (Fall 2008): 64.

84. Dionne L. Koller, "From Medals to Morality: Sportive Nationalism and the Problem of Doping in Sports," *Marquette Sports Law Review* 19, no. 1 (Fall 2008): 112-17.

85. *Flood*, 407 U.S. 258.

86. Curt Flood Act, 15 U.S.C. § 27a (1998).

87. Patsy Takemoto Mink Equal Opportunity in Education Act, 20 U.S.C. § 1681(a) (1972). The statute provides that "no person in the United States shall, on the basis of sex, be excluded from participation in, be denied the benefits of, or be subjected to discrimination under any education program or activity receiving Federal financial assistance."

88. "Athletics, Equal Opportunity," 45 C.F.R. § 86.41(c) (1975); "Athletics, Equal Opportunity," 34 C.F.R. § 106.41(c) (2020).

89. Dionne L. Koller, "Not Just One of the Boys: A Post-feminist Critique of Title IX's Vision for Gender Equity in Sports," *Connecticut Law Review* 43, no. 2 (December 2010): 403.

90. National Wrestling Coaches v. Department of Education, 366 F.3d. 930, 933 (D.C. Cir. 2004); Pederson v. Louisiana State University, 912 F. Supp. 892, 908 (M.D. La. 1996); Neal v. Board of Trustees of California State University, 198 F.3d 763, 771 (9th Cir. 1999); Cohen v. Brown University, 101 F.3d 155, 164 (1st Cir. 1996).

91. U.S. Department of Education National Coordinator for Title IX Athletics Dr. Mary Frances O'Shea to General Counsel of Bowling Green State University Nancy S. Footer, July 23, 1998, Office of Civil Rights, Department of Education, http://www.ed.gov/about/offices/list/ocr/docs/bowlgrn.html.

92. Assistant Secretary of Education for Civil Rights Russlynn Ali, Dear Colleague Letter, April 20, 2010 (Office of Civil Rights, Department of Education, https://www.ed.gov/sites/ed/files/about/offices/list/ocr/letters/colleague-20100420.pdf), stating that the Office of Civil Rights has explained that the three-part test allows institutions to "maintain flexibility and control over their athletic programs." See also Koller, "Not Just One of the Boys," 403.

93. Martin Barry Vinokur, *More than a Game: Sports and Politics* (Westport, CT: Praeger, 1988): 15.

94. Stephen Cormac Carlin and Christopher M. Fairman, "Squeeze Play: Workers' Compensation and the Professional Athlete," *University of Miami Entertainment and Sports Law Review* 12, no. 1 (January 1995): 95-96.

95. Brown v. Pro Football, Inc., 116 S. Ct. 2116 (1996).

4. THE LAW AND POLICY APPROACH TO YOUTH SPORT

1. B. David Ridpath, *Alternative Models of Sports Development in America: Solutions to a Crisis in Education and Public Health* (Athens: Ohio University Press, 2018),

xvi; U.S. Department of Health and Human Services, *National Youth Sports Strategy*, 46.

2. U.S. Department of Health and Human Services, *National Youth Sports Strategy* (Washington, DC, September 2019), 27 (funding and safety); Ridpath, *Alternative Models*, xvi (general availability).

3. For example, Consumer Product Safety Improvement Act, 15 U.S.C. § 2056b (2008), children's toys; Federal Hazardous Substances Labeling Act, 15 U.S.C. § 1278 (1960), children's toys; Children's Bicycle Helmet Safety Act, 15 U.S.C. §§ 6001-6006 (1993); Safe Sleep for Babies Act, 15 U.S.C. § 2057e (2021), crib bumpers; Agriculture, Rural Development, Food and Drug Administration, and Related Agencies Appropriations Act, 15 U.S.C. §§ 6501-6506 (1999), children's online privacy protection; Protecting Children in the 21st Century Act, 15 U.S.C. §§ 6551-6555 (2008), promoting a safe internet for children; Elementary and Secondary Education Act, 20 U.S.C. § 7293 (1965), establishing funding to create "Ready to Learn Programming," educational television to foster academic achievement; "Requirements for Rattles," 16 C.F.R. §§ 1510.1-1510.4 (1978); "Safety Standard for Booster Seats," 16 C.F.R. §§ 1237.1-1237.2 (2018); "Safety Standard for Stationary Activity Centers," 16 C.F.R. §§ 1238.1-1238.2 (2019); "Safety Standard for High Chairs," 16 C.F.R. §§ 1231.1-1231.2 (2018); "Safety Standard for Carriages and Strollers," 16 C.F.R. §§ 1227.1-1227.2 (2011); "Safety Standard for Toddler Beds," 16 C.F.R. §§ 1217.1-1217.2 (2011).

4. U.S. Department of Health and Human Services, *National Youth Sports Strategy*, 29.

5. "President's Council on Sports, Fitness and Nutrition," Health.gov, U.S. Department of Health and Human Services, updated February 26. 2024, http://www.fitness.gov.

6. "President's Council on Sports, Fitness and Nutrition"; 143 Cong. Rec. H4892 (daily ed. July 8, 1997) (statement of Representative Ron Kind on the National Youth Sports Program). The program was a public-private partnership that sought to benefit children through sports participation who were deemed "at risk" and "economically disadvantaged." The federal government eliminated the program in 2006.

7. "President's Council on Sports, Fitness and Nutrition."

8. "President's Council on Physical Fitness and Sports," Exec. Order No. 13265, 67 C.F.R., 39841-42 (June 6, 2002).

9. See *Amateur Sports Act: Hearing Before the Subcommittee on Consumer Affairs, Foreign Commerce, and Tourism of the Senate Committee on Commerce, Science, and Transportation*, 104th Cong. (October 18, 1995) (testimony of Tom McMillen).

10. See Tom Farrey, *Game On: How the Pressure to Win at All Costs Endangers Youth Sports and What Parents Can Do about It* (New York: ESPN Books, 2008),

75-76, describing the President's Council on Physical Fitness as a "barely funded, strictly advisory committee that works with the Department of Health and Human Services to recommend programs to encourage sports participation."

11. Council of Economic Advisers, *The Potential for Youth Sports to Improve Childhood Outcomes* (Washington, D.C., May 2018).

12. Office of Disease Prevention and Health Promotion, "Increase the Proportion of Children and Adolescents Who Play Sports—PA-12," Healthy People 2030, accessed August 20, 2023, https://health.gov/healthypeople/objectives-and-data/browse-objectives/physical-activity/increase-proportion-children-and-adolescents-who-play-sports-pa-12.

13. U.S. Department of Health and Human Services, *National Youth Sports Strategy* (Washington, DC, September 2019), 54, 3.

14. "Congressional Caucus on Youth Sports," National Council of Youth Sports, accessed March 11, 2022, https://ncys.org/advocacy/congressional-caucus-on-youth-sports/. For examples of resolutions, see Recognizing the millions of youth in this Nation benefitting from youth sports and the parents, volunteers, and local national organizations that make youth sports in this country possible, and for other purposes, H.R. Res. 435, 115th Cong. (2017); A resolution recognizing "National Youth Sports Week" and the efforts by parents, volunteers, and national organizations in their efforts to promote healthy living and youth development, S. Res. 227, 115th Cong. (2017); Expressing the sense of the House of Representatives that a National Youth Sports Week should be established, H.R. Res. 442, 110th Cong. (2007); PLAYS in Youth Sports Act, H.R. 2932, 114th Cong. (2015).

15. 134 Cong. Rec. 29166 (daily ed. October 6, 1988) (statement of Representative Charles B. Rangel on the National Youth Sports Program); Special Program of Recreational Training Act, H.R. 4711, 101st Cong. (1990).

16. National Youth Sports Program Revitalization Act, H.R. 4480, 111th Cong. (2010).

17. Expressing the sense of the House of Representatives that a National Youth Sports Week should be established, H.R. Res. 442, 110th Cong. (2007); 158 Cong. Rec. E671 (daily ed. April 26, 2012) (statement of Representative Mike McIntyre on Youth Sports Safety Month 2012); 155 Cong. Rec. E1930 (daily ed. July 24, 2009) (statement of Representative Mike McIntyre on National Youth Sports Week 2009).

18. COVID-19 Youth Sports and Healthy Working Families Relief Act, H.R. 7562, 116th Cong. (2020); COVID-19 Youth Sports and Working Families Relief Act, H.R. 6912, 116th Cong. (2020).

19. An Act to Revise, Codify, and Enact . . . Laws, Related to Patriotic and National Observances, Ceremonies, and Organizations . . . , 36 U.S.C. § 130502

(1998), explaining that Little League's purposes include promoting the game of baseball, "developing qualities of citizenship and sportsmanship," and using baseball to "teach spirit and competitive will to win, physical fitness through individual sacrifice, the values of team play, and wholesome well being."

20. Volunteer Protection Act, 42 U.S.C. § 14501 (1997).

21. Internal Revenue Code § 501(j) (1982).

22. "Allred Introduces Bipartisan Bill to Support Nonprofits, like the YMCA, in Efforts to Bolster Sports Participation for Young People," media release, U.S. Congressman Colin Allred, July 13, 2023, https://allred.house.gov/media/press-releases/allred-introduces-bipartisan-bill-support-nonprofits-ymca-efforts-bolster.

23. 20 Ill. Comp. Stat. 4107/5 (Westlaw through P.A. 103-586 of 2024 Reg. Sess.).

24. Md. Code Ann., Econ. Dev. § 10-612.1 (Westlaw through 2024 Reg. Sess.).

25. Mona Mirehie et al., "Towards an Understanding of Family Travel Decision-Making Processes in the Context of Youth Sport Tourism," *Journal of Destination Marketing and Management* 21, no. 2 (September 2021): 100644.

26. See, for example, Wash. Rev. Code § 43.388.040 (Westlaw through 2024 Reg. Sess.), Washington State's "Sports Mentoring Program," which seeks to "provide opportunities for underserved youth to join sports teams"; "Governor Newsom Promotes Physical Fitness and Mental Well-Being with Advisory Council," media release, Governor Gavin Newsom, January 31, 2022, https://www.gov.ca.gov/2022/01/31/governor-newsom-promotes-physical-fitness-and-mental-well-being-with-advisory-council/.

27. Dennis Gildea, "Youth Sports," in *The Routledge History of American Sport*, edited by Linda J. Borish, David K. Wiggins, and Gerald R. Gems (London: Routledge, 2017), 91.

28. Jay Coakley, *Sports in Society: Issues and Controversies*, 13th ed. (New York: McGraw-Hill, 2021), 86-89; U.S. Department of Health and Human Services, *National Youth Sports Strategy*, 21.

29. *Amateur Sports Act*, 104th Cong. (October 18, 1995) (testimony of Richard Schultz, Executive Director, United States Olympic Committee).

30. *Amateur Sports Act of 1978: Hearing Before the Committee on Commerce, Science, and Transportation*, 95th Cong. 12-13 (March 21, 1978) (letter from F. Don Miller, Executive Director of the U.S. Olympic Committee, to Senator Ted Stevens).

31. Amateur Sports Act, 36 U.S.C. §§ 220503(2), 220503(6), 220503(9) (1978).

32. Dionne L. Koller, "A Twenty-First-Century Olympic and Amateur Sports Act," *Vanderbilt Journal of Entertainment and Technology Law* 20, no. 4 (Summer 2018): 1049-50.

33. Koller, "Twenty-First-Century Olympic and Amateur Sports Act," 1047-48.

34. Dionne L. Koller, "Amateur Regulation and the Unmoored United States Olympic and Paralympic Committee," *Wake Forest Law Review Online* 9 (2019): 98-99.

35. *Amateur Sports Act*, 104th Cong. (October 18, 1995) (testimony of LeRoy T. Walker, President, United States Olympic Committee).

36. *Amateur Sports Act*, 104th Cong. (October 18, 1995) (testimony of LeRoy T. Walker).

37. *Amateur Sports Act*, 104th Cong. (October 18, 1995) (testimony of Tom McMillen; emphasis in original).

38. See, for example, 9 R.I. Gen. Laws § 9-1-48 (Westlaw through Ch. 24 of 2024 Reg. Sess.), which states that "no person who, without compensation and as a volunteer, renders services . . . in a youth sports program organized and conducted by or under the auspices of a nonprofit corporation . . . shall be liable to any person for any civil damages . . . unless the acts or omissions of the person were committed in willful, wanton, or reckless disregard for the safety of the participants. It shall be insufficient to impose liability upon any such person to establish only that the conduct of the person fell below ordinary standards of care"; Ala. Code § 6-5-344 (Westlaw through Act 2024-244); Del. Code Ann. title 16 § 6836 (Westlaw through ch. 261 of 152d Gen. Assem. 2023-24); Ga. Code Ann. § 51-1-20.1 (Westlaw through 2023); 745 Ill. Comp. Stat. § 80/1 (Westlaw through P.A. 103-586 of 2024 Reg. Sess.); Kan. Stat. Ann. § 60-3601 (Westlaw through 2024 Reg. Sess.).

39. AB Staff, "How Concussion Legislation Is Failing Young Athletes," *Athletic Business*, April 20, 2020.

40. Or. Rev. Stat. § 418.696 (Westlaw through 2024 Reg. Sess.), encouraging "youth sports provider[s]" to adopt a list of crimes that would disqualify an individual from coaching and completing criminal background checks.

41. See, for example, N.J. Rev. Stat. § 5:17-2 (Westlaw through L. 2023, c. 280 & J.R. No. 18), granting power to the school board to ban any student, coach, parent, or game official who violates the athletic code of conduct; Ga. Code Ann. § 20-2-319.2 (Westlaw through 2023 Reg. Sess.), requiring a physical examination to participate in extracurricular sports; Md. Code Ann., Educ. § 7-436 (Westlaw through 2024 Reg. Sess.), mandating cardiac arrest awareness.

42. 820 Ill. Comp. Stat. 205/2.5 (Westlaw through P.A. 103-586 of 2024 Reg. Sess.).

43. Md. Code Ann., Educ. § 7-436 (Westlaw through 2024 Reg. Sess.); Ohio Rev. Code Ann. § 3313.5310 (Westlaw through File 25, 135th Gen. Assem. 2023-24).

44. Va. Code Ann. § 58.1-4039 (Westlaw through 2024 Reg. Sess.).

45. See Ariz. Rev. Stat. Ann. § 15-120.02 (Westlaw through Second Reg. Sess. 56th legislature 2024); Ark. Code Ann. § 6-1-107 (Westlaw through 2024 Fiscal Sess. 94th Ark. Gen. Assem.). See also Idaho Code § 33-6202 (Westlaw through Second Reg. Sess. 67th Idaho legislature).

46. Cal. Health & Safety Code § 124241 (West 2021).

47. Kyle D. Logue, "Coordinating Sanctions in Tort," *Cardozo Law Review* 31, no. 6 (January 2010).

48. Alfred C. Yen and Matthew Gregas, "Liability Waivers and Participation Rates in Youth Sports: An Empirical Investigation," *Arizona State Sports and Entertainment Law Journal* 10, no. 1 (Fall 2020): 2, 7. The study Yen and Gregas conducted tested this proposition and the underlying belief that enforcement of liability waivers ultimately will increase sports opportunities for children. They conclude that the "major argument given by courts for enforcing youth sports releases lacks empirical support." The authors further report "no statistically significant relationship between enforceability of youth sports releases and participation rates."

49. Woodman v. Kera LLC, 785 N.W.2d 1 (Mich. 2010).

50. This is also true with respect to level of play. Thus, considerations of what is "part of the game" generally refer to the professional, adult version of the relevant sport. See Avila v. Citrus Community College District, 131 P.3d 383 (Cal. 2006).

51. Campagna-McGuffin v. Diva Gymnastics Academy, Inc., 199 N.E.3d 1034 (Ohio Ct. App. 2022).

52. Sam C. Ehrlich, "Swimming against the Current: *Mayall v. USA Water Polo* and Its Potential Impact on Overseeing Athletic Organizations," *Virginia Sports and Entertainment Law Journal* 19, no. 1 (Fall 2019): 19.

53. Kahn v. East Side Union High School District, 75 P.3d 30 (Cal. 2003).

54. Nabozny v. Barnhill, 334 N.E.2d 258, 260 (Ill. App. 1975).

55. Karas v. Strevell, 884 N.E.2d 122 (Ill. 2008).

56. Megenity v. Dunn, 68 N.E.3d 1080, 1084 (Ind. 2017).

57. Kabella v. Bouschelle, 672 P.2d 290, 294 (N.M. App. 1983).

58. Borella v. Renfro, 137 N.E.3d 431 (2019).

59. *Borella*, 137 N.E.3d at 444.

60. Doe v. U.S. Youth Soccer Association, Inc., 8 Cal. App. 5th 1118 (Cal. Ct. App. 2017).

61. Brown v. U.S.A. Taekwondo, 40 Cal. App. 5th 1077 (Cal. Ct. App. 2019).

62. Mayall v. U.S. Water Polo, Inc., 909 F.3d 1055 (9th Cir. 2018).

63. See, for example, R.K. v. United States Bowling Congress, 531 P.3d 901 (Wash. Ct. App. 2023); Annie G. v. Glacial Garden Skating Arenas, No. B293351

(Cal. Ct. App. Sept. 17, 2020); J.G. v. Pop Warner Little Scholars, Inc., E068611 (Cal. Ct. App. Aug. 22, 2019).

64. Lloyd Freeburn, *Regulating International Sport: Power, Authority, and Legitimacy* (Leiden, Germany: Brill Nijhoff, 2018), 6.

65. Matthew J. Mitten, Timothy Davis, N. Jeremi Duru, and Barbara Osborne, *Sports Law and Regulation: Cases, Materials, and Problems,* 5th ed. (Frederick, MD: Aspen, 2020).

66. Tennessee Secondary School Athletic Association v. Brentwood Academy, 531 U.S. 288 (2007).

67. For example, Menard v. Louisiana High School, 30 So.3d 790 (La. Ct. App. 2010); Taylor v. Enumclaw School District, 133 P.3d 492, 497 (2006); Mancuso v. Massachusetts Interscholastic Athletic Association, 900 N.E.2d 518, 527-28 (2009); Johansen v. Louisiana High School Athletic Association, 916 So.2d 1081 (La. Ct. App. 2005); Indiana High School Athletic Association v. Carlberg, 694, N.E.2d 222, 228 (Ind. 1997); Letendre v. Missouri State High School Activities Association, 86 S.W.3d 63, 67 (Mo. Ct. App. 2002); Tiffany v. Arizona Interscholastic Association, Inc., 726 P.2d at 234 (Ariz. 1986); Brands v. Sheldon Community School, 671 F. Supp. 627, 631 (N.D. Iowa 1987).

68. Vernonia School District 47J v. Acton, 515 U.S. 646, 661 (1995).

69. *Vernonia School District*, 515 U.S. at 657, 663.

70. *Vernonia School District*, 515 U.S. at 657.

71. Mahanoy Area School District v. B.L., 141 S. Ct. 2038 (2021).

72. See, for example, *Brentwood*, 551 U.S. 291.

73. Menora v. Illinois High School Association, 683 F.2d 1030 (7th Cir. 1982).

74. Wildman v. Marshalltown School District, 249 F.3d 768 (8th Cir. 2001).

75. Lowery v. Euverard, 497 F.3d 584 (6th Cir. 2007).

76. Brian L. Porto, "Unfinished Business: The Continuing Struggle for Equal Opportunity in College Sports on the Eve of Title IX's Fiftieth Anniversary," *Marquette Sports Law Review* 32, no. 1 (Fall 2021): 259-303.

77. B.P.J. v. West Virginia State Board of Education, 550 F. Supp. 3d 347 (S.D. W. Va. 2021).

78. Women's Sports Foundation, *50 Years of Title IX: We're Not Done Yet* (New York, 2022).

79. Knapp v. Northwestern University, 101 F.3d 473 (7th Cir. 1996).

80. Holzmueller v. Illinois High School Association, 881 F.3d 587 (7th Cir. 2018).

81. McFadden v. Grasmick, 485 F. Supp. 2d 642 (D. Md. 2007).

82. Sharon v. City of Newton, 769 N.E.2d 738 (Mass. 2002).

83. Coakley, *Sports in Society*, 534.

84. Ridpath, *Alternative Models*, 33; Joshua Newman and Kyle Bunds, "Special Issue Foreword: On the Political Economy of Amateur Athletics," *Journal of Amateur Sport* 2, no. 1 (February 2016): 10, stating that "most opportunities for individuals in public schools are for those who compete in highly competitive sports activities."

85. "PONY Baseball Inc. Agrees to Provide Equal Opportunity to Players with Disabilities," media release, U.S. Department of Justice, August 17, 2006, https://www.justice.gov/archive/opa/pr/2006/August/06_crt_549.html.

86. Hosea H. Harvey, "Refereeing the Public Health," *Yale Journal of Health Policy* 14, no. 1 (Winter 2014): 99.

87. Harvey, "Refereeing the Public Health," 102.

88. Harvey, 102, 86.

89. Harvey, 89–90.

90. Dionne L. Koller, "Putting Public Law into Private Sport," *Pepperdine Law Review* 43, no. 3 (April 2016): 681–744.

91. Kerri McGowan Lowrey and Stephanie R. Morain, "State Experiences Implementing Youth Sports Concussion Laws: Challenges, Successes, and Lessons for Evaluating Impact," *Journal of Law, Medicine, and Ethics* 42, no. 3 (September 2014): 290, 294.

92. Koller, "Putting Public Law into Private Sport."

93. *Mayall*, 174 F. Supp. 3d 1220. The court's holding was reversed by the Ninth Circuit on appeal.

5. THE POLITICS OF YOUTH SPORT

1. Daniel A. Grano and Michael L. Butterworth, eds., *Sport, Rhetoric, and Political Struggle* (New York: Peter Lang, 2019): 1. See also David L. Andrews, "Sport, Culture, and Late Capitalism," in *Marxism, Cultural Studies, and Sport*, ed. Ben Carrington and Ian McDonald (London: Routledge, 2009): 228.

2. Flood v. Kuhn, 407 U.S. 258, 267 (1972).

3. Conor Friedersdorf, "When Sports and Politics Mix," *The Atlantic*, June 29, 2023.

4. Jay Coakley, "Assessing the Sociology of Sport: On Cultural Sensibilities and the Great Sport Myth," *International Review for the Sociology of Sport* 50, nos. 4–5 (June–August 2015): 403. Coakley explains that sport's relationship to politics helps perpetuate the belief that sport is, inherently and in all forms, good and that this assumption makes critical research and scholarship on sport difficult. He also notes "the pervasiveness of the [Great Sport Myth] and the way it is strategically nurtured by self-interested political and economic elites" (405).

5. Barbara J. Keys, ed., *The Ideals of Global Sport: From Peace to Human Rights* (Philadelphia: University of Pennsylvania Press, 2019), 1.

6. Matthew J. Mitten, Timothy Davis, N. Jeremi Duru, and Barbara Osborne, *Sports Law and Regulation: Cases, Materials, and Problems*, 5th ed. (Frederick, MD: Aspen, 2020), 17.

7. Grano and Butterworth, *Sport, Rhetoric, and Political Struggle*, 1 (emphasis omitted).

8. Robert L. Simon, "Internalism and Internal Values in Sport," *Journal of the Philosophy of Sport* 27, no. 1 (May 2000): 1 (quotation); Peter Donnelly and Michael Atkinson, "Where History Meets Biography: Toward a Public Sociology of Sport," in *Playing for Change: The Continuing Struggle for Sport and Recreation*, edited by Russell Field (Toronto: University of Toronto Press, 2015), 375.

9. Mitten et al., *Sports Law and Regulation*, 16-19.

10. Ian McDonald, "One-Dimensional Sport: Revolutionary Marxism and the Critique of Sport," in *Marxism, Cultural Studies, and Sport*, ed. Ben Carrington and Ian McDonald (London: Routledge, 2009): 44; D. Stanley Eitzen, *Fair and Foul: Beyond the Myths and Paradoxes of Sport*, 6th ed. (Lanham, MD: Rowman and Littlefield, 2016), 1-2.

11. Ben Carrington and David L. Andrews, "Introduction: Sport as Escape, Struggle, and Art," in *A Companion to Sport*, ed. David L. Andrews and Ben Carrington (Malden, MA: Wiley Blackwell, 2013), 10; McDonald, "One-Dimensional Sport," 44.

12. Douglas Booth, "Constructing Knowledge: Histories of Modern Sport," in *A Companion to Sport*, ed. David L. Andrews and Ben Carrington (Malden, MA: Wiley Blackwell, 2013), 36; Ken Roberts, *Social Theory, Sport, Leisure* (London: Routledge, 2016), 131.

13. See Roberts, *Social Theory*, 121, explaining Foucault's theory that "discourses simultaneously impose limits on what can be thought, expressed and understood by others. It is the discourses we have acquired that allow us to think that sport might benefit our health and strengthen a nation's prestige and identity."

14. Matthew T. Bowers and Thomas M. Hunt, "The President's Council on Physical Fitness and the Systematisation of Children's Play in America," *International Journal of the History of Sport* 28, no. 11 (August 2011): 1496-1511.

15. Bowers and Hunt, "President's Council on Physical Fitness," 1496.

16. Centre for Sport and Human Rights, *Child Labour in Sport: Protecting the Rights of Child Athletes* (Durban, South Africa, 2022).

17. Kathleen E. Bachynski, "Competitive Youth Sports, Pediatricians, and Gender in the 1950s," in *Pink and Blue: Gender, Culture, and the Health of Children*, ed. Elena Conis, Sandra Eder, and Aimee Medeiros (New Brunswick, NJ: Rutgers University Press, 2021), chapter 9.

18. Department of Housing and Urban Development, Public and Indian Housing Youth Sports Program, 56 Fed. Reg. 66484-01 (December 23, 1991).

19. Proclamation No. 6576, 58 Fed. Reg. 36117 (July 1, 1993).

20. Donnelly and Atkinson, "Where History Meets Biography," 375; Douglas E. Abrams, "The State of Concussion: Protecting Athletes through Advances in Law, Public Health, and Science," *Journal of Business and Technology Law* 10, no. 1 (January 2015): 13, quoting President Barack Obama stating, "Sport is . . . fundamental to who we are as Americans."

21. Donnelly and Atkinson, "Where History Meets Biography," 374.

22. Jeffrey Montez de Oca, "Paradox of Privilege: Sport, Masculinities, and the Commodified Body," in *A Companion to Sport*, ed. David L. Andrews and Ben Carrington (Malden, MA: Wiley Blackwell, 2013): 149, 157.

23. Kathleen E. Bachynski, *No Game for Boys to Play: The History of Youth Football and the Origins of a Public Health Crisis* (Chapel Hill: University of North Carolina Press, 2019), 6.

24. See Emma Rich and John Evans, "Physical Culture, Pedagogies of Health, and the Gendered Body," in *A Companion to Sport*, ed. David L. Andrews and Ben Carrington (Malden, MA: Wiley Blackwell, 2013), 179–80; Michael L. Silk and David L. Andrews, "Sport and the Neoliberal Conjecture: Complicating the Consensus," in *Sport and Neoliberalism: Politics, Consumption, and Culture*, ed. David L. Andrews and Michael L. Silk (Philadelphia: Temple University Press, 2012), 8. Sport is advanced as a solution for numerous children's issues, from lack of physical fitness to crime. See also Caroline Fusco, "Governing Play: Moral Geographies, Healthification, and Neoliberal Urban Imaginaries," in *Sport and Neoliberalism: Politics, Consumption, and Culture*, ed. David L. Andrews and Michael L. Silk (Philadelphia: Temple University Press, 2012): 145–49. In this view, initiatives such as the NYSS and the President's Physical Fitness Award are part of the state's attempt to "ideologize the young," with childhood obesity recast as a failure of the individual to, among other things, participate in sport. See also Toby Miller, "Michel Foucault and the Critique of Sport," in *Marxism, Cultural Studies, and Sport*, ed. Ben Carrington and Ian McDonald (London: Routledge, 2009), 188.

25. Silk and Andrews, "Sport and the Neoliberal Conjecture," 15. According to this view, sport facilitates "an economy of affect through which power, privilege, politics, and position are (re)produced." See also Silk and Andrews, "Sport and the Neoliberal Conjecture," 5; Simon, "Internalism and Internal Values," 1; Alan G. Ingham, "The Sportification Process: A Bibliographical Analysis Framed by the Work of Marx, Weber, Durkheim, and Freud," in *Sport and Modern Social Theorists*, ed. Richard Giulianotti (London: Palgrave MacMillan, 2004): 14, explaining that capitalism "became so naturalized that it influenced production in other spheres (such as sport) and became hegemonic"; Eitzen, *Fair and Foul*, 125–26, stating that sport is a form of "ideological control"; and Claudio Colaguori, *Agon Culture: Competition, Conflict, and the Problem of Domination*

(Whitby, Ontario: De Sitter, 2012), 22. Colaguori argues that sport helps achieve hegemony by fostering societal buy-in "to the dominant project of power."

26. Roberts, *Social Theory*, 59. See also Matthew Atencio, Becky Beal, E. Missy Wright, and ZáNean McClain, *Moving Boarders: Skateboarding and the Changing Landscape of Urban Youth Sports* (Fayetteville: University of Arkansas Press, 2018): 29.

27. Steven J. Overman, *Youth Sports Crisis: Out-of-Control Adults, Helpless Kids* (Santa Barbara, CA: Praeger, 2014), 6.

28. Jay Coakley, *Sports in Society: Issues and Controversies*, 13th ed. (New York: McGraw-Hill, 2021), 88; Atencio et al., *Moving Boarders*, 30.

29. Colaguori, *Agon Culture*, 29, vii; Anouk Bélanger, "The Urban Sport Spectacle: Towards a Critical Political Economy of Sports," in *Marxism, Cultural Studies, and Sport,* ed. Ben Carrington and Ian McDonald (London: Routledge, 2009): 63, stating that sport is a "politicized cultural form"; Silk and Andrews, "Sport and the Neoliberal Conjecture," 5.

30. Robert J. Brustad, Runar Vilhjalmsson, and Antonio Manuel Fonseca, "Organized Sport and Physical Activity Promotion," in *Youth Physical Activity and Sedentary Behavior: Challenges and Solutions*, ed. Alan L. Smith and Stuart J. H. Biddle (Champaign, IL: Human Kinetics, 2008): 353.

31. Colaguori, *Agon Culture*, 25. See also Coakley, "Positive Youth Development," 24. Sport's ability to condition children to accept agonistic values and the dominant political discourse as natural, or "the way the world is," is heightened, scholars theorize, because sport is not just associated with childhood: children's sports opportunities are provided in schools. See B. David Ridpath, *Alternative Models of Sports Development in America: Solutions to a Crisis in Education and Public Health* (Athens: Ohio University Press, 2018), 33.

32. Richard Giulianotti, "Sport and Social Theorists—A Plurality of Perspectives," in *Sport and Modern Social Theorists,* ed. Richard Giulianotti (London: Palgrave MacMillan, 2004), 7. Participating in sport to compete and win and not, for instance, for play or fitness is a hallmark of U.S. sport. See also Eitzen, *Fair and Foul*, 5.

33. Donnelly and Atkinson, "Where History Meets Biography," 366.

34. Bachynski, "Competitive Youth Sports," 155.

35. Bachynski, 169.

36. Nancy Fraser, *Fortunes of Feminism: From State-Managed Capitalism to Neoliberal Crisis* (London: Verso, 2013): 209.

37. Fraser, *Fortunes of Feminism*, 210, 211. See also Grant Jarvie, "Sport, New Social Divisions, and Social Inequality," in *Inclusion and Exclusion through Youth Sport*, ed. Symeon Dagkas and Kathleen Armour (London: Routledge, 2012): 63, stating that "feminist ideals of gender inequality now sit squarely in the social mainstream but have yet to be fully realized in practice."

38. Elizabeth Mensch, "The History of Mainstream Legal Thought," in *The Politics of Law: A Progressive Critique,* 3rd ed., ed. David Kairys (New York: Basic Books, 1998), 35.

39. David A. Rochefort and Roger W. Cobb, eds., *The Politics of Problem Definition: Shaping the Policy Agenda* (Lawrence: University Press of Kansas, 1994), vii, 4; Frank R. Baumgartner and Bryan D. Jones, "Attention, Boundary Effects, and Large-Scale Policy Change in Air Transportation Policy," in *The Politics of Problem Definition: Shaping the Policy Agenda*, ed. David A. Rochefort and Roger W. Cobb (Lawrence: University Press of Kansas, 1994), 53.

40. Rochefort and Cobb, *Politics of Problem Definition*, 4; John W. Kingdon, *Agendas, Alternatives, and Public Policies*, 2nd ed. (New York: HarperCollins, 1995): 198.

41. B. Dan Wood and Alesha Doan, "The Politics of Problem Definition: Applying and Testing Threshold Models," *American Journal of Political Science* 47, no. 4 (October 2003): 640-53; Taleed El-Sabawi, "Defining the Opioid Epidemic: Congress, Pressure Groups, and Problem Definition, *Memphis Law Review*, 48, no. 4 (2018): 1357-1413.

42. Kingdon, *Agendas, Alternatives, and Public Policies*, 109.

43. Deborah Stone, *Policy Paradox: The Art of Political Decision Making*, 3rd ed. (New York: W. W. Norton, 2012): 133.

44. David A. Rochefort and Roger W. Cobb, "Problem Definition, Agenda Access, and Policy Choice," *Policy Studies Journal* 21, no. 1 (March 1993): 56-71.

45. Stone, *Policy Paradox*, 247.

46. Hugh D. Hindman, *Child Labor: An American History* (London: Routledge, 2015), 303.

47. Betsy Wood, *Upon the Altar of Work: Child Labor and the Rise of New American Sectionalism* (Urbana: University of Illinois Press, 2020), 2.

48. Hindman, *Child Labor*, 303.

49. Bowers and Hunt, "President's Council on Physical Fitness," 1497, 1498.

50. Bowers and Hunt, 1500.

51. Bachynski, "Competitive Youth Sports," 169-70.

52. American Academy of Pediatrics, "Tackling in Youth Football," *Pediatrics* 36, no. 5 (November 2015): e1419-e1430.

53. "Allred Introduces Bipartisan Bill to Support Nonprofits, like the YMCA, in Efforts to Bolster Sports Participation for Young People," media release, U.S. Congressman Colin Allred, July 13, 2023, https://allred.house.gov/media/press-releases/allred-introduces-bipartisan-bill-support-nonprofits-ymca-efforts-bolster.

54. "Participation Trends," State of Play 2023 Report, Aspen Institute Project Play, accessed May 24, 2024, https://projectplay.org/state-of-play-2023/participation.

55. Such proposals have been made in the past. See *Amateur Sports Act: Hearing Before the Subcommittee on Consumer Affairs, Foreign Commerce, and Tourism of the Senate Committee on Commerce, Science, and Transportation*, 104th Cong. (October 18, 1995) (testimony of Tom McMillen, Co-chair, President's Council on Physical Fitness and Sports); and *Amateur Sports Act: Hearing Before the Subcommittee on Consumer Affairs, Foreign Commerce, and Tourism of the Senate Committee on Commerce, Science, and Transportation*, 104th Cong. (October 18, 1995) (testimony of Jeff Darman, President, Road Runners Club of America), urging Congress to support additional funding for grassroots sports programs.

56. See *Amateur Sports Act: Hearing Before the Subcommittee on Consumer Affairs, Foreign Commerce, and Tourism of the Senate Committee on Commerce, Science, and Transportation* (October 18, 1995) (testimony of Jeff Darman), stating that the government should "try dramatic new approaches" to stimulating grassroots sports participation; ibid., 89 (testimony of Tom McMillen).

57. Commission on the State of U.S. Olympics and Paralympics, *Passing the Torch: Modernizing Olympic, Paralympic, and Grassroots Sports in America* (Washington, DC, March 2024).

58. See James R. Andrews, "Why Are There So Many Injuries to Our Young Athletes? Professionalization and Specialization in Youth Sport," *University of Baltimore Law Review* 40, no. 4 (Summer 2011): 575-86; Mark Hyman, *Until It Hurts: America's Obsession with Youth Sports and How It Harms Our Kids* (Boston: Beacon Press, 2009).

59. Karas v. Strevell, 884 N.E.2d 122 (Ill. 2008).

60. Coakley, *Sports in Society*, 93 ("exception").

61. One exception was the effort in a few states to legislate limits on, or to outright ban, tackle football for children in response to the rash of sports concussions. See Courtney Annway, "Series: Legislation Banning Youth Tackle Football—Part 3: Taking Steps in Response to Recent TBI Studies—Banning Youth Tackle Football," *University of Buffalo Sports and Entertainment Forum* (blog), February 1, 2020, accessed April 10, 2022, https://ublawsportsforum.com/2020/02/01/series-legislation-banning-youth-tackle-football-part-3-taking-steps-in-response-to-recent-tbi-studies-banning-youth-tackle-football/. Only California enacted such a statute, the California Youth Football Act (Cal. Health & Safety Code § 124241 [West 2021]), which affirmed the importance of the game but limited youth football programs' ability to conduct full contact practices and required coaches to be certified in proper tackling, blocking, and concussion management.

62. For instance, the Council of Europe and European Union launched a Child Safeguarding in Sport initiative; "Child Safeguarding in Sport," European Union and Council of Europe, accessed April 10, 2022, https://pjp-eu.coe.int/en

/web/pss. France regulates sport training centers and requires a written contract between the training centers, parents, and schools to specify the child's maximum weekly number of hours devoted to training and competing. See Paulo David, *Human Rights in Youth Sport* (London: Routledge, 2005): 145-47. In 2007, Norway created, and then updated in 2015, its Children's Rights in Sport document to guide how youth sport is provided; Norwegian Olympic and Paralympic Committee and Confederation of Sports, *Children's Rights in Sports* (Oslo, 2015). Japan's Committee for UNICEF initiated the *Children's Rights in Sports Principles*, 2nd ed. (Tokyo, December 2018), which are based on the United Nations Convention on the Rights of the Child.

63. Howard Davidson, "Does the U.N. Convention on the Rights of the Child Make a Difference?" *Michigan State International Law Review* 22, no. 2 (2014): 504-05; Martha Minow, "Whatever Happened to Children's Rights?" *Minnesota Law Review* 80, no. 2 (December 1995): 267.

64. United Nations, Convention on the Rights of the Child, art. 31(1).

65. UNICEF Innocenti Research Centre, *Protecting Children from Violence in Sport*, vii, stating that "UNICEF has long recognized that there is great value in children's sport and play, and has been a consistent proponent of these activities."

66. Japan Committee for UNICEF, *Children's Rights in Sports Principles*, ii.

67. See, for example, "What We Do," Centre for Sport and Human Rights, accessed April 6, 2022, https://www.sporthumanrights.org/what-we-do, describing the group's work "with all actors in sport" to support children's rights; David, *Human Rights in Youth Sport*, 145-47; Inger Eliasson, "The Gap between Formalised Children's Rights and Children's Real Lives in Sport," *International Review for the Sociology of Sport* 52, no. 4 (October 2015): 470-96; Melanie Lang and Mike Hartill, eds., *Safeguarding, Child Protection, and Abuse in Sport: International Perspectives in Research, Policy, and Practice* (London: Routledge, 2015), 2; Daniel Rhind and Frank Owusu-Sekyere, *International Safeguards for Children in Sport: Developing and Embedding a Safeguarding Culture* (London: Routledge, 2018).

68. Centre for Sport and Human Rights, *Child Labour in Sport*, 30, 32.

69. Tom Farrey, "Does Norway Have the Answer to Excesses in Youth Sports?" *New York Times*, April 28, 2019; Norwegian Olympic and Paralympic Committee and Conference of Sports, *Children's Rights in Sports*; N. Jeremi Duru, "It's Not Child's Play: A Regulatory Approach to Reforming American Youth Sports," *Virginia Sports and Entertainment Law Journal* 20, no. 1 (Spring 2021): 44; Coakley, *Sports in Society*, 94.

70. Matthew Futterman, "It's Norway's Games Again: What's Its Secret?" *New York Times*, February 18, 2022; Jan Emil Ellingsen and Anne G. Danielsen,

"Norwegian Children's Rights in Sport and Coaches' Understanding of Talent," *International Journal of Children's Rights* 25, no. 2 (August 2017): 412.

71. Norwegian Olympic and Paralympic Committee and Conference of Sports, *Children's Rights in Sports*, 5.

72. Norwegian Olympic and Paralympic Committee and Conference of Sports, *Children's Rights in Sports*, 9, 10.

73. Futterman, "It's Norway's Games Again"; Norwegian Olympic and Paralympic Committee and Conference of Sports, *Children's Rights in Sports*, stating that 8 out of 10 children participate in sports.

74. Futterman, "It's Norway's Games Again," explaining that Norway has "doubled down on its commitments under its Children's Rights in Sports document," which includes an emphasis on "participation and socialization rather than hard-core competition." Of course, a youth sport model need not produce Olympic champions to be considered effective.

75. Carrington and Andrews, "Introduction," 9, stating that "Western definitions of sport tend to assume that *competition* is axiomatic but this may be to unduly privilege a particular concept of sport" (emphasis in original). See also Daniel Gould, "Professionalization of Youth Sport: It's Time to Act!" *Clinical Journal of Sports Medicine* 19, no. 2 (March 2009): 81, 82, pinpointing the incorrect assumption of most youth sport parents and coaches that one cannot develop as an athlete in "an enjoyable, fun-filled atmosphere."

76. See Coakley, "Positive Youth Development," 27, stating that there is a "near universal belief that sport participation automatically produces positive development outcomes for participants"; Donnelly and Atkinson, "Where History Meets Biography," 374, stating, "The list of claims deriving from the notion of 'sport for good' is extensive, but research results regarding the use of sport to achieve these social goals are often equivocal and inconclusive"; Peter A. Harmer, "Injury Research in Pediatric and Adolescent Sports," in *Injury in Pediatric and Adolescent Sports: Epidemiology, Treatment, and Prevention*, ed. Dennis Caine and Laura Purcell (Cham, Switzerland: Springer, 2016): 234, stating that "it is clear that the very nature of competitive sport entails potential harm that threatens to undermine the value of participation."

6. THE YOUTH SPORT SURPLUS

1. Dionne L. Koller, "Putting Public Law into Private Sport," *Pepperdine Law Review* 43, no. 3 (April 2016): 687.

2. See, for example, N.J. Rev. Stat. § 5:17-1 (Westlaw through L. 2023, C.280 & J.R. No. 18), stating that "an athletic code of conduct" may be established by youth sport organizations that permit a person attending a "youth sports event" to be removed if the person "engages in verbal or physical threats or abuse" or

"initiates a fight or scuffle"; 105 Ill. Comp. Stat. § 5/24-24 (Westlaw through P.A. 103-586 of 2024 Reg. Sess.), authorizing schools to promulgate spectator codes of conduct for athletic events; "Sport Parent Code of Conduct," Little League, accessed April 10, 2022, https://www.littleleague.org/downloads/parent-code-conduct/.

3. Scott Kretchmar, "Formalism and Sport," in *Routledge Handbook of the Philosophy of Sport*, ed. Mike McNamee and William J. Morgan (London: Routledge, 2017): 19.

4. Zillah Eisenstein, "Constructing a Theory of Capitalist Patriarchy and Socialist Feminism," *Critical Sociology* 25, nos. 2-3 (March 1999): 209; Orly Lobel, "Class and Care: The Role of Private Intermediaries in the In-Home Care Industry in the U.S. and Israel," *Harvard Women's Law Journal* 24 (Spring 2001): 89; Taunya Lovell Banks, "Toward a Global Critical Feminist Vision: Domestic Work and the Nanny Tax Debate," *Journal of Gender, Race, and Justice* 3, no. 1 (Fall 1999): 6-8, stating that domestic work was not considered "real work"; Reva B. Siegal, "Home as Work: The First Women's Rights Claims Concerning Wives' Household Labor, 1850-1880," *Yale Law Journal* 103, no. 5 (March 1994): 1088, explaining women's "uncompensated labor" in the home.

5. Robin West, *Caring for Justice* (New York: New York University Press, 1997), 111, arguing that "the harms that might be done women by virtue of their greater engagement in household tasks—their intimate altruism—are cast into a sort of definitional oblivion" because it is not identified as labor.

6. Katharine Silbaugh, "Turning Labor into Love: Housework and the Law," *Northwestern University Law Review* 91, no. 1 (Fall 1996): 5.

7. Silbaugh, "Turning Labor into Love."

8. Eisenstein, "Constructing a Theory," 210.

9. Silbaugh, "Turning Labor into Love," 26.

10. Joseph M. Turrini, *The End of Amateurism in American Track and Field* (Urbana: University of Illinois Press, 2010), 2.

11. Berger v. National Collegiate Athletic Association, 843 F3d 285 (7th Cir. 2016).

12. Eisenstein, "Constructing a Theory," 210.

13. See, for example, Collective Bargaining Agreement between Major League Baseball and the Major League Baseball Players Association, signed December 14, 2016; Collective Bargaining Agreement between the National Basketball Association and the National Basketball Players Association, signed January 19, 2017; Collective Bargaining Agreement between the National Football League and the National Football League Players Association, signed March 15, 2020 (https://www.mlbplayers.com/cba).

14. See, for example, National Collegiate Athletic Association v. Alston, 141 S. Ct. 2141 (2021); Ramogi Huma and Ellen J. Staurowsky, *How the NCAA's Empire Robs Predominantly Black Athletes of Billions in Generational Wealth* (Riverside, CA: National College Players Association, 2020); Memorandum from NLRB General Counsel Jennifer A. Abruzzo to All Regional Directors, Officers-in-Charge, and Resident Officers, No. GC 21-08, "Statutory Rights of Players at Academic Institutions (Student Athletes) under the National Labor Relations Act" (September 29, 2021).

15. U.S. Department of Health and Human Services, *National Youth Sports Strategy* (Washington, DC, September 2019), 60 ("individual"), 61-63.

16. See Janet Halley, Prabha Kotiswaran, Rachel Rebouché, and Hila Shamir, *Governance Feminism: An Introduction* (Minneapolis: University of Minnesota Press, 2018): 256, stating that "liberal and neoliberal economic theory—both based on neoclassical economics—assumes that free market exchanges motivated by individual preferences and unhampered by transaction costs leave all players better off" and that "liberal and neoliberal economic theory starts with an assumption that the distributions of the market are fair."

17. Beth A. Cianfrone, James Jianhui Zhang, Brenda Pitts, and Kevin K. Byon, "Identifying Key Market Demand Factors Associated with High School Basketball Tournaments," *Sports Marketing Quarterly* 24, no. 2 (June 2015): 91, stating that in the United States "interest in high school sporting events is at an all-time high" as demonstrated by, among other indicators, game attendance and media coverage. The authors state that the increased commercial appeal of high school sport has "led to an arms race of sorts, similar to college programs," as well as more emphasis on "winning."

18. Symeon Dagkas and Kathleen Armour, eds., *Inclusion and Exclusion through Youth Sport* (London: Routledge, 2012), xv.

19. Alan G. Ingham, "Sportification Process: A Bibliographical Analysis Framed by the Work of Marx, Weber, Durkheim, and Freud," in *Sport and Modern Social Theorists*, ed. Richard Giulianotti (London: Palgrave MacMillan, 2004), 18, stating that for the sports industry to exist, "structures have to be developed which insure its continued reproduction through the production of athletic labour power with high levels of skill"; Michael A. Messner and Michela Musto, "Introduction: Kids and Sport," in *Child's Play: Sport in Kids' Worlds*, ed. Michael A. Messner and Michela Musto (New Brunswick, NJ: Rutgers University Press, 2016), 5, stating that "the kids who play and watch sports today supply the demographic buoyancy for the future of sport."

20. Nathan Kalman-Lamb, "Athletic Labor and Social Reproduction," *Journal of Sport and Social Issues* 43, no. 6 (May 2019): 522, explaining that athletes'

physical labor in playing has an "emotional consequence for fans." Kalman-Lamb also notes that youth sports "produces meaning and rejuvenation" for parents (527). See also Mark Hyman, *Until It Hurts: America's Obsession with Youth Sports and How It Harms Our Kids* (Boston: Beacon Press, 2009), ix–x.

21. President's Council on Sports, Fitness, and Nutrition Science Board, "PCSFN Science Board Report on Youth Sports" (Washington, DC, September 17, 2020), 11, stating that "as the extrinsic rewards linked to youth sports success have increased . . . the market has responded."

22. Halley et al., *Governance Feminism*, 256, explaining that in exploring "surplus," we ask "what gain in human welfare—quantifiable like profits or non-quantifiable like pleasure or prestige—does a given struggle produce?" Halley and colleagues also state that "this analysis starts by identifying not the injury . . . in a given setting but the *surplus* it generates" (256; emphasis in original).

23. Jayati Ghosh, "Capital," in *The Elgar Companion to Marxist Economics*, ed. Ben Fine and Alfredo Saad-Filho (Cheltenham, UK: Edward Elgar, 2012): 28, 29.

24. Gunther Teubner, "The Constitution of Non-monetary Surplus Values," *Social and Legal Studies* 30, no. 4 (August 2021): 4.

25. Teubner, "Constitution of Non-monetary Surplus Values," 2–3.

26. Halley et al., *Governance Feminism*, 256, stating that "Marxist economic theory posits that market exchanges produce a *surplus*—value over and above the bare costs of production—that can be appropriated by players with superior social power" (emphasis in original).

27. See Johnson v. National Collegiate Athletic Association, 556 F. Supp. 3d 491 (E.D. Pa. 2021).

28. Randolph Feezel, "A Pluralist Conception of Play," in *The Philosophy of Play*, ed. Emily Ryall, Wendy Russell, and Malcolm MacLean (London: Routledge, 2013): 11, explaining that "the philosophical and scientific literature on play is extensive, and the approaches to the study, description and explanation of play are diverse"; Henning Eichberg, *Play in Philosophy and Social Thought*, ed. Signe Højbjerre Larsen (London: Routledge, 2019), 160–61, arguing that classic definitions of play are "stiff" and overly rational. See Ben Carrington and David L. Andrews, "Introduction: Sport as Escape, Struggle, and Art," in *A Companion to Sport*, ed. David L. Andrews and Ben Carrington (Malden, MA: Wiley Blackwell, 2013), 9–10, explaining that "the lines between what is merely 'play' . . . and what constitutes a sport" are not always "clear-cut."

29. Feezel, "Pluralist Conception of Play," 29, describing sport as "in the neighbourhood of play."

30. See Carrington and Andrews, "Introduction," 9.

31. John W. Loy and W. Robert Morford, "The Agon Motif Redux: A Study of the Contest Element in Sport," *Physical Culture and Sport* 82, no. 1 (June 2019): 12.

32. Johan Huizinga, "The Nature of Play," in *Philosophic Inquiry in Sport*, ed. William J. Morgan and Klaus V. Meier (Champaign, IL: Human Kinetics, 1995), 5.

33. Klaus Meier, "Triad Trickery: Playing with Sports and Games," in *Philosophic Inquiry in Sport*, ed. William J. Morgan and Klaus V. Meier (Champaign, IL: Human Kinetics, 1995), 32.

34. Ingham, "Sportification Process," 15.

35. Huizinga, "Nature of Play," 5.

36. Carrington and Andrews, "Introduction," 10.

37. Carrington and Andrews, "Introduction," 9; Bernard Suits, "Tricky Triad: Games, Play, and Sport," in *Philosophic Inquiry in Sport*, ed. William J. Morgan and Klaus V. Meier (Champaign, IL: Human Kinetics, 1995), 21-22.

38. Yvonne Williams, "Protecting Children from Violence in Sport: A UNICEF Report," *Entertainment and Sports Law Journal* 9, no. 1 (June 2011): 72-75.

39. Stephen H. Hardy, "Entrepreneurs, Organizations, and the Sports Marketplace," in *The New American Sport History: Recent Approaches and Perspectives*, ed. S. W. Pope (Urbana: University of Illinois Press, 1997), 343-44, 344-45, explaining that "rulemakers create a special product—the game form—that may exist as a commodity" and that "game forms are usually played in a situation that involves more than simple, expressive use-value for the players."

40. Kalman-Lamb, "Athletic Labor and Social Reproduction," 518 ("social reproduction"; "needs"), 522. Kalman-Lamb goes on to assert that sport is important to capitalism because athletes create value not just as laborers in their sport but as performers of that sport, so that they "produce the capacity for value by affectively reproducing the labor power of others" (527).

41. Kalman-Lamb, "Athletic Labor and Social Reproduction," 527. Indeed, at least one researcher refers to U.S. youth sport as an "elite entertainment model." See Daniel Gould, "Professionalization of Youth Sport: It's Time to Act!" *Clinical Journal of Sports Medicine* 19, no. 2 (March 2009), 154.

42. Kimberly S. Schimmel, "Sport and International Political Economy: An Introduction," in *The Political Economy of Sport*, ed. John Nauright and Kimberly S. Schimmel (London: Palgrave MacMillan, 2005): 1.

43. Hardy, "Entrepreneurs," 344 ("triple commodity"), 345.

44. Hardy, 344-45, 346.

45. Lincoln Allison, *Amateurism in Sport: An Analysis and Defense* (London: Routledge, 2001), 79-80.

46. Toby Miller, "Michel Foucault and the Critique of Sport," in *Marxism, Cultural Studies, and Sport*, ed. Ben Carrington and Ian McDonald, 181-94 (London: Routledge, 2009), quoted in Carrington and Andrews, "Introduction," 6.

47. Ronald McKinney, "Toward a Post-post-modern Philosophy of Play," *Philosophy Today* 64, no. 1 (Winter 2020): 161.

48. Suits, "Tricky Triad," 21–22.

49. Ingham, "Sportification Process," 18.

50. Ingham, 18.

51. Ingham, "Sportification Process," 29, explaining the difference between play and work as "human *being*" and "self as human *doing.*" Indeed, the difference between play and sport is currently seen in the incorporation of break dancing, surfing, and skateboarding into Olympic sports, with at least some who participate in these activities noting the changes it will mean, especially with respect to the toll on their bodies from needing to "train." See Rick Maese, "How Breakdancing Made the Leap from 80s Pop Culture to the Olympic Stage," *Washington Post*, February 9, 2021.

52. Ingham, "Sportification Process," 17.

53. Jean Côté, Colleen Coakley, and Mark Bruner, "Children's Talent Development in Sport: Effectiveness or Efficiency?" in *Inclusion and Exclusion through Youth Sport*, ed. Symeon Dagkas and Kathleen Armour (London: Routledge, 2012), 180. Play is considered so important that it is asserted to be a child's right in the U.N. Convention on the Rights of the Child.

54. Heather Macpherson Parrott and Lynn E. Cohen, "Advocating for Play: The Benefits of Unstructured Play in Public Schools," *School Community Journal* 30, no. 2 (Fall–Winter 2020): 229.

55. Côté, Coakley, and Bruner, "Children's Talent Development," 180.

56. UNICEF Innocenti Research Centre, *Protecting Children from Violence in Sport: A Review with a Focus on Industrialized Countries* (Florence, Italy: UNICEF, July 2010), 3.

57. Jay Coakley, *Sports in Society: Issues and Controversies*, 13th ed. (New York: McGraw-Hill, 2021), 87.

58. Robert J. Brustad, Runar Vilhjalmsson, and Antonio Manuel Fonseca, "Organized Sport and Physical Activity Promotion," in *Youth Physical Activity and Sedentary Behavior: Challenges and Solutions*, ed. Alan L. Smith and Stuart J. H. Biddle (Champaign, IL: Human Kinetics, 2008), 351.

59. D. Stanley Eitzen, *Fair and Foul: Beyond the Myths and Paradoxes of Sport*, 6th ed. (Lanham, MD: Rowman and Littlefield, 2016), 113; see Steven J. Overman, *Youth Sports Crisis: Out-of-Control Adults, Helpless Kids* (Santa Barbara, CA: Praeger, 2014), 2, distinguishing the "game" of baseball from the "sport" of baseball by the presence of adults who direct and supervise the activity with formal rules and procedures.

60. Overman, *Youth Sports Crisis*, 7.

61. Hyman, *Until It Hurts*, 114; Melanie Lang and Mike Hartill, *Safeguarding, Child Protection, and Abuse in Sport: International Perspectives in Research, Policy, and Practice* (London: Routledge, 2015), 1.

62. Hyman, *Until It Hurts*, xii; Gould, "Professionalization of Youth Sport," 82, stating that the "single biggest problem" in youth sport is the adoption of a "professional" model. See also Messner and Musto, "Introduction," 8, stating that "researchers have begun to explore how commercial sport organizations and sports media have at times routinized, rationalized, and commercialized kid-created street sports"; Ingham, "Sportification Process," 17; Charles A. Popkin, Ahmad F. Bayomy, and Christopher S. Ahmad, "Early Sport Specialization," *Journal of the American Academy of Orthopaedic Surgeons* 27, no. 22 (November 15, 2019): 996, explaining that adults involved in youth sport frequently believe that sport specialization is better than simple "play."

63. Overman, *Youth Sports Crisis*, 2.

64. Eitzen, *Fair and Foul*, 121. See also Douglas E. Abrams, "The Challenge Facing Parents and Coaches in Youth Sports: Assuring Children Fun and Equal Opportunity," *Villanova Sports and Entertainment Law Journal* 8, no. 2 (January 2002), 265–66, describing some youth travel teams as having "grueling" schedules that would "exhaust adult professionals" and arguing that "youngsters before puberty are often treated as commodities"; Dennis Caine and Laura Purcell, "The Exceptionality of the Young Athlete," in *Injury in Pediatric and Adolescent Sports: Epidemiology, Treatment, and Prevention*, ed. Dennis Caine and Laura Purcell (Cham, Switzerland: Springer, 2016): 3, stating that it is "not uncommon . . . for children as young as six to play organized sports and travel with select teams to compete against other teams"; Joshua Newman and Kyle: Bunds, Special Issue Foreword: On the "Political Economy of Amateur Athletes," *Journal of Amateur Sport* 2, no. 1 (February 2016): 8, describing the "hyper-commodification of youth sports"; Hardy, "Entrepreneurs," 359, urging sports historians to consider whether the commodification of sport has "strangulat[ed] sport as play"; University of Kansas School of Education and Human Sciences, "The Commercialization of Youth Sports," *University of Kansas School of Education and Human Sciences* (blog), December 23, 2020, accessed April 23, 2022, https://onlinesportmanagement.ku.edu/community/commercialization-of-youth-sports.

7. YOUTH SPORT'S BENEFICIARIES

1. David Kennedy, *A World of Struggle: How Power, Law, and Expertise Shape Global Political Economy* (Princeton, NJ: Princeton University Press, 2016), 58–59, explaining that proponents of certain societal arrangements may "obscure the distributional significance of what they seek by emphasizing the benefits that will accrue to all mankind. . . . When claims are framed this way, it is easy to overlook" the distributional consequences.

2. Kennedy, *World of Struggle*, 59. Similarly, Carrington and Andrews state with respect to sport specifically that "scholars of sport need to situate the 'study

of play, games, and sports in the context of understanding the historical struggle over the control of rules and resources in social life.'" See Ben Carrington and David L. Andrews, "Introduction: Sport as Escape, Struggle, and Art," in *A Companion to Sport*, edited by David L. Andrews and Ben Carrington (Malden, MA: Wiley Blackwell, 2013), 10 (quoting Richard Gruneau, *Class, Sports, and Social Development* [Amherst: University of Massachusetts Press, 1983], 28).

3. Research shows that fitness and fun with friends, and not playing to win, are the primary motivations for children to participate in sport. See Gretchen Kerr and Ashley Stirling, "Putting the Child Back in Children's Sport: Nurturing Young Talent in a Developmentally Appropriate Manner," in *Ethics in Youth Sport: Policy and Pedagogical Applications*, ed. Stephen Harvey and Richard L. Light (London: Routledge, 2013), 27.

4. U.S. Department of Health and Human Services, *National Youth Sports Strategy* (Washington, DC, September 2019), 3; Laura Newberry, "Kids are Losing Interest in Organized Sports; Why That Matters," *Los Angeles Times*, December 6, 2021.

5. U.S. Department of Health and Human Services, *National Youth Sports Strategy*, 22.

6. Mark Rerick, "Making Cuts on Athletic Teams—The Necessary Evil," National Federation of State High School Associations, October 28, 2015, https://www.nfhs.org/articles/making-cuts-on-athletic-teams-the-necessary-evil/, explaining the need to cut athletes at the high school level: "As much as we'd like to base our entire program in just meeting our three department goals (having fun, learning how to compete, and learning the sport), the reality of an athletic department is that all of our stakeholders—athletes, coaches, parents, public—still expect us to be able to compete with the intent to win games."

7. "Sports," Gallup Historical Trends, Gallup, accessed April 23, 2022, https://news.gallup.com/poll/4735/sports.aspx, citing 2015 survey data.

8. Nathan Kalman-Lamb, "Athletic Labor and Social Reproduction," *Journal of Sport and Social Issues* 43, no. 6 (May 2019): 527.

9. Paulo David, *Human Rights in Youth Sport* (London: Routledge, 2005), 144, stating, "Modern sport needs a continual succession of attractive entertainers capable of exciting supporters and TV viewers alike with their skill and outstanding results."

10. Alan G. Ingham, "The Sportification Process: A Bibliographical Analysis Framed by the Work of Marx, Weber, Durkheim, and Freud," in *Sport and Modern Social Theorists*, ed. Richard Giulianotti (London: Palgrave MacMillan, 2004), 18, stating that "the sports feeder system is instrumentally rational."

11. Robert H. Frank and Philip J. Cook, *The Winner-Take-All Society: Why the Few at the Top Get So Much More than the Rest of Us* (New York: Penguin Books, 1995), 102.

12. Frank and Cook, *Winner-Take-All Society*, 29, stating that athletics is a "quintessential winner-take-all" market.

13. Doune MacDonald et al., "The Will for Inclusion: Bothering the Inclusion/Exclusion Discourses of Sport," in *Inclusion and Exclusion through Youth Sport*, ed. Symeon Dagkas and Kathleen Armour (London: Routledge, 2012), 21.

14. B. David Ridpath, *Alternative Models of Sports Development in America: Solutions to a Crisis in Education and Public Health* (Athens: Ohio University Press, 2018), 67–68.

15. Ann Skelton, Paul Singh, and Steve Cornelius, "Protection of Young Athletes," in *Handbook on International Sports Law*, ed. James A. R. Nafziger and Ryan Gauthier (Cheltenham, UK: Edward Elgar, 2022): 403.

16. Alan Bairner, "Sportive Nationalism and Nationalist Politics: A Comparative Analysis of Scotland, the Republic of Ireland, and Sweden," *Journal of Sport and Social Issues* 20, no. 3 (August 1996): 314.

17. Tom Weir, "Breaking Down USA's 1,000 Summer Olympic Gold Medals," *Bleacher Report*, August 13, 2016.

18. Nicholas Dixon, "On Winning and Athletic Superiority," *Journal of the Philosophy of Sport* 26, no. 1 (1999): 10–26.

19. Lawrence J. Hatab, "The Drama of Agonistic Embodiment: Nietzschean Reflections on the Meaning of Sports," *International Studies in Philosophy* 30, no. 3 (1998): 103–4.

20. Steven J. Overman, *The Youth Sports Crisis: Out-of-Control Adults, Helpless Kids* (Santa Barbara, CA: Praeger, 2014), 42.

21. For instance, the state of Maryland has a program to bring more youth sports events to the state and "attract sports fans" and "tourists." See Md. Code Ann., Econ. Dev. § 10-612.1 (West 2023). See also Iowa Code § 15E.321 (2022), promoting "youth sports" and "sports tourism."

22. See Overman, *Youth Sports Crisis*, 43.

23. Mona Mirehie et al., "Towards an Understanding of Family Travel Decision-Making Processes in the Context of Youth Sports Tourism," *Journal of Destination Marketing and Management* 21, no. 2 (September 2021): 100644.

24. Dionne L. Koller, "The Pipeline to Title IX," *Marquette Sports Law Review* 33, no. 1 (Fall 2022): 76.

25. Eric Hungenberg, Tommy Aicher, and Taylor Sawyer, "A Glimpse into the Experience of a Youth Sport Tourism Consumer: An Analysis of Parents vs. Coaches," *Journal of Sport and Tourism* 26, no. 1 (January 2022): 43.

26. Long v. Napolitano, 53 P.3d 172 (Ariz. Ct. App. 2002).

27. Town of Sterlington v. East Ouachita Recreation District No. 1, 215 So. 3d 381 (La. Ct. App. 2017).

28. *Town of Sterlington*, 215 So. 3d at 388.

29. Amy Chan Hyung Kim et al., "Social Geographies at Play: Mapping the Spatial Politics of Community-Based Youth Sport Participation," *Journal of Amateur Sport* 41, no 1 (February 2016): 41.

30. Bill Pennington, "Parents Behaving Badly: A Youth Sports Crisis Caught on Video," *New York Times*, July 18, 2019; Meredith Deliso, "Over 20 Incidents Involving Guns at Youth Sporting Events in Recent Weeks, Gun Safety Group Finds," *ABC News*, September 30, 2021. See also Dianna K. Fiore, "Parental Rage and Violence in Youth Sports: How Can We Prevent 'Soccer Moms' and 'Hockey Dads' from Interfering in Youth Sports and Causing Games to End in Fistfights Rather than Handshakes?" *Villanova Sports and Entertainment Law Journal* 10, no. 1 (January 2003): 103–29.

31. Kim et al., "Social Geographies at Play," 46.

32. Travis E. Dorsch et al., "A History of Parental Involvement in Organized Youth Sport: A Scoping Review," *Sport, Exercise, and Performance Psychology* 10, no. 4 (June 2021): 536–37 (term "sport parenting"), 548.

33. Kim et al., "Social Geographies at Play," 44; Dorsch et al., "History of Parental Involvement," 540.

34. Michael A. Messner and Michela Musto, "Introduction: Kids and Sport," in *Child's Play: Sport in Kids' Worlds*, ed. Michael A. Messner and Michela Musto (New Brunswick, NJ: Rutgers University Press, 2016), 12.

35. Jay Coakley, "Positive Youth Development through Sport: Myths, Beliefs, and Realities," in *Positive Youth Development through Sport*, ed. Nicholas L. Holt (London: Routledge, 2016), 25 ("good"), explaining that "parental moral worth came to be linked with parents' efforts to enlist their children in visible, achievement-oriented, and culturally valued activities" such as youth sport.

36. Dorsch et al., "History of Parental Involvement," 544.

37. Overman, *Youth Sports Crisis*, 50.

38. Messner and Musto, "Introduction," 12.

39. D. Stanley Eitzen, *Fair and Foul: Beyond the Myths and Paradoxes of Sport*, 6th ed. (Lanham, MD: Rowman and Littlefield, 2016), 204–5.

40. Phoebe Friesen, Bethany Saul, Lisa Kearns, Kathleen Bachynski, and Arthur Caplan, "Overuse Injuries in Youth Sports: Legal and Social Responsibility," *Journal of Legal Aspects of Sport* 28, no. 2 (2018): 153, 154.

41. Overman, *Youth Sports Crisis*, 29 ("perform").

42. Overman, *Youth Sports Crisis*, 7.

43. Ian R. Tofler, Penelope Krener Knapp, and Martin Drell, "Achievement by Proxy Spectrum in Youth Sports: A Distorted Mentoring of High-Achieving Youth; Historical Perspectives and Clinical Intervention with Children, Adolescents, and Their Families," *Sport Psychiatry* 7, no. 1 (October 1998): 804, 807 ("normal pride").

44. Tofler, Knapp, and Drell, "Achievement by Proxy Spectrum," 544, 808.
45. Tofler, Knapp, and Drell, 808.
46. Tofler, Knapp, and Drell, 809.
47. Tofler, Knapp, and Drell, 810.
48. Tofler, Knapp, and Drell, 809. See also Mark Hyman, *Until It Hurts: America's Obsession with Youth Sports and How It Harms Our Kids* (Boston: Beacon Press, 2009), ix.
49. James R. Andrews, "Why Are There So Many Injuries to Our Young Athletes? Professionalization and Specialization in Youth Sport," *University of Baltimore Law Review* 40, no. 4 (Summer 2011): 577.
50. Overman, *Youth Sports Crisis*, 42.
51. Dorsch et al., "History of Parental Involvement," 540.
52. Anne C. Dailey and Laura A. Rosenbury, "The New Parental Rights," *Duke Law Journal* 71, no. 1 (October 2021): 75n222.
53. Kalman-Lamb, "Athletic Labor and Social Reproduction," 527.
54. "NCAA Recruiting Facts," National Collegiate Athletic Association, accessed April 13, 2022, https://ncaaorg.s3.amazonaws.com/compliance/recruiting/NCAA_RecruitingFactSheet.pdf.
55. "Student-Athletes," National Collegiate Athletic Association, accessed April 13, 2022, https://www.ncaa.org/sports/2021/7/22/student-athletes.aspx (500,000 figure); Saahil Desai, "College Sports Are Affirmative Action for Rich White Students," *The Atlantic*, October 23, 2018.
56. U.S. House Committee on Energy and Commerce (Majority Staff), *Nassar and Beyond: A Review of the Olympic Community's Efforts to Protect Athletes from Sexual Abuse* (Washington, DC: December 20, 2018), 11-15.
57. See, for example, National Collegiate Athletic Association v. Alston, 141 S. Ct. 2141 (2021), noting that the NCAA is a "massive business" and that "those who run this enterprise profit in a different way than the student-athletes whose activities they oversee"; Otis B. Grant, "African American College Football Players and the Dilemma of Exploitation, Racism, and Education: A Socio-economic Analysis of Sports Law," *Whittier Law Review* 24, no. 3 (Spring 2003): 645-62; David J. Berri, "Paying NCAA Athletes," *Marquette Sports Law Review* 26, no. 2 (2016): 479-91, describing "exploitation" of college athletes; Anne Marie Lofaso, "Groomed for Exploitation! How Applying the Statutory Definition of Employee to Cover Division IA College Football Players Disrupts the Student-Athlete Myth," *West Virginia Law Review* 119, no. 3 (April 2017): 957-97.
58. There are many questions, though, about the extent of the benefit to children from participating in sports, at least under the current U.S. sport model. One scholar concluded that, while youth sport has the "potential" to contribute to a healthy, physically active lifestyle, the current model generally makes only a

"small" contribution. See Toben F. Nelson, "Sport and the Childhood Obesity Epidemic," in *Child's Play: Sport in Kids' Worlds*, ed. Michael A. Messner and Michela Musto (New Brunswick, NJ: Rutgers University Press, 2016), 91. Nelson further states that there is "insufficient evidence to conclude that sport participation" helps lower the risk of a child being overweight or obese (85). See also Kerr and Stirling, "Putting the Child Back in Children's Sport," 27, stating that youth sport that is not provided in a "developmentally appropriate" way can be harmful.

59. Ingham, "Sportification Process," 18 ("payment"); Messner and Musto, "Introduction," 13 (emphasis in original).

60. Messner and Musto, "Introduction," 13.

61. Andrews, "Why Are There So Many Injuries to Our Young Athletes?" 583.

62. Emma Kavanagh et al., "Managing Abuse in Sport: An Introduction to the Special Issue," *Sport Management Review* 23, no. 1 (February 2020): 1–7; Friesen et al., "Overuse Injuries," 156.

63. See David, *Human Rights in Youth Sport*, 181.

64. Nicholas Dixon, "Sport, Parental Autonomy, and Children's Rights to an Open Future," *Journal of the Philosophy of Sport* 34, no. 2 (October 2007): 153 (emphasis in original).

65. Ramogi Huma and Ellen J. Staurowsky, *How the NCAA's Empire Robs Predominantly Black Athletes of Billions in Generational Wealth* (Riverside, CA: National College Players Association, 2020).

66. U.S. Department of Health and Human Services, *National Youth Sports Strategy*, 35.

67. Alana Semuels, "The White Flight from Football," *The Atlantic*, February 1, 2019; Vivian E. Hamilton, "Play Now, Pay Later? Youth and Adolescent Collision Sports," *Hastings Law Journal* 71, no. 1 (2020): 172–73, stating that "Black youth and men are overrepresented in . . . tackle football and basketball" and that this "makes them disproportionately likely to suffer the effects of injury" from concussions.

68. Eitzen, *Fair and Foul*, 207.

69. Messner and Musto, "Introduction," 11.

70. Coakley, "Positive Youth Development," 26.

71. See Brian L. Porto, "Unfinished Business: The Continuing Struggle for Equal Opportunity in College Sports on the Eve of Title IX's Fiftieth Anniversary," *Marquette Sports Law Review* 32, no. 1 (Fall 2021): 259–303.

72. See U.S. House Committee on Energy and Commerce, *Nassar and Beyond*, 11–15.

73. Paul S. Carbone et al., "Promoting the Participation of Children and Adolescents with Disabilities in Sports, Recreation, and Physical Activity," *Pediatrics* 148, no. 6 (December 2021): 1.

74. Carbone et al., "Promoting the Participation of Children and Adolescents with Disabilities," 3.

75. Carbone et al., 4, 5.

76. Carbone et al., 5.

77. Messner and Musto, "Introduction," 8, stating that through a conservative lens these children are "lazy couch potatoes" or "losers," and in the liberal narrative they are "underprivileged" and "'at-risk' kids" because they are not involved in sport.

78. Carbone et al., "Promoting the Participation of Children and Adolescents with Disabilities," 12, stating that a system that emphasized inclusion and provided developmentally appropriate opportunities would provide "substantial" benefits to children with disabilities.

79. Carbone et al., "Promoting the Participation of Children and Adolescents with Disabilities," 1, explaining the relative lack of research on youth sport exploring "to what extent youth sports participation is part of the problem or part of the solution when it comes to concerns about children's health"; Jay Coakley, "Assessing the Sociology of Sport: On Cultural Sensibilities and the Great Sport Myth," *International Review for the Sociology of Sport* 50, nos. 4–5 (June–August 2015): 405, stating that the pervasive assumption that sport is inherently good "consistently undermines critical discussions and research on the culture and social organization of sports"; Dorsch et al., "History of Parental Involvement," 549, stating that there are "gaps" in the research on parental involvement in youth sports and that future research is warranted.

80. Messner and Musto, "Introduction," 1.

81. Messner and Musto, "Introduction," 2–5, 6–7.

82. Martha Minow, "Preface," in *The Oxford Handbook of Children's Rights Law*, ed. Jonathan Todres and Shani M. King (Oxford: Oxford University Press, 2020): ix–x; Melanie Lang and Mike Hartill, *Safeguarding, Child Protection, and Abuse in Sport: International Perspectives in Research, Policy, and Practice* (London: Routledge, 2015), 1, stating that in youth sport children "are often viewed as miniature adults, as athletes first and children second, and as objects by the adults around them who have a stake in their success."

CONCLUSION

1. Memorandum from NLRB General Counsel Jennifer A. Abruzzo to All Regional Directors, Officers-in-Charge, and Resident Officers, "Statutory Rights of Players at Academic Institutions (Student Athletes) under the National Labor Relations Act," No. GC 21-08 (September 29, 2021), 1n1.

2. Memorandum No. GC 21-08, "Statutory Rights of Players," 1n1.

3. Miranda Fricker, *Epistemic Injustice: Power and the Ethics of Knowing* (Oxford: Oxford University Press, 2007), 1 (epistemic injustice), 9–11.

4. R. Scott Kretchmar, "Why a Focus on Sporting Tests Would Reveal an Alternate Story and Raise Ethical Questions about Agon: A Commentary," *Physical Culture and Sport* 82, no. 1 (June 2019): 57.

SELECTED BIBLIOGRAPHY

This listing includes books, book chapters, journal articles, and government and national governing body reports. It does not include court cases, statutes, legislative hearing transcripts, or newspaper or magazine articles.

Abrams, Douglas E. "The Challenge Facing Parents and Coaches in Youth Sports: Assuring Children Fun and Equal Opportunity." *Villanova Sports and Entertainment Law Journal* 8, no. 2 (January 2002): 253-92.
———. "References to Baseball in Judicial Opinions and Written Advocacy." *Journal of the Missouri Bar* 72, no. 5 (September-October 2016): 268-74.
———. "References to Football in Judicial Opinions and Written Advocacy." *Journal of the Missouri Bar* 73, no. 1 (January-February 2017): 34-38.
———. "The State of Concussion: Protecting Athletes through Advances in Law, Public Health, and Science." *Journal of Business and Technology Law* 10, no. 1 (January 2015): 1-14.
Allison, Lincoln. *Amateurism in Sport: An Analysis and Defense.* London: Routledge, 2001.
American Law Institute. *Restatement of the Law Third, Torts: Liability for Physical and Emotional Harm.* St. Paul, 2010.
American Academy of Pediatrics. "Tackling in Youth Football." *Pediatrics* 36, no. 5 (November 2015): e1419-e1430.
Anderson, Elizabeth. *Agents of Reform: Child Labor and the Origins of the Welfare State.* Princeton, NJ: Princeton University Press, 2021.
Andrews, David L. "Sport, Culture, and Late Capitalism." In *Marxism, Cultural Studies, and Sport,* edited by Ben Carrington and Ian McDonald, 213-31. London: Routledge, 2009.
Andrews, David L., and Ben Carrington, eds. *A Companion to Sport.* Malden, MA: Wiley Blackwell, 2013.

Andrews, James R. "Why Are There So Many Injuries to Our Young Athletes? Professionalization and Specialization in Youth Sport." *University of Baltimore Law Review* 40, no. 4 (Summer 2011): 575–86.

Atencio, Matthew, Becky Beal, E. Missy Wright, and ZáNean McClain. *Moving Boarders: Skateboarding and the Changing Landscape of Urban Youth Sports*. Fayetteville: University of Arkansas Press, 2018.

Bachynski, Kathleen E. "Competitive Youth Sports, Pediatricians, and Gender in the 1950s." In *Pink and Blue: Gender, Culture, and the Health of Children*, edited by Elena Conis, Sandra Eder, and Aimee Medeiros, chapter 9. New Brunswick, NJ: Rutgers University Press, 2021.

———. *No Game for Boys to Play: The History of Youth Football and the Origins of a Public Health Crisis*. Chapel Hill: University of North Carolina Press, 2019.

Bairner, Alan. "Sportive Nationalism and Nationalist Politics: A Comparative Analysis of Scotland, the Republic of Ireland, and Sweden." *Journal of Sport and Social Issues* 20, no. 3 (August 1996): 314–30.

Banks, Taunya Lovell. "Toward a Global Critical Feminist Vision: Domestic Work and the Nanny Tax Debate." *Journal of Gender, Race, and Justice* 3, no. 1 (Fall 1999): 1–44.

Baumgartner, Frank R., and Bryan D. Jones. "Attention, Boundary Effects, and Large-Scale Policy Change in Air Transportation Policy." In *The Politics of Problem Definition: Shaping the Policy Agenda*, edited by David A. Rochefort and Roger W. Cobb, 50–66. Lawrence: The University Press of Kansas, 1994.

———, eds. *Agendas and Instability in American Politics*. 2nd ed. Chicago: University of Chicago Press, 2009.

Bélanger, Anouk. "The Urban Sport Spectacle: Towards a Critical Political Economy of Sports." In *Marxism, Cultural Studies, and Sport*, edited by Ben Carrington and Ian McDonald, 51–67. London: Routledge, 2009.

Berri, David J. "Paying NCAA Athletes." *Marquette Sports Law Review* 26, no. 2 (2016): 479–91.

Berryman, Jack W., and Roberta J. Park, eds. *Sport and Exercise Science: Essays in the History of Sports Medicine*. Champaign: University of Illinois Press, 1992.

Bloodworth, Andrew, Mike McNamee, and Richard Bailey. "Sport, Physical Activity, and Well-Being: An Objectivist Account." *Sport, Education, and Society* 17, no. 4 (August 2012): 497–514.

Booth, Douglas. "Constructing Knowledge: Histories of Modern Sport." In *A Companion to Sport*, edited by David L. Andrews and Ben Carrington, 23–40. Malden, MA: Wiley Blackwell Publishing, 2013.

Bowers, Matthew T., and Thomas M. Hunt. "The President's Council on Physical Fitness and the Systematisation of Children's Play in America." *International Journal of the History of Sport* 28, no. 11 (August 2011): 1496–1511.

Boykoff, Jules. *Power Games: A Political History of the Olympics.* New York: Verso Books, 2016.

Brewer, Scott. "Summing Up So Far, Looking Forward: What Is a Jurisprudence of Excellence?" Lecture at Harvard Law School, Cambridge, MA, November 9, 2021.

Britton, Tess. "Predictions vs. Reality: The Economic Impact of COVID-19 on Sports." *Michigan Journal of Economics*, March 31, 2021. https://sites.lsa.umich.edu/mje/2021/03/31/predictions-vs-reality-the-economic-impact-of-covid-19-on-sports/.

Brustad, Robert J., Runar Vilhjalmsson, and Antonio Manuel Fonseca. "Organized Sport and Physical Activity Promotion." In *Youth Physical Activity and Sedentary Behavior: Challenges and Solutions*, edited by Alan L. Smith and Stuart J. H. Biddle, 351-76. Champaign, IL: Human Kinetics, 2008.

Buss, Emily. "'Parental' Rights." *Virginia Law Review* 88, no. 3 (May 2002): 635-83.

Cahn, Naomi R. "Models of Family Privacy." *George Washington Law Review* 67, nos. 5-6 (June-August 1999): 1225-46.

Caine, Dennis, and Laura Purcell. "The Exceptionality of the Young Athlete." In *Injury in Pediatric and Adolescent Sports: Epidemiology, Treatment, and Prevention*, edited by Dennis Caine and Laura Purcell, 3-14. Cham, Switzerland: Springer, 2016.

Camiré, Martin, and Fernando Santos. "Promoting Positive Youth Development and Life Skills in Youth Sport: Challenges and Opportunities amidst Increased Professionalization." *Journal of Sport Pedagogy and Research* 5, no. 1 (August 2019): 27-34.

Carbone, Paul S., Peter J. Smith, Charron Lewis, and Claire LeBlanc. "Promoting the Participation of Children and Adolescents with Disabilities in Sports, Recreation, and Physical Activity." *Pediatrics* 148, no. 6 (December 2021). https://doi.org/10.1542/peds.2021-054664.

Carlin, Stephen Cormac, and Christopher M. Fairman. "Squeeze Play: Workers' Compensation and the Professional Athlete." *University of Miami Entertainment and Sports Law Review* 12, no. 1 (January 1995): 95-127.

Carrington, Ben, and David L. Andrews. "Introduction: Sport as Escape, Struggle, and Art." In *A Companion to Sport*, edited by David L. Andrews and Ben Carrington, 1-16. Malden, MA: Wiley Blackwell, 2013.

Carter, W. Burlette. "Introduction: What Makes a Field a Field." *Virginia Journal of Sports and the Law* 1, no. 2 (Fall 1999): 235-45.

Centre for Sport and Human Rights. *Child Labour in Sport: Protecting the Rights of Child Athletes.* Durban, South Africa, 2022.

Chun, Benjamin J., Troy Furutani, Ross Oshiro, Casey Young, Gale Prentiss, and Nathan Murata. "Concussion Epidemiology in Youth Sports: Sports Study of a Statewide High School Sports Program." *Sports Health* 13, no. 1 (January-February 2021): 18-24.

Cianfrone, Beth A., James Jianhui Zhang, Brenda Pitts, and Kevin K. Byon. "Identifying Key Market Demand Factors Associated with High School Basketball Tournaments." *Sports Marketing Quarterly* 24, no. 2 (June 2015): 91-104.

Coakley, Jay. "Assessing the Sociology of Sport: On Cultural Sensibilities and the Great Sport Myth." *International Review for the Sociology of Sport* 50, nos. 4-5 (June-August 2015): 402-6.

———. "Positive Youth Development through Sport: Myths, Beliefs, and Realities." In *Positive Youth Development through Sport*, edited by Nicholas L. Holt, 21-33. London: Routledge, 2016.

———. *Sports in Society: Issues and Controversies*. 13th ed. New York: McGraw-Hill, 2021.

Colaguori, Claudio. *Agon Culture: Competition, Conflict, and the Problem of Domination*. Whitby, Ontario: De Sitter, 2012.

Commission on the State of U.S. Olympics and Paralympics. *Passing the Torch: Modernizing Olympic, Paralympic, and Grassroots Sports in America*. Washington, DC, March 2024.

Côté, Jean, Colleen Coakley, and Mark Bruner. "Children's Talent Development in Sport: Effectiveness or Efficiency?" In *Inclusion and Exclusion through Youth Sport*, edited by Symeon Dagkas and Kathleen Armour, 172-85. London: Routledge, 2012.

Council of Economic Advisers. *Economic Report of the President and The Annual Report of the Council of Economic Advisors*. Washington, D.C., February 2018.

———. *The Potential for Youth Sports to Improve Childhood Outcomes*. Washington, D.C., May 2018.

Dagkas, Symeon, and Kathleen Armour, eds. *Inclusion and Exclusion through Youth Sport*. London: Routledge, 2012.

Dailey, Anne C., and Laura A. Rosenbury. "The New Law of the Child." *Yale Law Journal* 127, no. 6 (April 2018): 1448-1537.

———. "The New Parental Rights." *Duke Law Journal* 71, no. 1 (October 2021): 75-165.

David, Paulo. *Human Rights in Youth Sport*. London: Routledge, 2005.

Davidson, Howard. "Does the U.N. Convention on the Rights of the Child Make a Difference?" *Michigan State International Law Review* 22, no. 2 (2014): 498-530.

Davis, Samuel M., Elizabeth S. Scott, Lois A. Weithorn, and Walter Wadlington, eds. *Children in the Legal System*. 6th ed. St. Paul: Foundation Press, 2020.

Diekmann, Sydney, Christine Egan, Carly Rasmussen, and Francis X. Shen. "The Failure of Youth Sports Concussion Laws and the Limits of Legislating

Health Education." *Yale Journal of Health Policy, Law, and Ethics* 19, no. 1 (2019): 1-214.

Dixon, Nicholas. "On Winning and Athletic Superiority." *Journal of the Philosophy of Sport* 26, no. 1 (1999): 10-26.

———. "Sport, Parental Autonomy, and Children's Rights to an Open Future." *Journal of the Philosophy of Sport* 34, no. 2 (October 2007): 147-59.

Donnelly, Peter, and Michael Atkinson. "Where History Meets Biography: Toward a Public Sociology of Sport." In *Playing for Change: The Continuing Struggle for Sport and Recreation*, edited by Russell Field, 363-88. Toronto: University of Toronto Press, 2015.

Dorsch, Travis E., Alan L. Smith, Jordan A. Blazo, Jay Coakley, Jean Coté, Christopher R. D. Wagstaff, Stacy Warner, and Michael Q. King. "Toward an Integrated Understanding of the Youth Sport System." *Research Quarterly for Exercise and Sport* 93, no. 1 (March 2022): 105-19.

Dorsch, Travis E., Emily Wright, Valeria C. Eckardt, Sam Elliott, Sam Thrower, and Camilla J. Knight. "A History of Parental Involvement in Organized Youth Sport: A Scoping Review." *Sport, Exercise, and Performance Psychology* 10, no. 4 (June 2021): 536-57.

Duru, N. Jeremi. "It's Not Child's Play: A Regulatory Approach to Reforming American Youth Sports." *Virginia Sports and Entertainment Law Journal* 20, no. 1 (Spring 2021): 25-55.

Edelman, Marc. "Disarming the Trojan Horse of the UAAA and SPARTA: How America Should Reform its Sports Agent Laws to Conform with True Agency Principles." *Harvard Journal of Sports and Entertainment Law* 4, no. 2 (Spring 2013): 145-89.

———. "A Prelude to *Jenkins v. NCAA:* Amateurism, Antitrust Law, and the Role of Consumer Demand in a Proper Rule of Reason Analysis." *Louisiana Law Review* 78, no. 1 (Fall 2017): 227-44.

———. "A Short Treatise on Amateurism and Antitrust Law: Why the NCAA's No Pay Rules Violate Section 1 of the Sherman Act." *Case Western Reserve Law Review* 64, no. 1 (2013).

Ehrlich, Sam C. "Swimming against the Current: *Mayall v. USA Water Polo* and Its Potential Impact on Overseeing Athletic Organizations." *Virginia Sports and Entertainment Law Journal* 19, no. 1 (Fall 2019): 1-28.

Eichberg, Henning. *Play in Philosophy and Social Thought.* Edited by Signe Højbjerre Larsen. London: Routledge, 2019.

Eisenstein, Zillah. "Constructing a Theory of Capitalist Patriarchy and Socialist Feminism." *Critical Sociology* 25, nos. 2-3 (March 1999): 196-217.

Eitzen, D. Stanley. *Fair and Foul: Beyond the Myths and Paradoxes of Sport.* 6th edition. Lanham, MD: Rowman and Littlefield, 2016.

Eliasson, Inger. "The Gap between Formalised Children's Rights and Children's Real Lives in Sport." *International Review for the Sociology of Sport* 52, no. 4 (October 2015): 470-96.

Ellingsen, Jan Emil, and Anne Greta Danielsen. "Norwegian Children's Rights in Sport and Coaches' Understanding of Talent." *International Journal of Children's Rights* 25, no. 2 (August 2017): 412-37.

El-Sabawi, Taleed. "Defining the Opioid Epidemic: Congress, Pressure Groups, and Problem Definition. *Memphis Law Review* 48, no. 4 (2018): 1357-1413.

Farrey, Tom. *Game On: How the Pressure to Win at All Costs Endangers Youth Sports and What Parents Can Do about It*. New York: ESPN Books, 2008.

Feezel, Randolph. "A Pluralist Conception of Play." In *The Philosophy of Play*, edited by Emily Ryall, Wendy Russell, and Malcolm MacLean, 11-31. London: Routledge, 2013.

Feldman, Gabe. "A Modest Proposal for Taming the Antitrust Beast." *Pepperdine Law Review* 41, no. 2 (February 2014): 249-66.

Fiore, Dianna K. "Parental Rage and Violence in Youth Sports: How Can We Prevent 'Soccer Moms' and 'Hockey Dads' from Interfering in Youth Sports and Causing Games to End in Fistfights Rather than Handshakes?" *Villanova Sports and Entertainment Law Journal* 10, no. 1 (January 2003): 103-29.

Frank, Robert H., and Philip J. Cook. *The Winner-Take-All Society: Why the Few at the Top Get So Much More than the Rest of Us*. New York: Penguin Books, 1995.

Fraser, Nancy. *Fortunes of Feminism: From State-Managed Capitalism to Neoliberal Crisis*. London: Verso, 2013.

Freeburn, Lloyd. *Regulating International Sport: Power Authority, and Legitimacy*. Leiden, Germany: Brill Nijhoff, 2018.

Fricker, Miranda. *Epistemic Injustice: Power and the Ethics of Knowing*. Oxford: Oxford University Press, 2007.

———. "Powerlessness and Social Interpretation." *Episteme: A Journal of Social Epistemology* 3, nos. 1-2 (2006): 96-108.

Friesen, Phoebe, Bethany Saul, Lisa Kearns, Kathleen Bachynski, and Arthur Caplan. "Overuse Injuries in Youth Sports: Legal and Social Responsibility." *Journal of Legal Aspects of Sport* 28, no. 2 (2018): 151-69.

Fusco, Caroline. "Governing Play: Moral Geographies, Healthification, and Neoliberal Urban Imaginaries." In *Sport and Neoliberalism: Politics, Consumption, and Culture*, edited by David L. Andrews and Michael L. Silk, 143-59. Philadelphia: Temple University Press, 2012.

Ghosh, Jayati. "Capital." In *The Elgar Companion to Marxist Economics*, edited by Ben Fine and Alfredo Saad-Filho, 28-33. Cheltenham, UK: Edward Elgar, 2012.

Gildea, Dennis. "Youth Sports." In *The Routledge History of American Sport*, edited by Linda J. Borish, David K. Wiggins, and Gerald R. Gems, 82–94. London: Routledge, 2017.

Giulianotti, Richard. "Sport and Social Theorists—A Plurality of Perspectives." In *Sport and Modern Social Theorists*, edited by Richard Giulianotti, 1–10. London: Palgrave MacMillan, 2004.

GLSEN Research Institute. *LGBTQ Students and School Sports Participation*. New York, 2021.

Gould, Daniel. "The Current Youth Sport Landscape: Identifying Critical Research Issues." *Kinesiology Review* 8, no. 3 (August 2019): 150–61.

———. "The Professionalization of Youth Sport: It's Time to Act!" *Clinical Journal of Sports Medicine* 19, no. 2 (March 2009): 81–82.

Grano, Daniel A., and Michael L. Butterworth, eds. *Sport, Rhetoric, and Political Struggle*. New York: Peter Lang, 2019.

Grant, Otis B. "African American College Football Players and the Dilemma of Exploitation, Racism, and Education: A Socio-economic Analysis of Sports Law." *Whittier Law Review* 24, no. 3 (Spring 2003): 645–62.

Halley, Janet, Prabha Kotiswaran, Rachel Rebouché, and Hila Shamir. *Governance Feminism: An Introduction*. Minneapolis: University of Minnesota Press, 2018.

Hamilton, Vivian E. "Play Now, Pay Later? Youth and Adolescent Collision Sports." *Hastings Law Journal* 71, no. 1 (2020): 151–96.

Hardy, Stephen H. "Entrepreneurs, Organizations, and the Sports Marketplace." In *The New American Sport History: Recent Approaches and Perspectives*, edited by S. W. Pope, 341–65. Urbana: University of Illinois Press, 1997.

Harmer, Peter A. "Injury Research in Pediatric and Adolescent Sports." In *Injury in Pediatric and Adolescent Sports: Epidemiology, Treatment, and Prevention*, edited by Dennis Caine and Laura Purcell, 233–42. Cham, Switzerland: Springer, 2016.

Harvey, Hosea H. "Refereeing the Public Health." *Yale Journal of Health Policy* 14, no. 1 (Winter 2014): 66–121.

Hatab, Lawrence J. "The Drama of Agonistic Embodiment: Nietzschean Reflections on the Meaning of Sports." *International Studies in Philosophy* 30, no. 3 (1998): 97–107.

Henning, Kristin. "The Fourth Amendment Rights of Children at Home: When Parental Authority Goes Too Far." *William and Mary Law Review* 53, no. 1 (October 2011): 55–109.

Hill, B. Jessie. "Medical Decision Making by and on Behalf of Adolescents: Reconsidering First Principles." *Journal of Health Care Law and Policy* 15, no. 1 (January 2012): 37–73.

Hindman, Hugh D. *Child Labor: An American History*. London: Routledge, 2015.

Huizinga, Johan. "The Nature of Play." In *Philosophic Inquiry in Sport*, edited by William J. Morgan and Klaus V. Meier, 5–7. Champaign, IL: Human Kinetics, 1995.

Huma, Ramogi, and Ellen J. Staurowsky. *How the NCAA's Empire Robs Predominantly Black Athletes of Billions in Generational Wealth*. Riverside, CA: National College Players Association, 2020.

Hungenberg, Eric, Tommy Aicher, and Taylor Sawyer. "A Glimpse into the Experience of a Youth Sport Tourism Consumer: An Analysis of Parents vs. Coaches." *Journal of Sport and Tourism* 26, no. 1 (January 2022): 43–63.

Huntington, Clare, and Elizabeth S. Scott. "Conceptualizing Legal Childhood in the Twenty-First Century." *Michigan Law Review* 118, no. 7 (May 2020): 1371–1458.

———. "The Enduring Importance of Parental Rights." *Fordham Law Review* 90, no. 6 (2022): 2529–40.

Hyman, Mark. *Until It Hurts: America's Obsession with Youth Sports and How It Harms Our Kids*. Boston: Beacon Press, 2009.

Ingham, Alan G. "The Sportification Process: A Bibliographical Analysis Framed by the Work of Marx, Weber, Durkheim, and Freud." In *Sport and Modern Social Theorists*, edited by Richard Giulianotti, 11–32. London: Palgrave MacMillan, 2004.

Japan Committee for UNICEF. *Children's Rights in Sports Principles*. 2nd ed. Tokyo, December 2018.

Jarvie, Grant. "Sport, New Social Divisions, and Social Inequality." In *Inclusion and Exclusion through Youth Sport*, edited by Symeon Dagkas and Kathleen Armour, 57–71. London: Routledge, 2012.

Kalman-Lamb, Nathan. "Athletic Labor and Social Reproduction." *Journal of Sport and Social Issues* 43, no. 6 (May 2019): 515–30.

Kavanagh, Emma, Adi Adams, Daniel Lock, Carly Stewart, and Jamie Cleland. "Managing Abuse in Sport: An Introduction to the Special Issue." *Sport Management Review* 23, no. 1 (February 2020): 1–7.

Kennedy, David. *A World of Struggle: How Power, Law, and Expertise Shape Global Political Economy*. Princeton, NJ: Princeton University Press, 2016.

Kennedy, Duncan. "The Stakes of Law, or Hale and Foucault!" *Legal Studies Forum* 15, no. 4 (1991): 327–66.

Kerr, Gretchen, and Ashley Stirling. "Putting the Child Back in Children's Sport: Nurturing Young Talent in a Developmentally Appropriate Manner." In *Ethics in Youth Sport: Policy and Pedagogical Applications*, edited by Stephen Harvey and Richard L. Light, 25–39. London: Routledge, 2013.

Keys, Barbara J., ed. *The Ideals of Global Sport: From Peace to Human Rights*. Philadelphia: University of Pennsylvania Press, 2019.

Kim, Amy Chan Hyung, Joshua I. Newman, Minjung Kim, Christopher Coutts, and Simon Brandon-Lai. "Social Geographies at Play: Mapping the Spatial Politics of Community-Based Youth Sport Participation." *Journal of Amateur Sport* 41, no 1 (February 2016): 39-72.

Kim, Sungwon, Daniel Connaughton, John Spengler, and Joon Hoon Lee. "Legislative Efforts to Reduce Concussions in Youth Sports: An Analysis of State Concussion Statutes." *Journal of Legal Aspects of Sport* 27, no. 2 (August 2017): 162-86.

Kingdon, John W. *Agendas, Alternatives, and Public Policies*. 2nd ed. New York: HarperCollins, 1995.

Koller, Dionne L. "Amateur Regulation and the Unmoored United States Olympic and Paralympic Committee." *Wake Forest Law Review Online* 9 (2019): 88-103.

———. "From Medals to Morality: Sportive Nationalism and the Problem of Doping in Sports." *Marquette Sports Law Review* 19, no. 1 (Fall 2008): 91-124.

———. "Frozen in Time: The State Action Doctrine's Application to Amateur Sports." *St. John's Law Review* 82, no. 1 (Winter 2008): 183-233.

———. "How the Expressive Power of Title IX Dilutes Its Promise." *Harvard Journal of Sports and Entertainment Law* 3, no. 1 (Winter 2012): 103-58.

———. "How the United States Government Sacrifices Athletes' Constitutional Rights in the Pursuit of National Prestige." *Brigham Young University Law Review* 2008, no. 5 (2008): 1465-1544.

———. "Not Just One of the Boys: A Post-feminist Critique of Title IX's Vision for Gender Equity in Sports." *Connecticut Law Review* 43, no. 2 (December 2010): 401-56.

———. "The Obese and the Elite: Using the Law to Reclaim School Sports." *Oklahoma Law Review* 67, no. 3 (Spring 2015): 383-441.

———. "The Pipeline to Title IX." *Marquette Sports Law Review* 33, no. 1 (Fall 2022): 51-81.

———. "Putting Public Law into Private Sport." *Pepperdine Law Review* 43, no. 3 (April 2016): 681-744.

———. "A Twenty-First-Century Olympic and Amateur Sports Act." *Vanderbilt Journal of Entertainment and Technology Law* 20, no. 4 (Summer 2018): 1027-72.

Kretchmar, R. Scott. "Why a Focus on Sporting Tests Would Reveal an Alternate Story and Raise Ethical Questions about Agon: A Commentary." *Physical Culture and Sport* 82, no. 1 (June 2019): 53-58.

———. "Formalism and Sport." In *Routledge Handbook of the Philosophy of Sport*, edited by Mike McNamee and William J. Morgan, 11-21. London: Routledge, 2017.

Landry, James, and Thomas A. Baker III. "Change or Be Changed: A Proposal for the NCAA to Combat Corruption and Unfairness by Proactively Reforming Its Regulation of Athlete Publicity Rights." *New York University Journal of Intellectual Property and Entertainment Law* 9, no. 1 (February 2020): 1–61.

Lang, Melanie, and Mike Hartill, eds. *Safeguarding, Child Protection, and Abuse in Sport: International Perspectives in Research, Policy, and Practice*. London: Routledge, 2015.

Laufer-Ukeles, Pamela. "The Relational Rights of Children." *Connecticut Law Review* 48, no. 3 (February 2016): 741–816.

LeRoy, Michael H. "Courts and the Future of 'Athletic Labor' in College Sports." *Arizona Law Review* 57, no. 2 (2015): 475–521.

Lindquist, Eric, Katrina N. Mosher-Howe, and Xinsheng Liu. "Nanotechnology . . . What Is It Good For? (Absolutely Everything): A Problem Definition Approach." *Review of Policy Research* 27, no. 3 (May 2010): 255–71.

Lobel, Orly. "Class and Care: The Role of Private Intermediaries in the In-Home Care Industry in the U.S. and Israel." *Harvard Women's Law Journal* 24 (Spring 2001): 89–137.

Lofaso, Anne Marie. "Groomed for Exploitation! How Applying the Statutory Definition of Employee to Cover Division IA College Football Players Disrupts the Student-Athlete Myth." *West Virginia Law Review* 119, no. 3 (April 2017): 957–97.

Logan, Kelsey, Steven Cuff, and American Association of Pediatrics Council on Sports Medicine and Fitness. "Organized Sports for Children, Preadolescents, and Adolescents." *Pediatrics* 143, no. 6 (June 2019): e20190997.

Logue, Kyle D. "Coordinating Sanctions in Tort." *Cardozo Law Review* 31, no. 6 (January 2010): 2313–64.

LoMonte, Frank D. "Fouling the First Amendment: Why Colleges Can't and Shouldn't Control Student Athletes' Speech on Social Media." *Business and Technology Law Journal* 9, no. 1 (January 2014): 1–50.

Lowe, Stephen R. *The Kid on the Sandlot: Congress and Professional Sports, 1910–1992*. Bowling Green, OH: Popular Press, 1995.

Lowrey, Kerri McGowan, and Stephanie R. Morain. "State Experiences Implementing Youth Sports Concussion Laws: Challenges, Successes, and Lessons for Evaluating Impact." *Journal of Law, Medicine, and Ethics* 42, no. 3 (September 2014): 290–96.

Loy, John W., and W. Robert Morford. "The Agon Motif Redux: A Study of the Contest Element in Sport." *Physical Culture and Sport* 82, no. 1 (June 2019): 10–45.

MacDonald, Doune, Bonnie Pang, Kelly Knez, Alison Nelson, and Louise McCuaig. "The Will for Inclusion: Bothering the Inclusion/Exclusion Discourses of Sport." In *Inclusion and Exclusion through Youth Sport,* edited by Symeon Dagkas and Kathleen Armour, 9-23. London: Routledge, 2012.

MacKinnon, Catharine A. "Feminism, Marxism, Method, and the State: An Agenda for Theory." *Signs* 7, no. 3 (Spring 1982): 515-44.

Malagrino, Dylan Oliver, and Christopher Davis Jr. "Hold Your Fire: The Injustice of NCAA Sanctions on Innocent Student Athletes." *Virginia Sports and Entertainment Law Journal* 11, no. 2 (Spring 2012): 432-59.

Masterson, Marina A. "When Play Becomes Work: Child Labor Laws in the Era of 'Kidfluencers.'" *University of Pennsylvania Law Review* 169, no. 2 (2021): 577-607.

McDonald, Ian. "One-Dimensional Sport: Revolutionary Marxism and the Critique of Sport." In *Marxism, Cultural Studies, and Sport,* edited by Ben Carrington and Ian McDonald, 32-48. London: Routledge, 2009.

McKinney, Ronald. "Toward a Post-post-modern Philosophy of Play." *Philosophy Today* 64, no. 1 (Winter 2020): 159-71.

Meier, Klaus. "Triad Trickery: Playing with Sports and Games." In *Philosophic Inquiry in Sport,* edited by William J. Morgan and Klaus V. Meier, 23-25. Champaign, IL: Human Kinetics, 1995.

Mensch, Elizabeth. "The History of Mainstream Legal Thought." In *The Politics of Law: A Progressive Critique,* 3rd ed., edited by David Kairys, 23-53. New York: Basic Books, 1998.

Messner, Michael A., and Michela Musto. "Introduction: Kids and Sport." In *Child's Play: Sport in Kids' Worlds,* edited by Michael A. Messner and Michela Musto, 1-22. New Brunswick, NJ: Rutgers University Press, 2016.

Miller, Toby. "Michel Foucault and the Critique of Sport." In *Marxism, Cultural Studies, and Sport,* edited by Ben Carrington and Ian McDonald, 181-94. London: Routledge, 2009.

Minnich, Mikayla. "That's Just Show Business: Relying on Industrial Revolution Solutions for a 'Kidfluencer' Problem." *University of Louisville Law Review* 62, no. 2 (Spring 2024): 523-50.

Minow, Martha. "Preface." In *The Oxford Handbook of Children's Rights Law,* edited by Jonathan Todres and Shani M. King, ix-xiv. Oxford: Oxford University Press, 2020.

———. "What Ever Happened to Children's Rights?" *Minnesota Law Review* 80, no. 2 (December 1995): 267-98.

Mirehie, Mona, Heather J. Gibson, Richard J. Buning, Cassandra Coble, and Meredith Flaherty. "Towards an Understanding of Family Travel

Decision-Making Processes in the Context of Youth Sport Tourism." *Journal of Destination Marketing and Management* 21, no. 2 (September 2021): 100644.

Mitten, Matthew J., Timothy Davis, N. Jeremi Duru, and Barbara Osborne. *Sports Law and Regulation: Cases, Materials, and Problems*. 5th ed. Frederick, MD: Aspen, 2020.

Montez de Oca, Jeffrey. "Paradox of Privilege: Sport, Masculinities, and the Commodified Body." In *A Companion to Sport*, edited by David L. Andrews and Ben Carrington, 149-63. Malden, MA: Wiley Blackwell, 2013.

Moskowitz, Seymour. "Save the Children: The Legal Abandonment of American Youth in the Workplace." *Akron Law Review* 43, no. 1 (2010): 107-61.

Nelson, Toben F. "Sport and the Childhood Obesity Epidemic." In *Child's Play: Sport in Kids' Worlds,* edited by Michael A. Messner and Michela Musto, 82-101. New Brunswick, NJ: Rutgers University Press, 2016.

Newman, Joshua, and Kyle Bunds. "Special Issue Foreword: On the Political Economy of Amateur Athletics." *Journal of Amateur Sport* 2, no. 1 (February 2016): 1-11.

Norwegian Olympic and Paralympic Committee and Confederation of Sports. *Children's Rights in Sports*. Oslo, 2015.

Novkov, Julie. "Historicizing the Figure of the Child in Legal Discourse: The Battle over the Regulation of Child Labor." *American Journal of Legal History* 44, no. 4 (October 2000): 369-404.

Office of Special Education and Rehabilitative Services, Office of Special Education Programs. *Creating Equal Opportunities for Children and Youth with Disabilities to Participate in Physical Education and Extracurricular Athletics*. Washington, D.C.: U.S. Department of Education, 2011.

Olsen, Frances. "The Family and the Market: The Study of Ideology and Legal Reform." *Harvard Law Review* 96, no. 7 (May 1983): 1497-1578.

Overman, Steven J. *The Youth Sports Crisis: Out-of-Control Adults, Helpless Kids*. Santa Barbara, CA: Praeger, 2014.

Parrott, Heather Macpherson, and Lynn E. Cohen. "Advocating for Play: The Benefits of Unstructured Play in Public Schools." *School Community Journal* 30, no. 2 (Fall-Winter 2020): 229-54.

Physical Activity Alliance. *2022 U.S. Report Card on Physical Activity for Children and Youth*. Washington, D.C., 2022.

Popkin, Charles A., Ahmad F. Bayomy, and Christopher S. Ahmad. "Early Sport Specialization." *Journal of the American Academy of Orthopaedic Surgeons* 27, no. 22 (November 15, 2019): 995-1000.

Porto, Brian L. "Unfinished Business: The Continuing Struggle for Equal Opportunity in College Sports on the Eve of Title IX's Fiftieth Anniversary." *Marquette Sports Law Review* 32, no. 1 (Fall 2021): 259-303.

President's Commission on Olympic Sports. *The Final Report of the President's Commission on Olympic Sports*. Washington, DC: Government Printing Office, January 1977.

———. *First Report to the President*. Washington, DC: Government Printing Office, February 1976.

President's Council on Sports, Fitness, and Nutrition Science Board. *Benefits of Youth Sports*. Washington, D.C., September 17, 2020.

———. "PCSFN Science Board Report on Youth Sports." Washington, DC, September 17, 2020.

Rhind, Daniel, and Frank Owusu-Sekyere. *International Safeguards for Children in Sport: Developing and Embedding a Safeguarding Culture*. London: Routledge, 2018.

Rich, Emma, and John Evans. "Physical Culture, Pedagogies of Health, and the Gendered Body." In *A Companion to Sport*, edited by David L. Andrews and Ben Carrington, 179-95. Malden, MA: Wiley Blackwell, 2013.

Ridpath, B. David. *Alternative Models of Sports Development in America: Solutions to a Crisis in Education and Public Health*. Athens: Ohio University Press, 2018.

Roberts, Ken. *Social Theory, Sport, Leisure*. London: Routledge, 2016.

Rochefort, David A., and Roger W. Cobb, eds. *The Politics of Problem Definition: Shaping the Policy Agenda*. Lawrence: University Press of Kansas, 1994.

———. "Problem Definition, Agenda Access, and Policy Choice." *Policy Studies Journal* 21, no. 1 (March 1993): 56-71.

Rosentraub, Mark S. *Major League Losers: The Real Cost of Sports and Who's Paying for It*. Rev. ed. New York: Basic Books, 1999.

Schimmel, Kimberly S. "Sport and International Political Economy: An Introduction." In *The Political Economy of Sport*, edited by John Nauright and Kimberly S. Schimmel, 1-18. London: Palgrave MacMillan, 2005.

Scott, Elizabeth S. "Comment on Part 4 Essays: Goodwin and Dailey and Rosenbury." *University of Chicago Law Review* 91, no. 2 (2024): 633-49.

Shropshire, Kenneth L. "Legislation for the Glory of Sport: Amateurism and Compensation." *Seton Hall Journal of Sport Law* 1, no. 1 (1991): 7-27.

Siegal, Reva B. "Home as Work: The First Women's Rights Claims Concerning Wives' Household Labor, 1850-1880." *Yale Law Journal* 103, no. 5 (March 1994): 1073-1217.

Silbaugh, Katharine. "The Legal Design for Parenting Concussion Risk." *UC Davis Law Review* 53, no. 1 (November 2019): 197-269.

———. "Turning Labor into Love: Housework and the Law." *Northwestern University Law Review* 91, no. 1 (Fall 1996): 1-86.

Silk, Michael L., and David L. Andrews. "Sport and the Neoliberal Conjecture: Complicating the Consensus." In *Sport and Neoliberalism: Politics, Consumption, and Culture*, edited by David L. Andrews and Michael L. Silk, 1–22. Philadelphia: Temple University Press, 2012.

Simon, Robert L. "Internalism and Internal Values in Sport." *Journal of the Philosophy of Sport* 27, no. 1 (May 2000): 1–16.

Sinnard, Holden C. "Family Time Is Money: Modernizing Iowa's Child Labor Laws." *Iowa Law Review* 109, no. 3 (March 2024): 1361–97.

Skelton, Ann, Paul Singh, and Steve Cornelius. "Protection of Young Athletes." In *Handbook on International Sports Law*, edited by James A. R. Nafziger and Ryan Gauthier, 403–22. Cheltenham, UK: Edward Elgar, 2022.

Stone, Deborah. *Policy Paradox: The Art of Political Decision Making*. 3rd ed. New York: W. W. Norton, 2012.

Straubel, Michael. "The International Convention against Doping in Sport: Is It the Missing Link to USADA Being a State Actor and WADC Coverage of U.S. Pro Athletes?" *Marquette Sports Law Review* 19, no. 1 (Fall 2008): 63–89.

Suits, Bernard. "Tricky Triad: Games, Play, and Sport." In *Philosophic Inquiry in Sport*, edited by William J. Morgan and Klaus V. Meier, 16–22. Champaign, IL: Human Kinetics, 1995.

Teubner, Gunther. "The Constitution of Non-monetary Surplus Values." *Social and Legal Studies* 30, no. 4 (August 2021): 501–21.

Tofler, Ian R., Penelope Krener Knapp, and Martin Drell. "Achievement by Proxy Spectrum in Youth Sports: A Distorted Mentoring of High-Achieving Youth; Historical Perspectives and Clinical Intervention with Children, Adolescents, and Their Families." *Sport Psychiatry* 7, no. 1 (October 1998): 803–20.

Trivedi, Shanta. "The Harm of Child Removal." *New York University Review of Law and Social Change* 43, no. 3 (2019): 523–80.

Turrini, Joseph M. *The End of Amateurism in American Track and Field*. Urbana: University of Illinois Press, 2010.

Tygart, Travis T. "Winners Never Dope and Finally, Dopers Never Win: USADA Takes Over Drug Testing of United States Olympic Athletes." *DePaul Journal of Sports Law and Contemporary Problems* 1, no. 2 (Fall 2003): 124–38.

UNICEF Innocenti Research Centre. *Protecting Children from Violence in Sport: A Review with a Focus on Industrialized Countries*. Florence, Italy: UNICEF, July 2010.

U.S. Department of Health and Human Services. *National Youth Sports Strategy*. Washington, DC, September 2019.

U.S. Government Accountability Office. *K-12 Education: High School Sports Access and Participation*. GAO-17-754R. Washington, D.C., September 14, 2017. https://www.gao.gov/assets/gao-17-754r.pdf.

Vinokur, Martin Barry. *More Than a Game: Sports and Politics*. Westport, CT: Praeger, 1988.

West, Robin. *Caring for Justice*. New York: New York University Press, 1997.

Wiggins, David K. "A Worthwhile Effort? History of Organized Youth Sport in the United States." *Kinesiology Review* 2, no. 1 (February 2013): 65–75.

Wilhelm, Ben. *The United States Olympic and Paralympic Committee: A Primer*. CRS Report R47850. Washington, DC: Library of Congress, Congressional Research Service, 2023.

Williams, Yvonne. "Protecting Children from Violence in Sport: A UNICEF Report." *Entertainment and Sports Law Journal* 9, no. 1 (June 2011): 72–75.

Women's Sports Foundation. *50 Years of Title IX: We're Not Done Yet*. New York, 2022.

Wood, B. Dan, and Alesha Doan. "The Politics of Problem Definition: Applying and Testing Threshold Models." *American Journal of Political Science* 47, no. 4 (October 2003): 640–53.

Wood, Betsy. *Upon the Altar of Work: Child Labor and the Rise of New American Sectionalism*. Urbana: University of Illinois Press, 2020.

Yen, Alfred C., and Matthew Gregas. "Liability Waivers and Participation Rates in Youth Sports: An Empirical Investigation. *Arizona State Sports and Entertainment Law Journal* 10, no. 1 (Fall 2020): 1–50.

INDEX

achievement by proxy, 135
"Active People, Healthy Nation" initiative (Centers for Disease Control and Prevention), 26
age of majority: and children's rights, 41; state law on, 16
Allison, Lincoln, 116–17
Amateur Athletic Union (AAU), 17, 18, 53, 54, 99
amateur sport: college sports as amateur athletics, 111–12; defining concept of, 16–18; NCAA's amateurism model, 4–7, 17, 145–46n6; problem definition and politics of sport, 99; state laws on, 73–74; and youth sport as hidden labor, 111–12. *See also* Amateur Athletic Union (AAU); Ted Stevens Olympic and Amateur Sports Act (1978)
American Academy of Pediatrics (AAP), 16, 19, 27–28, 96–101
American College of Sports Medicine, 21
Americans with Disabilities Act (ADA, 1990), 59–61, 64, 86
Andrews, David L., 48
Andrews, James R., 135
antitrust law: Flood's claim against MLB, 51–52, 66–67, 91, 98–99; law and policy approach to sport, 51–52, 60, 61, 66–69; and NCAA's amateurism model, 4–7, 17, 145–46n6

Arizona, youth sport tourism of, 131
Aspen Institute, 25, 29, 101
athletic code of conduct, 179–80n2
Atkinson, Michael, 95
Avila v. Citrus Community College District (Cal. 2006), 58

Bachynski, Kathleen, 22, 94, 95–96, 101
baseball (Little League), 11, 64, 73, 76, 168n19
baseball (professional): law and policy approach to sport, 51–52, 66–67; MLB, 60, 65, 66–68; reserve clause, 66
basketball (college), scholarships/admission for athletes, 136–37
Bellotti v. Baird (U.S. 1979), 154n1
beneficiaries of youth sport, 121–40; children as, 109–10, 136–40; future elite athletes as, 129–30; parents as, 133–36; play-based sport approach, defined, 122; professional sports leagues as, 126–27; school-based sports programs as, 125–26; and social struggle of youth sport, 121–22; society at large as, 124–25; sports medicine physicians as, 132–33; state and local governments as, 130–32; U.S. Olympic Movement as, 127–29; U.S. Paralympic Movement as, 129; youth sport industry as, 122–24

Berger v. NCAA (7th Cir. 2016), 54, 111–12
Berryman, Jack, 21–22
Biedinger v. Quinnipiac University (2nd Cir. 2012), 14
Biles, Simone, 129, 130
Bloom v. NCAA (Colo. App. 2004), 54
Borella v. Renfro (Mass. App. Ct. 2019), 79
Bowers, Matthew, 93, 99
Brentwood Academy v. Tennessee Secondary School Athletic Association (U.S. 2001), 40
Brown v. Pro Football, Inc. (U.S. 1996), 68
Brown v. U.S.A. Taekwondo (Cal. 2021), 79, 80
Brundage, Avery, 53
bullying and hazing in sport, 27–28, 61–62
Bush, George W., 72

California: child labor in, 45; tort liability and youth sport, 77–80; Youth Football Act (2019), 158n86, 177n61
Campagna-McGuffin v. Diva Gymnastics Academy, Inc. (Ohio Ct. App., 2022), 3, 78
Carrington, Ben, 48
Carter, Burlette, 52–53
Centers for Disease Control and Prevention, 26
Centre for Sport and Human Rights, 93, 105, 115
cheer, and Title IX, 14
child abuse: bullying and hazing in sport, 27–28, 61–62; and misplaced motivation of sport parents, 135–36; SafeSport, 56, 61–63, 65, 81, 82; sexual abuse, law and policy approach to sport, 61–62; sexual abuse, tort liability and youth sport, 79
child and family, law of. *See* law of child and family
child labor: and Fair Labor Standards Act (FLSA, 1938), 43–45, 54, 111–12; history of, 42–47; law and policy approach to sport and collective bargaining, 68–69; and National Labor Relations Act (NLRA, 1935), 63; and problem definition theory, 98–99; and youth sport as hidden labor, 110–12. *See also* law of child and family
children, sports as benefit to: children as the beneficiaries of youth sport, 109–10, 136–40; and fun of youth sport, 122, 123, 137, 139–40; and "Great Sport Myth," 91, 96, 106, 172n4, 191n79; mental health importance of sport participation, 4, 27, 28; and substance use avoidance, 27; "youth-sport-is-good" narrative, 3–5. *See also* children's fitness
children's fitness: and military readiness, 21; Sports and Fitness Industry Association, 25; *Sports Illustrated* on, 99; as youth sport benefit, 122, 123, 189–90n58. *See also* Cold War mentality of U.S. sport; medical issues; presidential awards/commissions for fitness
children's rights: *Children's Rights in Sports Principles*, 2nd ed. (Japan), 178n62; children's status, legal history, 33, 34–35; and decision making by children, 39–42; law and policy approach to youth sport on, 80–81; law of child and family on, 39–42, 157n57; U.N. Convention on the Rights of the Child, 104–5, 184n53. *See also* law of child and family
Child Safeguarding in Sport initiative (Council of Europe and European Union), 177–78n62
civil rights: and children's status under law, 34–35; and law and policy approach to sport, 57–58, 165n92; and NGB-affiliated youth sport, 84. *See also* children's rights; race
Clinton, William J., 33, 94
coaching in sport: research on, 28; sponsor-coach-athlete hierarchy, 7, 13; state statutes on, 14, 15, 17; training for, 20, 25–26
Coakley, Jay: amateur athletes defined by, 17; on competitive nature of sports, 86;

on "Great Sport Myth," 91, 96, 106, 172n4, 191n79; sport defined by, 13; on United States' lack of regulation, 104; on youth sport increased participation, 22, 26; youth sport models defined by, 19; on youth sport participation, 21; on youth sport skills and excellence model, 19, 26

code of conduct, athletic, 179–80n2

Cold War mentality of U.S. sport: children's fitness and military readiness, 21; government goals for youth sport, 90–91; and government's hands-off approach, 53, 55; problem definition and politics of sport, 99; and Soviet-era sportive nationalism, 68, 93

college attendance, youth sport correlation to, 12, 89, 119

college sports: colleges as beneficiaries of, 125–26; covert politics of, 93; fans of, 23; and government's hands-off approach, 52, 54; law and policy approach to sport, 56–57; scholarships and admission for athletes, 136–37; surplus value of, 111–13. *See also* National Collegiate Athletic Association (NCAA); *individual names of legal cases*

Colorado, law and policy approach to sport, 54

Commission on Amateur Sports Act (Illinois), 73

concussion injury and management: and law and policy approach to sport, 164n74; and law and policy of youth sport, 77, 80, 81, 87–89; law of child and family, 48–50, 159n97; and political goals for sport, 100; racial disparity of, 190n67; research on, 24–25; and youth sport definitions, 14, 15

Congress, U.S.: Americans with Disabilities Act (ADA, 1990), 59–61, 64, 86; "Congressional Caucus on Youth Sports" (National Council of Youth Sports), 73, 167n14; Congressional Research Service, 55; Consumer Product Safety Improvement Act (1972), 166n3; Curt Flood Act (1998), 66; Fair Labor Standards Act (FLSA, 1938), 43–45; law and policy approach to sport, 54–55, 56, 57, 60–62, 65, 66; on law and policy approach to sport, 55–57, 61–63; on law and policy approach to youth sport, 71, 73, 74–75; National Labor Relations Act (NLRA, 1935), 63; National Youth Sports Week proposal, 167n14; PLAYS in Youth Sports Act proposal, 73; PLAY Sports Coalition, 101; and politics of youth sport, 93, 94, 99, 101, 102; Rehabilitation Act (1973), 57–58, 84–85, 104; Youth Sport Program funding by, 94. *See also* Ted Stevens Olympic and Amateur Sports Act (1978)

Constitution, U.S.: Commerce Clause, 71; First Amendment, 40, 41, 83; Fourth Amendment, 83; Fourteenth Amendment, 35, 155n25

Consumer Product Safety Improvement Act (1972), 166n3

contract law, and children's rights, 39–40

Cook, Philip, 125

Council of Economic Advisers, 72, 94, 109

Council of Europe, 177–78n62

coverture doctrine, 36

criminal law, and children's rights, 40

Curt Flood Act (1998), 66, 67

Dailey, Anne C., 36–37, 42, 48, 157n57

data on youth sport, 22–26

Declaration on Sport (International Council on Sport and Physical Education and UNESCO), 90

Department of Defense, U.S., 92

Department of Education, U.S., 28

Department of Health and Human Services, U.S. (HHS): Healthy People 2030 program, 25, 72; Office of Disease Prevention and Health Promotion, 25, 72. *See also* National Youth Sports Strategy (NYSS)

Department of Justice, U.S., 86
Department of Labor, U.S., 43–45
disabled persons: Americans with Disabilities Act (ADA, 1990), 59–61, 64, 86; and politics of youth sport, 97; Rehabilitation Act (1973), 57–58, 84–85, 104; U.S. Paralympic Movement as beneficiary of youth sport, 129; youth sport opportunities as limited for, 139. *See also* U.S. Olympic and Paralympic Committee
distributive consequences of youth sport. *See* beneficiaries of youth sport; youth sport surplus
Doe v. U.S. Youth Soccer Association (Cal. Ct. App. 2017), 79, 80
Donnelly, Peter, 95
Due Process Clause (Fourteenth Amendment), 155n25

economic disparity: and accessibility of youth sport, 5, 12, 20–21, 25, 26, 146n12; and exploitation of youth athletes, 138–39; and politics of youth sport, 94, 95, 97
economic surplus. *See* youth sport surplus
education: "academically unsound" education for athletes, 59; homeschooling of youth athletes, 136; law and policy approach to sport, 64; and NGB-affiliated youth sport, 82–86; politics of youth sport and need for regulation, 103–4; "redshirting," 48; school-based sports programs as beneficiaries of youth sport, 125–26; transgender children and state laws on school sports, 77; youth sport and college attendance correlation, 12, 89, 119. *See also* college sports; high school sports
Eisenhower, Dwight, 11, 72, 99
Eitzen, Stanley, 118
elite athletes, as beneficiaries of youth sport, 129–30
Equal Pay for Team USA Act (2022), 62
European Union, on Child Safeguarding in Sport initiative, 177–78n62

executive branch of government. *See* presidential awards/commissions for fitness; *individual names of presidents*

Fair Labor Standards Act (FLSA, 1938), 43–45, 54, 111–12
family, law of. *See* law of child and family
fans of sports, and sports revenue, 22–23
Farrey, Tom, 5
Federal Baseball Club v. National League (U.S. 1922), 51
Fédération Internationale de Gymnastique (FIG), 82
feminism: on family as private, 36; neoliberalism and politics of youth sport, 96–97; on women's labor, 110–11
financial issues: capitalism, neoliberal political values, and youth sport, 94–97, 174–75n25; capitalism and sport as "triple commodity," 116; federal funding and USOPC, 18; "paid patriotism" and sports, 92; play-based sport model and loss of jobs in sports, 126; spending by families of youth athletes, 23; U.S. sports share of world's sports revenue, 22; youth sport industry revenue, 122–23. *See also* beneficiaries of youth sport; youth sport surplus
First Amendment, 40, 41
Flake, Jeff, 92
Flanagan, Linda, 5
Flood, Curt, 51–52, 66–67, 91, 98–99
Flood v. Kuhn (U.S. 1972), 51–52, 66–67
Florida, youth sport tourism by, 74
football (college): law and policy approach to sport, 56–57; scholarships and admission for athletes, 136–37
football (professional), 65, 87, 101
football (youth), tackle regulations, 95–96, 177n61
Ford, Gerald R., 54, 93
Foucault, Michel, 173n13
Fourth Amendment, 83

Fourteenth Amendment, 35, 155n25
"Framework for Understanding Youth Sports Participation" (NYSS), 113
France, youth sport governed by, 178n62
Frank, Robert, 125
Fraser, Nancy, 96
Free Exercise and Establishment Clause (First Amendment), 41
Fricker, Miranda, 147n19

gambling on youth sport, 77
Game On (Farrey), 5
gender issues of sports: feminist theory about, 36, 96–97, 110–11; importance of girls' sport participation, 27; LGBTQ students, youth sport avoided by, 24; male authority in law of child and family, 34, 36, 111; participation data, boys' and girls' sports, 23–24; pay and sexual discrimination, 62; and politics of youth sport, 94, 96–97; of sport parenting, 133; transgender children and NGB-affiliated youth sport, 84; transgender children and state laws on school sports, 77. *See also* feminism; Title IX
Ginsberg v. New York (U.S. 1968), 38
GLSEN (formerly Gay, Lesbian, and Straight Education Network), 24
Gould, Daniel, 28
governing bodies of sport. *See* national governing bodies (NGBs)
Government Accountability Office, 26–27
government (U.S.) goals for youth sport. *See* Cold War mentality of U.S. sport
Gray v. Ferris (N.Y. App. Div. 1930), 53
"Great Sport Myth," 91, 96, 106, 172n4, 191n79
Gregas, Matthew, 170n48
gymnastics: *Campagna-McGuffin v. Diva Gymnastics Academy, Inc.* (Ohio Ct. App., 2022), 3, 78; governing bodies, 66, 82

hands-off approach to sport, by government. *See* law and policy approach to sport

Healthy People 2030 program (Department of Health and Human Services), 25, 72
hermeneutical injustice, 147n19
high school sports: National Federation of State High School Associations (NFHS), 23, 56; as spectacle, 114. *See also individual names of legal cases*
Hindman, Hugh, 43–45
Hollonbeck v. USOC (10th Cir. 2008), 57–58, 129
Holzmueller v. Illinois High School Association (7th Cir. 2018), 84–85
Huizinga, Johan, 115
Hunt, Thomas, 93, 99
Huntington, Clare, 34
Hyman, Mark, 5

Illinois: Commission on Amateur Sports Act, 73; tort liability and youth sport, 78; youth sport definition of, 14
Indiana: tort liability and youth sport, 79; youth sport definition of, 17; youth sport tourism by, 74
Internal Revenue Code, 73
International Council on Sport and Physical Education, 90
international federations (IFs), defined, 81–82
International Gymnastics Federation, 81–82
International Olympic Committee (IOC), 15, 53, 81
International Paralympic Committee (IPC), 15, 81

Japan, youth sport governed by, 178n62
Johnson, Lyndon, 72

Kabella v. Bouschelle (N.M. App. 1983), 79
Kaepernick, Colin, 92
Kahn v. East Side Union High School (Cal. 2003), 77–78
Kalman-Lamb, Nathan, 116
Karas v. Strevell (Ill. 2008), 70, 78, 79, 103
Kennedy, John F., 21, 93

Kennedy v. Bremerton School District (U.S. 2022), 41
Keys, Barbara, 91
"kidfluencers" (social media influencers), 45–46
Knapp v. Northwestern University (7th Cir. 1996), 57–58
Knight v. Jewett (Cal. 1992), 59

labor law. *See* child labor
law and policy approach to sport, 51–69; and ADA, 59–61, 64; and civil rights, 57–58; Congress on, 55–57; hands-off approach, exceptions, 61–63; hands-off approach, overview, 51–54; hands-off approach and politics of youth sport, 91–92, 97, 100, 106; lack of federal governing body, 15, 54–55, 70–71; and law in service of sport, 64–69; regulation vs. support of sport sponsors, 51, 63–64; state laws on, 61; and tort claims, 58–59. *See also* law and policy approach to youth sport
law and policy approach to youth sport, 70–89; lack of children's rights, 80–81; lack of governing body for, 15, 54–55, 70–71; lack of regulation, 3, 29, 76–80; NGB-affiliated youth sport, 81–89; promotion of youth sport by presidential administrations, 72–73; promotion of youth sport tourism, 73–74; reform needed for, 8, 10, 141–43; Ted Stevens Olympic and Amateur Sports Act and role in, 9; youth sport as privatized system, 74–76
law of child and family, 33–50; child and family as central to U.S. youth sport, 33–34; child labor example, 42–47; children's rights as limited, 39–42, 157n57; children's status, legal history, 33, 34–35; parental authority and privacy of family, 33, 35–38, 46–47, 110–12, 154n1, 155n26; and state authority to protect children, 33–34, 38–39; youth sport and effect of, 47–50, 158n86. *See also* children's rights

LGBTQ students, youth sport avoided by, 24
Little League baseball, 11, 64, 73, 76, 168n19
local governments: as beneficiaries of youth sport, 130–32; youth sport tourism of, 73–74, 130–32
Long v. Napolitano (Ariz. Ct. App. 2002), 131
Louisiana, youth sport tourism of, 131
Lowery v. Euverard (6th Cir. 2007), 84
Lystedt, Zackery, 49
"Lystedt Law," 49

MacDonald, Doune, 147n3
Mahanoy Area School District v. B. L. (2021), 83
Major League Baseball (MLB), 51–52, 60, 65, 66–68, 91, 98–99
Martin, Casey, 59–61, 64
Maryland: Youth and Amateur Sports Grants Program, 73–74; youth sport tourism of, 187n21
Massachusetts: law and policy approach to youth sport, 85–86; tort liability and youth sport, 79
Masterson, Marina, 45–46
Mayall v. U.S.A. Water Polo (9th Cir. 2018), 80, 88–89
McCain, John, 51, 52, 92
McCants v. NCAA (M.D.N.C. 2016), 59
McFadden v. Grasmick (D. Md. 2007), 85
McMillen, Tom, 76
medical issues: exploitation of youth athletes, 135, 137; government initiatives, 26; medical treatment for children, law of child and family, 37; overuse injuries in youth sport, 153n100; pediatricians' view of competitive youth sport, 95–96; and politics of youth sport, 101–6; Rehabilitation Act and civil rights, 57–58, 104; sport participation as beneficial to, 94, 174n24; sports medicine physicians as beneficiaries of youth sport, 132–33. *See also* American Academy of Pediatrics;

children's fitness; concussion injury and management; disabled persons
Megenity v. Dunn (Ind. 2017), 79
"Memorandum on Enhancing Efforts to Promote the Health of Our Young People through Physical Activity and Participation in Sports" (Clinton), 33
Menora v. Illinois High School Association (7th Cir. 1982), 83–84
mental health, importance of sport participation to, 4, 27, 28
Messner, Michael, 28, 137, 140
Miller v. Alabama (U.S. 2012), 40
Mississippi, youth sport tourism of, 131
Montana, youth sport definition of, 15
Muscular Christians, 20
Musto, Michela, 28, 137, 140

Nabozny v. Barnhill (Ill. App. 1975), 78
name, image, and likeness (NIL), 61
Nassar, Larry, 61, 66
National Athletic Trainers Association, 21
National Basketball Association (NBA), 15
National Collegiate Athletic Association (NCAA): antitrust law and amateurism model of, 4–7, 17, 145–46n6; as beneficiary of youth sport, 189n57; eligibility rules, 17; inception of, 56–57; law and policy approach to sport, 56–57, 59–61, 63, 65–66; SPARTA and UAAA, 65, 164n80
National Council of Youth Sports, 25, 73, 167n14
National Federation of State High School Associations (NFHS), 23, 56
National Football League (NFL), 65, 87, 101
national governing bodies (NGBs): and beneficiaries of youth sport, 128, 129; lack of single body for youth sport, 15, 54–55, 70–71; and lack of youth sport regulation, 102; and law and policy approach to sport, 55, 62, 65–66; law and policy approach to youth sport, 75, 79, 81–82; NGBs, defined, 15, 81–82; and private sector athlete development, 93; and private unaffiliated youth sport, 86–89; and sport in schools, 82–86
National Hockey League (NHL), 101
National Labor Relations Act (NLRA, 1935), 63
National Labor Relations Board (NLRB), 63
National Little League Baseball, 11. *See also* Little League baseball
National Sporting Goods Association, 25
National Youth Sports Program, 72, 166n6
National Youth Sports Strategy (NYSS, Department of Health and Human Services): on access to youth sport, 25, 26; and beneficiaries of youth sport, 124–26, 139; and concept of sport participation as beneficial, 174n24; on data for youth sport, 148n15, 151–52n80, 151n75; on definition for youth sport, 150n60; "Framework for Understanding Youth Sports Participation," 113; government's goal of, 72–73; on parental choice of youth sport, 119; politics of youth sport and attrition rate, 102; politics of youth sport and school-based sports regulation, 104; on retention in youth sport, 12, 126
NBA (National Basketball Association), 101
NCAA v. Alston (U.S. 2021), 6, 17, 59–61, 64, 112
NCAA v. Board of Regents of the University of Oklahoma (U.S. 1984), 5–6, 54
Nebraska, youth sport definition of, 14–15
neoliberal political values, and youth sport, 94–97, 174–75n25
New Mexico, tort liability and youth sport, 79
New York state, child labor in, 45
NGBs. *See* national governing bodies (NGBs)
Nixon, Richard, 93
Northwestern University, 57–58, 63
Norway, youth sport governed by, 105–6, 178n62, 179n74

Office of National Drug Control Policy (ONDCP), 56
Ohio, youth sport definition of, 14
Olsen, Frances, 36
Olympic Games: eligibility rules, 17; United States and overall medal counts, 128; U.S. Olympic Movement as beneficiaries of youth sport, 127–29; USOPC as only privately funded Olympic committee worldwide, 160n24. *See also* U.S. Olympic and Paralympic Committee
Oregon, youth sport definition of, 15

parens patrie powers, 34, 38, 71
parental authority: parents as beneficiaries of youth sport, 133–36; and politics of youth sport, 100, 102–3; and privacy of family, 33, 35–38, 46–47, 154n1, 155n26; tort law and parental waivers in youth sport, 3, 48, 77–78, 85–86, 170n48; and U.N. Convention on the Rights of the Child, 104–5; youth sport surplus and parent-child power balance, 119
Parham v. J. R. (U.S. 1979), 37, 39, 155n26
Park, Roberta, 21–22
pay-to-play model. *See* privatized structure of youth sport
PGA Tour v. Martin (2001), 59–61, 64
Phelps, Michael, 129, 130
Physical Activity Alliance (PAA), 25
play-based sport approach, defined, 122. *See also* beneficiaries of youth sport
PLAYS in Youth Sports Act proposal, 73
PLAY Sports Coalition, 101
play vs. sport, 115–19
politics of youth sport, 90–106; covert political features of youth sport, 92–97; football (youth) and tackle regulations, 95–96, 177n61; and government goals for youth sport, 90–91; and hands-off approach of government, 91–92, 97, 100, 106; as paradoxical, 92; and persistence of current approach, 97–106; and political nature of sport, 91–92

Pop Warner football, 76
power, in youth sport, 6–8, 13, 119–20. *See also* beneficiaries of youth sport; parental authority; youth sport surplus
prayer at sporting events, 40–41
presidential awards/commissions for fitness: Presidential Sports Award, 72; President's Commission on Olympic Sports, 54, 128; President's Council on Physical Fitness and Sports, 72, 76, 93; President's Council on Sports, Fitness and Nutrition, 26, 166n6; President's Council on Youth Fitness, 72, 93, 99; President's Physical Fitness Award, 174n24; promotion of youth sport by presidential administrations, 72–73. *See also individual names of presidents*
Prince v. Massachusetts (U.S. 1944), 38
private sport international federations (IFs), 81–82
privatized structure of youth sport: law and policy on, 6, 74–76, 86–89; law in service of sports, 64–69, 164n77; politics of, 93, 95
problem definition theory, 98–99
professionalization of youth sport: and play vs. sport, 118–19; and political goals for sport, 93, 100; pressure for children to specialize, 5, 27, 146n8; and youth sport as hidden labor, 110–11
professional sports: baseball, 51–52, 60, 65–68; as beneficiaries of youth sport, 126–27, 129–30; football, 65, 87, 101
Progressive-era reforms/initiatives, 20, 34, 43, 89, 99
Project Play (Aspen Institute), 101
Protecting Children from Violence in Sport (UNICEF), 178n65
Protecting Young Victims from Sexual Abuse and SafeSport Authorization Act (2017), 61–62. *See also* SafeSport

race issues of sports: and exploitation of youth athletes, 138–39; and politics of youth sport, 97; sport parenting

issues of, 134; and youth sport accessibility, 20–21
"redshirting," 48
regulation: of child labor, 42–47; politics of youth sport and need for regulation, 103–4; regulation vs. support of sport sponsors, 51, 63–64, 70; of youth sport, resistance to, 3, 29, 76–80. *See also* law and policy approach to sport
Rehabilitation Act (1973), 57–58, 84–85, 104
religion, First Amendment rights and youth sport, 83
"Report on Children and Sport" (UNICEF), 12
Ridpath, David, 13, 16
Roosevelt, Theodore, 56–57
Rosenbury, Laura A., 36–37, 42, 48, 157n57

SafeSport, 56, 61–63, 65, 81, 82
Santa Fe Independent School District v. Doe (U.S. 2000), 40–41
Santee v. Amateur Athletic Union (N.Y.S.2d 1956), 53
Santosky v. Kramer (U.S. 1982), 35
Scalia, Antonin, 64
Scott, Elizabeth S., 34
sexual abuse: law and policy approach to sport, 61–62; tort liability and youth sport, 79. *See also* child abuse
Sharon v. City of Newton (Mass. 2002), 85–86
Sherman Act. *See* antitrust law
Shirley Temple Act, 45. *See also* Fair Labor Standards Act (FLSA, 1938)
Silbaugh, Katharine, 48, 49–50, 81, 87, 111
social media influencers ("kidfluencers"), 45–46
society at large: as beneficiaries of youth sport, 124–25; social cohesion of youth sport, 131–32
sociology field: on youth sport and parental authority, 47; on youth sport models, 19

South Carolina, youth sport definition of, 15
South Dakota, youth sport definition of, 17
Soviet-era sportive nationalism, 68, 93. *See also* Cold War mentality of U.S. sport
Special Olympics, 139
sport, defined, 12–14. *See also* youth sport
sport, law and policy approach to. *See* law and policy approach to sport
Sport and Society program (Aspen Institute), 29
sportive nationalism, 128
Sports Agent Responsibility and Trust Act (SPARTA, 2004), 65, 164n80
Sports and Fitness Industry Association, 25, 101
Sports Illustrated, on children's fitness, 99
sports law: as academic field, 52–53; as marginalized field of law, 5
sports medicine field, inception of, 21–22
state and local governments: as beneficiaries of youth sport, 130–32; youth sport tourism of, 73–74, 130–32
state laws: on age of majority, 16; on child labor, 45; and children's rights, 40; on law and policy approach to sport, 61; on law and policy approach to youth sport, 71, 73–74, 75, 76–80, 82–89; parens patrie powers, 34, 38, 71; state authority to protect children, 33–34, 38–39; on youth sport concussions, 49; and youth sport definitions, 14–15, 17. *See also individual names of states*
Stone, Deborah, 98
substance use: and sport participation benefits, 27; United States Anti-Doping Agency (USADA) on, 56, 63, 65
Supreme Court, U.S.: on baseball's antitrust exemption, 99; on child labor, 43; on children's status under law, 34; and law and policy approach to sport, 51–53, 55–57, 59–61, 66–67, 68; on law and policy approach to

Supreme Court *(continued)*
  youth sport, 83; on parental authority, 35–37; on rights of children, 40–41; on state authority to protect children, 38–39. *See also* names of individual legal cases
surplus. *See* youth sport surplus

Take Back the Game (Flanagan), 5
taxes: IRS Private Letter Ruling, 121; law and policy approach to youth sport, 73; Nebraska and youth sport definition, 14–15; and youth sport tourism, 73–74, 130–32
Ted Stevens Olympic and Amateur Sports Act (1978): amateur athletes/athletic competition, defined, 17–18; and law and policy approach to sport, 54, 55, 62, 63, 160n22; and law and policy of youth sport, 74–75, 81, 82; and privatized structure of U.S. Olympic and Paralympic Movement sport, 93; and privatized structure of youth sport, 6, 74–76
Tennessee, on children's rights, 40
Title IX: and cheer, 14; enforcement of, 104, 138–39; and importance of girls' sport participation, 27; law and policy approach to sport, 52, 67–68; and NGB-affiliated youth sport, 84
tort law: and children's rights, 40; and law and policy approach to sport, 58–59; and law and policy of youth sport, 76–80; parental waivers in youth sport, 3, 48, 77–78, 85–86, 170n48; politics of youth sport and injuries to children, 103
tourism, youth sport, 73–74, 130–32
Town of Sterlington v. East Ouachita Recreation District (La. Ct. App. 2017), 131
transgender children: and NGB-affiliated youth sport, 84; state laws on school sports, 77
Troxel v. Granville (U.S. 2000), 37
Trump, Donald, 92
Turrini, Joseph, 53

Uniform Athlete Agent Act (UAAA, 2000), 65, 164n80
United Nations: Convention on the Rights of the Child, 16, 104–5, 117–18, 184n53; "Report on Children and Sport," 12; UNESCO, 90; UNICEF, 105, 117, 178n65
United States Anti-Doping Agency (USADA), 56, 63, 65
United States government. *See* Cold War mentality of U.S. sport; Congress, U.S.; law and policy approach to sport; law and policy approach to youth sport; law of child and family; politics of youth sport; presidential awards/commissions for fitness; Supreme Court, U.S.; *individual names of government agencies; individual names of presidents*
University of North Carolina, 59
Until It Hurts (Hyman), 5
U.S. Center for SafeSport (SafeSport), 56, 61–63, 65, 81, 82
U.S. Olympic and Paralympic Committee (USOPC): as beneficiary of youth sport, 128; dispute resolution process, 68; inception of, 17–18; law and policy of youth sport, 74–75, 79, 81, 82; mission of, 55–56, 62–63; Paralympic program management by, 58; and politics of youth sport, 93, 99, 102–3; private funding of, 160n24
U.S. Paralympic Movement: as beneficiaries of youth sport, 129; U.S. Paralympics Cycling, 15; USOPC management and, 58. *See also* U.S. Olympic and Paralympic Committee (USOPC)
U.S. Soccer, 62
U.S. Youth Soccer Association, 79
USADA (United States Anti-Doping Agency), 82
USA Gymnastics, 66, 82
USA Lacrosse, 18
USA Swimming, 15
USA Taekwondo, 79
USA Water Polo, 80

Vernonia School District v. Acton (U.S. 1995), 83
Vicksburg, Mississippi, and youth sport tourism, 131

Walker, LeRoy T., 75
Washington state, "Lystedt Law," 49
weight control. *See* children's fitness
Wiggins, David, 20-21
Wildman v. Marshalltown School District (8th Cir. 2001), 84
The Winner-Take-All Society (Frank & Cook), 125
Women's Sports Foundation (WSF), 24
Women's Tennis Association, 15
Wood, Betsy, 44
Woodman v. Kera (Mich. 2010), 77-78

Yen, Alfred C., 170n48
YMCA, 18
Youth and Amateur Sports Grants Program (Maryland), 73-74
Youth Football Act (California, 2019), 158n86, 177n61
youth sport, 3-10, 11-29; beneficial aspects, traditional discourse of, 11-12, 147n3; challenges of defining, 14-19; data on, 22-26; defined, for book's purposes, 19; goals (external) for, 13, 16; and "Great Sport Myth," 91, 96, 106, 172n4, 191n79; history of, 20-22; participation rate in, 25, 151-52n80, 151n75; play vs. sport, 115-19; power dynamics affecting children in, 6-8; research on youth sport experience, 26-29; retention in, 12, 26, 29, 101-2; sport, defined, 12-14; student-athletes (intercollegiate sport) and NCAA's amateurism model, 4-7; traditional discourse of, 8-9; youth sport industry as beneficiaries of, 122-24; "youth-sport-is-good" narrative of, 3-5. *See also* beneficiaries of youth sport; law and policy approach to youth sport; politics of youth sport; youth sport surplus
youth sport surplus, 109-20; as hidden labor, 110-12; and intentional approach to youth sport, 109-10; and play vs. sport, 115-19; and power systems, 119-20; sport as commodity, 116, 185n64; surplus, defined, 112-15

Founded in 1893,
UNIVERSITY OF CALIFORNIA PRESS
publishes bold, progressive books and journals
on topics in the arts, humanities, social sciences,
and natural sciences—with a focus on social
justice issues—that inspire thought and action
among readers worldwide.

The UC PRESS FOUNDATION
raises funds to uphold the press's vital role
as an independent, nonprofit publisher, and
receives philanthropic support from a wide
range of individuals and institutions—and from
committed readers like you. To learn more, visit
ucpress.edu/supportus.